Bank Regulation and Supervision a Decade after the Global Financial Crisis

GLOBAL FINANCIAL DEVELOPMENT REPORT 2019/2020

Bank Regulation and Supervision a Decade after the Global Financial Crisis

WORLD BANK GROUP

1 2 3 4 22 21 20 19

ISBN (paper): 978-1-4648-1447-1
ISBN (electronic): 978-1-4648-1496-9
ISSN: 2304-957X
DOI: 10.1596/978-1-4648-1447-1

Library of Congress Control Number: 2019952879

Cover image: © Shutterstock. Used with permission. Further permission required for reuse.
Cover design: Critical Stages, LLC.

This report reflects information available up to June 30, 2019.

Contents

BOXES

FIGURES

TABLES

Foreword

This *Global Financial Development Report* is a crucial contribution to the ongoing policy debate on the role of banking regulation and supervision in ensuring a banking sector that delivers stable and inclusive growth.

This report, the fifth in a series, marks a decade since the 2007–09 global financial crisis. The decade prior to the crisis was characterized by the deregulation of banking sectors in several geographies, especially in advanced economies. The onset of the crisis ushered in a period of intense reregulation of the banking sector, with several initiatives put in motion to address the flaws made so apparent during the crisis. The Financial Stability Board and the Basel Committee on Banking Supervision have built on a strong mandate from the Group of 20 to pioneer a global financial reform agenda to correct the mistakes made in advanced countries. Yet, in today's interconnected global financial system, regulatory changes do not recognize national boundaries and affect advanced and developing countries alike. The policy discussions regarding the right blend of regulation and supervision have become critical to the fate of billions of people in developing countries as these nations grapple with financial sector reforms shaped by the agendas of advanced economies.

This *Global Financial Development Report* offers new research and data that help fill gaps in the knowledge of banking regulation and supervision, while providing key insights into the policy discussion. The report documents emerging trends in the regulatory landscape and examines existing and new evidence on the benefits and pitfalls of bank regulation and supervision for a well-functioning banking system, which is vital for economic growth and poverty reduction.

For many years, the World Bank Group has provided crucial support to those developing countries that have sought to reap the benefits of financial development while also minimizing risks to financial stability. This work is becoming even more critical as the world seeks to avoid the devastating effects of future financial crises while utilizing the opportunities of modern financial services to meet the rising aspirations of the poor. This is possible only through efficient financial systems with stakeholders whose incentives are aligned with those of society as a whole. Crowding-in the private sector is crucial not only as an engine of growth in developing countries, but also as a foundation for the kind of market discipline that can prevent excessive risk-taking and put capital in the hands of the entrepreneurs who can invest in the future. The right regulatory and supervisory environment—accompanied by effective financial sector policies—is key to creating a financial system that can attract private capital and align private incentives with the public good.

We hope that this year's *Global Financial Development Report* will prove useful for a wide range of stakeholders, including governments, international financial institutions, nongovernmental organizations, think tanks, academics, the private sector, donors, and the broader development community.

Mahmoud Mohieldin
Senior Vice President
World Bank Group

Acknowledgments

Global Financial Development Report 2019/2020 reflects the efforts of a broad and diverse group of experts, both inside and outside the World Bank Group. The report was produced by the World Bank Research Department in collaboration with the Finance, Competitiveness, and Innovation Global Practice and the International Finance Corporation (IFC). Moreover, it includes inputs from a wide range of units within the World Bank Group.

Asli Demirgüç-Kunt was the report's director. Ata Can Bertay and Davide S. Mare were the task managers of the project. The main authors in charge of the chapters were Deniz Anginer, Robert J. Cull, and Davide S. Mare (chapter 1); Deniz Anginer and Ata Can Bertay (chapter 2); and Miriam Bruhn and Claudia Ruiz Ortega (chapter 3). Nan Zhou and Jinjing Liu were responsible for the statistical appendixes and completed the core team. Jinjing Liu provided excellent research assistance. Inputs were received from Cedric Mousset (box 1.2), Aurora Ferrari and Aquiles A. Almansi (box 1.3), Miquel Dijkman (box 1.4), and Nan Zhou (box 2.5).

Pinelopi Goldberg, Chief Economist, and Mahmoud Mohieldin, Senior Vice President, provided overall guidance and valuable advice. External advisers to the report included Franklin Allen, the Nippon Life Professor of Finance and Economics at the Wharton School of Business; James R. Barth, the Lowder Eminent Scholar in Finance at Auburn University; Thorsten Beck, Professor of Banking and Finance at Cass Business School in London; Allen Berger, Professor of Banking and Finance at the University of South Carolina; Charles Calomiris, Henry Kaufman Professor of Financial Institutions at Columbia University; Gerard Caprio, William Brough Professor of Economics at Williams College; Stijn Claessens, Head of Financial Stability Policy, Bank for International Settlements; Patrick Honohan, Senior Fellow at the Peterson Institute for International Economics and Former Governor of the Central Bank of Ireland; Harry Huizinga, Professor at Tilburg University; Edward Kane, Professor of Finance at the Carroll School of Management; and Ross Levine, Willis H. Booth Chair in Banking and Finance at the University of California at Berkeley.

The individual chapters of the report were presented at the Global Financial Development seminars. The seminars were presented by members of the core team and benefited from thorough discussions with Sebastian-A Molineus and Erik Feyen (chapter 1), Aurora Ferrari and Neil Gregory (chapter 2), Mario

Guadamillas and Alfonso Garcia Mora (chapter 3), and the participants in these seminars. Neil Gregory was the key contact at the IFC, and Ceyla Pazarbasioglu, Alfonso Garcia Mora, and Sebastian A. Molineus were the key contacts in the Finance, Competitiveness, and Innovation Global Practice. The authors benefited from informal discussions, and received valuable suggestions and other contributions, from Pietro Calice, Martin Čihák, and Martin Melecky.

In the bank-wide review of the concept note and of the report, substantial comments were received from Mahmoud Mohieldin (Senior Vice President); Tatiana Nenova and Ilias Skamnelos (both of the South Asia Region); Guillermo Beylis (of the Latin America and the Caribbean Region); Mohamed Gouled, Bachar Samra, Dan Goldblum, Jackie Irving, Jeff Anderson, and Sephooko Motelle (all from the IFC); Martin Raiser and Andrew Mason (both of the East Asia and Pacific Region); Alison Evans (Independent Evaluation Group); and Ceyla Pazarbasioglu (Equitable Growth, Finance and Institutions Gobal Practice).

The report would have not been possible without the production team, including Patricia Katayama (acquisitions editor for the report), Susan Graham (production editor), Orlando Mota (print and conversion coordinator), and Sabra Ledent (external editor). The communications team included Mark Edgar Felsenthal, Chisako Fukuda, and Ryan Douglas Hahn. Roula Yazigi assisted the team with the website. Excellent administrative and budget assistance was provided by Tourya Tourougui and Esther Landines.

The authors would like to thank the many country officials and other experts who participated in the surveys underlying this report, including the Financial Development Barometer and the Bank Regulation and Supervision Survey.

Financial support from the Knowledge for Change Program's research support budget is gratefully acknowledged.

Abbreviations and Glossary

AQR	asset quality review
AT1	additional Tier 1 capital
BCBS	Basel Committee on Banking Supervision
BIS	Bank for International Settlements
BRDD	Bank Recovery and Resolution Directive
BRSS	Bank Regulation and Supervision Survey
CBRC	China Banking Regulation Commission
CDS	credit default swap
CET1	common equity Tier 1 capital
CoCo	contingent convertible bond
D-SIB	domestic systemically important bank
EAP	East Asia and Pacific
EBA	European Banking Authority
ECA	Europe and Central Asia
ECB	European Central Bank
EU	European Union
FDIC	Federal Deposit Insurance Corporation (U.S.)
FSAP	Financial Sector Assessment Program
FSB	Financial Stability Board
GDP	gross domestic product
G-SIB	global domestic systemically important bank
IFRS	International Financial Reporting Standards
IMF	International Monetary Fund
IRB	internal ratings–based
LAC	Latin America and the Caribbean
LCR	liquidity coverage ratio
MENA	Middle East and North Africa
MES	marginal expected shortfall
MPOE	multiple points of entry
NPL	nonperforming loan
NSFR	net stable funding ratio
OECD	Organisation for Economic Co-operation and Development

OFC	offshore financial center
ROA	return on assets
ROE	return on equity
RWA	risk-weighted assets
RWR	risk-weighted ratio
SIB	systemically important bank
SIFI	systemically important financial institution
SPOE	single point of entry
SRM	Single Resolution Mechanism
SSA	Sub-Saharan Africa
TARP	Troubled Asset Relief Program
TBTF	too big to fail
TLAC	total loss-absorbing capacity
WMP	wealth management product

Note: All dollar amounts are U.S. dollars ($), unless otherwise indicated.

GLOSSARY

Additional Tier 1 capital	Capital instruments that meet the criteria for inclusion in the Tier 1 capital.
Bank	A service institution whose business is to receive deposits and/or close substitutes for deposits and grant credit and/or make investments in securities.
Bank capital	Equity owned by shareholders.
Bank regulation	Rules that regulate the establishment and operations of banks.
Bank supervision	Implementation of banking rules and regulations.
Banking sector	The collection of financial institutions provided with a bank charter.
Basel Accords	Global minimum standards for the prudential regulation of banks set by the Basel Committee on Bank Supervision, housed with the Bank for International Settlements. The Basel Accords do not have legal force. The standards need to be incorporated into local legal frameworks through each jurisdiction's rule-making process within the predefined time frame established by the Basel Committee on Bank Supervision. There are three main sets of these agreements, which are commonly known as Basel I, II, and III.
Capital requirement	The amount of capital required of banks by their financial regulator to fund their investments. It is commonly measured in the form of a ratio, where the numerator corresponds to the amount of regulatory capital and the denominator is a measure of either total assets (commonly known as unweighted regulatory capital ratio) or risk-weighted assets (commonly known as the risk-based regulatory capital ratio).
Common equity Tier 1 capital	Common shares and retained earnings.

Country	A territorial entity for which statistical data are maintained and provided internationally on a separate and independent basis (not necessarily a state as understood by international law and practice). The term, used interchangeably with *economy,* does not imply political independence or official recognition by the World Bank.
Deposit insurance	A form of financial safety net in which depositors are provided with a guarantee that their deposits will be paid partly or in full no matter what happens to the bank.
Economic capital	The amount of capital that a firm needs to hold to ensure that it stays solvent given its risk exposures.
Financial development	Conceptually, a process of reducing the costs of acquiring information, enforcing contracts, and making transactions.
Financial safety net	A government affords protection to bank creditors by providing direct compensation or a guarantee that a bank obligation would be fulfilled under specific circumstances.
Financial system	A country's financial institutions (banks, insurance companies, and other nonbank financial institutions) and financial markets (such as those in stocks, bonds, and financial derivatives). Also includes the financial infrastructure (for example, credit information–sharing systems and payments and settlement systems).
Institutional investors	Public and private pension funds, life insurance companies, non–life insurance companies, and mutual funds.
Internal ratings–based approach	Introduced with the Basel II capital accord, this approach allows banks, subject to previous supervisory approval, to use their own internal risk models to quantify the capital requirements for exposures to credit risk, operational risk, and market risk.
International bank	A bank with significant cross-border operations or international subsidiaries.
Leverage	A measure of how much of a bank's funding is in the form of bank capital. Commonly computed as bank capital divided by bank assets or bank assets divided by bank capital.
Limited liability	The obligation of an owner of a company is limited to the amount invested in the company.
Negative externalities	Costs borne by a third party for economic activities carried out by a company.
Nonbank financial institutions	Institutional investors and other nonbank financial intermediaries (such as leasing companies and investment banks).
Offshore financial center	A country or jurisdiction providing financial services to nonresidents beyond a scale commensurate with the size and financing of the domestic economy.

Regulatory capital	The amount of capital required of banks by their financial regulator to fund their investments, such as extending loans to borrowers or purchasing securities.
Risk-weighted assets	Assets weighted by their risk exposure. High risk corresponds to high weight.
Systematically important bank	Banks important on a system-wide level because of their size, interconnectedness, complexity, lack of substitutability, or global scope.
Systematically important financial institution	Financial institutions important on a system-wide level because of their size, interconnectedness, complexity, lack of substitutability, or global scope.

Overview

Over a decade has passed since the collapse of the U.S. investment bank Lehman Brothers marked the onset of the largest global economic crisis since the Great Depression. Drawing on 10 years of data and analysis, this report reflects on the causes of the crisis and the regulatory remedies adopted to prevent future financial troubles. Today, there is widespread agreement that the crisis was caused by excessive risk-taking by financial institutions. Financial intermediaries increased their leverage, drawing heavily on wholesale funding; they lowered their lending standards and, relying on inaccurate credit ratings, invested in complex structured instruments.

The crisis revealed major shortcomings in market discipline, regulation, and supervision, and reopened important policy debates on financial regulation.[1] Since the onset of the crisis, emphasis has been placed on better regulation of banking systems and on enhancing the tools available to supervisory agencies to oversee banks and intervene speedily in case of distress. Examining the key reforms in regulation and supervision since the crisis, specifically the experience of and lessons for developing countries, is what motivates this issue of the *Global Financial Development Report*.

After the onset of the crisis, there was much talk about using the crisis to push through difficult but needed regulatory reforms. At the global level, the G-20 has mandated the Financial Stability Board (FSB) to promote the coordinated development and implementation of effective regulatory, supervisory, and other financial sector policies. As part of this regulatory reform agenda, the Basel Committee on Banking Supervision (BCBS) prepared new capital and liquidity requirements for banks under the third Basel framework, Basel III. At the national level, many countries have enacted or are still in the process of adopting new laws and regulations in response to the lessons from the crisis. In addition to strengthening microprudential rules, many countries have stepped up efforts in the area of macroprudential policy, as well as put into effect better regimes for bank resolution and consumer protection.

Because the crisis emanated from advanced countries, much of the reform effort focused on reforms in that part of the world, with less emphasis on developing countries. Thus, there is a lack of systematic evidence on the detailed reforms undertaken by developing countries and on their impact on the stability and lending behavior of local banking sectors. Using new data from the World Bank's Bank Regulation and Supervision Survey (BRSS) around the world, a key objective of this report is to start filling these knowledge gaps.

Bank regulation and supervision—the rules of the game and how they are enforced—are paramount for the effective functioning of domestic banking systems. Banks are in the business of asset transformation and liquidity creation because they transform short-term liquid deposits into long-term illiquid assets. Imperfect information and a reliance on short-term funding, combined with high leverage and limited liability, create a potentially unstable system prone to runs, generating negative externalities that can affect the wider economy (Diamond and Dybvig 1983). Moreover, many bank creditors are unsophisticated depositors with a limited capacity to monitor bank operations. Thus, government represents these stakeholders, providing oversight through regulation and supervision (Dewatripont and Tirole 1994), as well as a safety net to protect them.

Incentives are critical in the financial sector. For effective bank regulation, it is important to complement government oversight with private monitoring. Such market discipline by outside parties capable of and incentivized to monitor bank operations reinforces government regulation. However, implicit and explicit government guarantees and wider safety net and resolution mechanisms intended to instill confidence and provide stability can also distort the incentives of bank managers and bank liability holders and make them prone to excessive risk-taking. The incentive distortions are twofold. First, government guarantees incentivize banks to take on riskier investments because the economic profits from higher risk-taking are privately captured by the bank, but losses are often socialized through the safety-net guarantees. Second, because in practice not only small depositors but also other bank liability holders are often protected when a bank fails, their incentives to monitor the financial condition of their bank are significantly reduced. Designing policies that align private incentives with the public interest to minimize these distortions is a key challenge of regulation and supervision, as well as of bank resolution regimes.

Where are reforms of bank regulation and supervision a decade after the global financial crisis? A renewed focus on systemic risks and macroprudential regulation, and the need to pay greater attention to incentives in the design of regulation and supervision, were among the early lessons of the crisis. New data from the BRSS (see box O.1 for a

BOX O.1 The World Bank's 2019 Bank Regulation and Supervision Survey

An important input into this report is the 2019 update of the World Bank's Bank Regulation and Supervision Survey (BRSS). The survey is a unique data set of bank regulation and supervision around the world. In the early 2000s, the World Bank created a global database of bank regulation and supervision (Barth, Caprio, and Levine 2001). The second update of the database was issued in 2003, the third in 2007, and the fourth in 2012. The current update represents the fifth wave and was completed in 2019.

This update of the survey encompasses information on 160 jurisdictions (including two monetary areas and the West African Economic and Monetary Union), 66 high-income countries, and 93 developing countries. These jurisdictions include all G-20 countries and countries from all the World Bank developing regions.

The survey went through a major revision for the 2012 update, but several questions from the 2007 survey were not changed for reasons of comparability. Other questions have been reformulated to generate more precise answers. Several questions were added, in particular on macroprudential regulation and consumer protection.

The current update of the survey questionnaire builds on previous waves by adding new questions on recent regulatory developments that characterized the period 2011–16, such as the Basel III capital

(box continued next page)

BOX O.1 The World Bank's 2019 Bank Regulation and Supervision Survey *(continued)*

FIGURE BO.1.1 Geographic Coverage of Bank Regulation and Supervision Survey, 2019

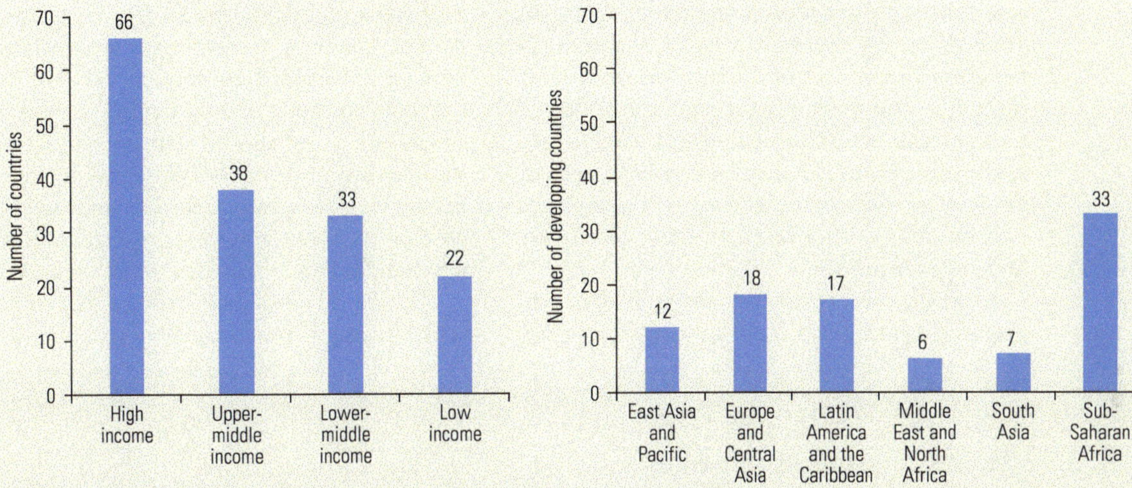

Source: Bank Regulation and Supervision Survey (BRSS), wave 5, https://www.worldbank.org/en/research/brief/BRSS.

and liquidity requirements, bank resolution mechanisms, and macroprudential supervision. Specifically, compared with the 2012 wave, the 2019 wave has 91 new questions and a new section on Islamic banking. Just two questions have been discontinued, and 12 questions in the two most recent surveys do not match exactly. The survey design and revisions mobilize the expertise of both supervisors and researchers. Most of the questions have been redrafted or changed to improve clarity and lessen measurement error concerns. The final list of questions included in the fifth wave of the BRSS reflects feedback from several banking experts, both within and outside the World Bank, who suggested rewording of questions from the previous wave and the inclusion of new questions.

The survey questionnaire was distributed in March 2017 using the survey platform Qualtrics. It was sent to the directors of bank supervision units or relevant officials within bank supervisory authorities. Thirty agencies opted to submit their answers on a hard copy of the questionnaire. To limit coding errors, the survey team regularly communicated with the national authorities and clarified the intended meaning of the BRSS questions. Each submission has been checked by the survey team, and there has been follow-up with the relevant agencies to clarify any issues arising from conflicting answers to diverse questions, or consistency between responses in the current survey and the preceding one. The data were finalized in 2019.

For an in-depth description of changes in bank regulation and supervision and an empirical analysis of what drove those changes, see Anginer et al. (2019) and box 1.6 in chapter 1. The sections of BRSS 2019 are as follows:

1. Entry into banking	4. Activities	7. Liquidity and diversification requirements	10. Accounting/information disclosure	13. Banking sector characteristics
2. Ownership	5. External auditing requirements	8. Depositor (savings) protection schemes	11. Discipline/problem institutions/exit	14. Consumer protection
3. Capital	6. Bank governance	9. Asset classification, provisioning, and write-offs	12. Supervision	15. Islamic banking

description of the database) provide an assessment of progress with the reforms since the crisis. This report examines these new data and both new and existing evidence on bank regulation and supervision to inform policy makers. Because regulatory reform is a very broad topic with many dimensions, the analysis mostly focuses on two key areas: the progress and impact of the reforms on market discipline and bank capital regulation. Nevertheless, the database being released along with this report is comprehensive, and its analysis over the coming years will likely shed light on many other facets of bank regulation and supervision.

Overall, this report sifts through data and research evidence to shed light on important policy concerns. To what extent are regulatory reforms designed with high-income countries in mind appropriate for developing countries? What has been the impact of reforms on market discipline and bank capital? How should countries balance the political and social demands for a safety net for users of the financial system with potentially severe moral hazard consequences? Are higher capital requirements damaging to the flow of credit? How should capital regulation be designed to improve stability and access? The report provides a synthesis of what we know, as well as areas where more evidence is still needed. Box O.2 provides the main messages.

The views of policy makers and other financial sector practitioners are split on the

BOX O.2 Main Messages of This Report

The 2007–09 global financial crisis has called into question the role of financial policy in general, especially in banking, revealing major shortcomings in market discipline, regulation, and supervision. The decade following the crisis was characterized by intense regulation of banking sectors across the world, especially in advanced countries. The crisis has also reignited the debate about the right blend of regulation and market discipline to ensure the safety and efficient functioning of banking systems.

A key challenge of bank regulation is to align private incentives with the public interest without taxing or subsidizing private risk-taking. Incentives are critical in the banking sector. Effective regulation and supervision need to harness the power of market discipline to curb excessive risk-taking by private parties. Design of safety nets and guarantees, availability of information, and capital regulation—all play a very important role in reinforcing or undermining market discipline.

Government interventions and the expansion of safety nets may have undermined market discipline. The crisis led to widespread government interventions to rescue insolvent banks, reinforcing too-big-to-fail subsidies. Since the crisis, deposit insurance systems around the world have expanded and have become more generous. The availability and quality of information disclosure have not improved significantly. These developments may have undermined market discipline, damaging both the incentives and ability of market participants to monitor financial institutions and making the job of regulators more challenging. Although, after the crisis, new regulations were put in place to improve resolution of systemically important banks, cross-border resolution systems remain underdeveloped and many of these mechanisms are untested. Moreover, despite these efforts to address too-big-to-fail issues, large banks have continued to become larger and more complex, and systemically important banks' share of global banking assets has increased in recent years.

The Basel III framework and capital regulations after the crisis were intended to increase both the quantity and quality of capital. Regulatory capital ratios are at their highest since the crisis, but analyzing data for 158 jurisdictions and 20,000 banks reveals that this has been driven mainly by a shift toward asset categories with lower risk weights. Thus for many banks, improvements in capital hinge on the extent to which risk weights reflect actual risk across different asset classes. In addition, most

(box continued next page)

BOX O.2 Main Messages of This Report *(continued)*

authorities now allow a wider array of instruments to satisfy Tier 1 capital—a regulatory capital component that is supposed to have the greatest capacity for loss absorption. This issue is important since it may lead to deterioration of the quality of capital in the future. Furthermore, noncash assets, including borrowed funds, are increasingly being permitted as initial bank capital in developing countries. Therefore, while on the surface it looks like banks may now be holding more equity and safer assets than before the crisis, the numbers may be providing a false sense of security.

After the crisis, bank regulations became more complex, potentially reducing transparency, increasing regulatory arbitrage, and taxing supervisory resources and capacity. Overall, a growing number of countries have adopted components of Basel II and III since the crisis. Developing countries have been shifting out of Basel I, and nearly 40 percent have adopted some aspects of Basel III. Many, however, have also been selective in their adoption, eschewing some of the more complicated aspects, such as using internal models to assess bank risk. Supervisory capacity in the developing world did not improve to keep up with the increasing complexity of bank regulations.

When it comes to regulation, one size does not fit all. This is the "principle of proportionality" in regulatory jargon. The level of public intervention should not exceed what is appropriate to achieve the social objectives. Thus, regulation and supervision need to be appropriate for the institutional environment, strength of market discipline, supervisory capacity, and business models of banks in a given country.

Less can be more. Especially in developing countries, adoption of sophisticated rules designed for developed countries may not be beneficial. Less complex regulations may mean more effective enforcement by supervisors and better monitoring by stakeholders. Within banking sectors, proportionality would suggest the application of simplified prudential regulations for small or noncomplex institutions to reduce excessive compliance costs.

Regulations also need to be compatible with incentives. Working with the market instead of against it is essential for effective regulation. Generating and incentivizing markets to provide signals would reinforce official supervision. Transparency, disclosure, and incentive compatibility of regulations would harness market forces and improve the effectiveness of regulation. Government interventions in finance need to be incentive-compatible to be effective, but designing and enforcing such regulations are complex tasks, particularly where sophisticated markets do not exist and institutions are underdeveloped. Globalization and technological change are important trends that make it even more challenging to provide effective oversight of banks.

net impact of postcrisis regulatory changes on developing countries. In the latest rounds of the Financial Development Barometer—an informal poll of policy makers in developing countries undertaken for this *Global Financial Development Report* (see box O.3)—most respondents signal that reforms were effective in enhancing financial stability by reducing the transmission of international shocks. Nevertheless, close to 70 percent of the respondents are also concerned that more restrictive regulations have led to regulatory arbitrage and shifted financial intermediation and risks to the unregulated shadow-banking industry. Moreover, two in five respondents think that risk-weighted capital requirements are too low to ensure financial stability, suggesting that the debate regarding the optimal level of bank capital is far from over. Finally, 55 percent of the respondents believe postcrisis regulations in developing countries either will have no impact or will be detrimental for those countries. Some of these conflicting responses reflect the lack of systematic data on the progress of reform efforts in developing countries. This *Global Financial Development Report 2019/2020: Bank Regulation and Supervision a Decade after the Global Financial*

BOX O.3 Views on Regulation and Supervision by Practitioners: Financial Development Barometer

To examine trends and sentiments on key financial sector policy issues, the *Global Financial Development Report* team has used the Financial Development Barometer survey since 2012. The barometer is an informal global poll of financial sector practitioners focusing on development issues. This poll examines trends and sentiments on financial sector issues that are under policy debate. The latest two rounds of the barometer, conducted in 2017 and 2018, include questions on current bank regulations and the efficacy of regulatory changes enacted after the global financial crisis. The responses to these polls reveal interesting insights from central bankers, finance ministry officials, regulatory and supervisory authorities, market participants, and international financial organization practitioners. For the 2017 and 2018 barometers, 179 individuals were polled and 102 responded—on average, for most questions, 42 developed and 60 developing countries responded.

Responses to the barometer questions (figure BO.3.1) suggest that over 80 percent of respondents consider the postcrisis financial reforms to have mitigated the transmission of international shocks. However, almost 70 percent of respondents also think that postcrisis financial regulations have led to more regulatory arbitrage within the regulated financial system. Another 68 percent believe the new regulations have shifted financial intermediation to entities outside the regulated financial system to shadow banks. Similarly, 68 percent consider the postcrisis regulations to be too burdensome/costly for financial institutions, leading to inefficiencies in financial intermediation. Also, only 62 percent of respondents think the current minimum capital requirement for financial institutions is enough to ensure financial stability.

Participants also have different attitudes toward the likely net impact of regulatory changes enacted after the global financial crisis on the sustainability of financial sector development in developing countries. As reported in table BO.3.1, 19 percent of respondents think that recent regulatory changes are mostly detrimental for developing countries, with another 36 percent believing there will be little impact. Only 45 percent are hopeful that the net impact of the regulatory changes will be mostly positive for developing countries.

FIGURE BO.3.1 Views on Postcrisis Regulations

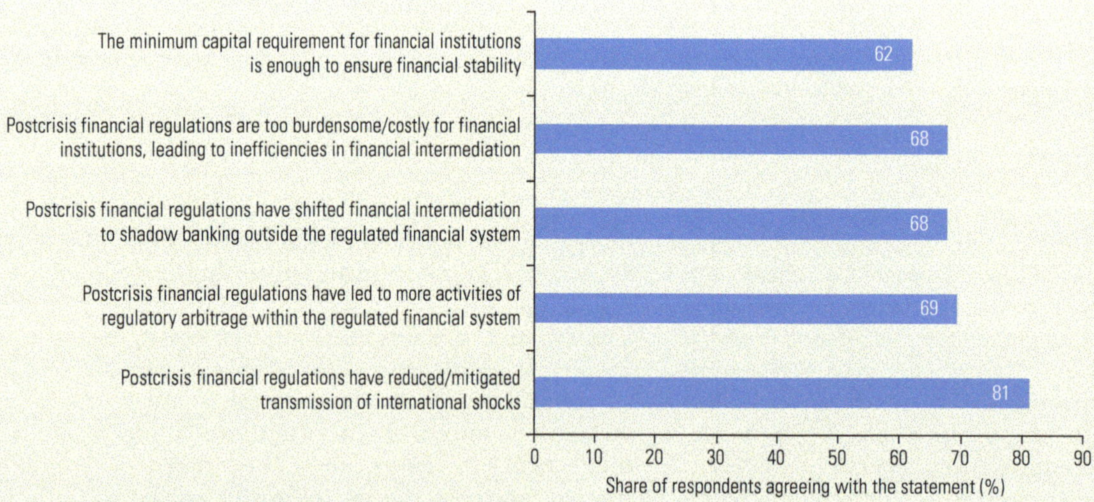

Source: Financial Development Barometer, 2017–18 (database, World Bank).

(box continued next page)

BOX O.3 Views on Regulation and Supervision by Practitioners: Financial Development Barometer *(continued)*

TABLE BO.3.1 Views on Net Impact of Postcrisis Regulatory Changes

What is your view on the likely net impact of regulatory changes postcrisis for developing countries?

The likely net impact of regulatory changes after crisis for developing countries is	Percentage of respondents agreeing with the statement
Mostly detrimental	19
Little impact	36
Mostly positive	45

Source: Financial Development Barometer, 2017–18 (database, World Bank).

Crisis brings new data and research and draws on available insights and experience to inform the policy discussion.

THE RATIONALE FOR REGULATION AND SUPERVISION

Government's role as regulator and supervisor of banking is key for promoting the stable and efficient functioning of the financial system. Economic theory provides several good reasons for this role. One central reason is the existence of "market imperfections," such as the costs and uncertainties associated with acquiring and processing information that influence all financial contracts and transactions. These imperfections often cause the actions of a few people or institutions to adversely affect many others throughout society. Preventing such externalities is one reason that government's role as regulator and supervisor can improve the functioning of the financial system.

How do these information issues motivate government oversight? Consider the case of "contagion," where the failure of one bank or weakness in one part of the financial system can cause distress in other banks or parts of the financial system. For example, when one bank fails, depositors and creditors may become nervous about the health of other banks. They may seek to withdraw their investments from these otherwise healthy banks, triggering a cascade of failures—that is, a classic bank run. In this way, weakness in one part of the financial system can stress healthy parts of the system, leading to problems for both individuals and firms that rely on those institutions.

There are also externalities associated with risk-taking that motivate government oversight. For example, cars and trucks rolling down a busy road are more likely to get into a crash when they travel too fast, resulting in costs for all innocent parties involved in the crash. Likewise, financial institutions that take excessive risks are more likely to fail and cause problems for the rest of the system. The larger the truck and the faster it goes, the more costly the crash is likely to be. Thus another way to think of bank regulation is as a "speed limit" or a "speed bump" that limits excessive risk-taking, particularly for large institutions whose crashes are likely to be most costly.

There are additional reasons for imposing such limits. Governments are often forced to bail out troubled banks, which means that financial institutions often do not bear the full risk of their activities. For example, when a large bank makes risky investments, and the bets pay off, the gains are private, in that the bank's owners reap the profits. However, when such gambles fail, the losses are often socialized—that is, the government pays for some of the losses. Bailouts of troubled banks through guarantees and inefficient resolution practices spread the costs of failed gambles to taxpayers who had no part in the original risky bets. Society often demands some protection, particularly for those depositors who are unable to assess risks by themselves, despite the fact that such protection may make banks even more likely to take excessive risks—a behavior associated with "moral hazard." This is another reason governments intervene and introduce speed bumps and limits.

Aside from unsophisticated depositors' inability to assess risk and monitor financial institutions, the complexity of financial instruments, the inability to appreciate the possibility of rare and extreme events, and the tendency of some people to follow the crowd (herding) can lead even sophisticated investors to make systematic mistakes. Such behavior can jeopardize the stability of the economy and can again cascade through to people with no part in or influence over the initial investments. This is another reason governments may take an active role in regulating financial institutions and markets.

Regulation and supervision can constrain the adverse implications of market failures. Governments can limit excessive risk-taking to prevent externalities associated with financial fragility. They can also design the safety nets, associated guarantees, and insolvency resolution systems needed to protect unsophisticated depositors and meet the social demands for a safety net, and yet minimize the moral hazard that arises from such protection by leaving large depositors, creditors, and investors unprotected so they are incentivized to monitor the institutions. Importantly, the authorities can promote information disclosure and transparency to facilitate more informed financial decisions and monitoring by all market participants. They can even regulate financial products—much like that for food and drugs—to protect the consumers of these products. These are all valid and important reasons for regulation and supervision.

However, just because governments can address market failures and improve the functioning of the financial system does not mean they will. Governments can fail as well. Correcting for market imperfections is complicated, and measuring risks and enforcing risk-based regulations are far from straightforward. Some regulations that reduce one market imperfection can create other distortions. For example, when governments insure the liabilities of banks to reduce the likelihood of bank runs, the insured investors of banks may no longer monitor the banks and bank management, potentially leading to excessive risk-taking and greater instability. Regulators could require banks to hold capital as large as their loans, which would minimize the risk of failures, but then financial intermediation would grind to a halt, because banks would not be able to lend.

An even more complicated issue is whether the government has sufficient incentives to address market imperfections. Governments and regulatory officials do not always use their powers to promote the public's interests. Sometimes, they use the power of the state to achieve different objectives, such as helping friends, family, cronies, and political constituents. Such government failures—or "regulatory capture," when they happen—can cause serious harm in the financial sector. This also suggests a wariness about relying solely on the government and the political system's ability to promote the public good.

Regulatory reform is also a slow-moving process that does not match the speed at which the private sector innovates. This leads to a continuous process of regulation, regulatory arbitrage (through which the private sector finds ways to circumvent the reforms), and re-regulation to close the new loopholes. Regulators and supervisors are at a disadvantage when it comes to catching up with profit-motivated financial institutions. Moreover, in many countries supervisory capacity is quite limited.

To overcome these challenges, effective regulation should cultivate and harness the power of market discipline. A clear lesson from research and practice is that banking regulation and supervision need to be supplemented by the use of incentives and information to maximize the number of well-informed, well-motivated monitors of financial intermediaries. Who are these private monitors? The first group includes the owners and senior management of the bank, whose net worth should depend on the prudent performance of the institution. The second group comprises all outside creditors, investors, large depositors, and counterparties that should be incentivized to monitor the institution because they cannot be certain they will be "bailed out" in case of failure. For market discipline to be effective, market participants should have not only the incentives to monitor banks, but also access to relevant and timely information and the ability to influence banks' risk-taking behavior. Official regulators and supervisors are the third group of monitors, which should—through information availability and design of policies—both incentivize the first two groups to be effective monitors and use the signals generated by them to strengthen their own oversight. Effective market discipline can work as a powerful restraining device and complement the government's regulatory oversight of banks.

Within this broader context, this overview continues with a discussion of recent reforms and trends in the evolution of market discipline and bank capital, and it highlights the relevant background research. The last section reviews the adoption of reforms by developing countries and discusses policies for an integrated framework of regulation and supervision. To navigate the rest of the report, see the outline in box O.4.

BOX O.4 Navigating This Report

The rest of this report consists of three chapters that cover important elements of bank regulation and supervision, some key facts, and general guidelines for the role of policy. Within this broad topic, the report focuses on two issues—market discipline and bank capital regulation—and tracks their evolution since the crisis using new data and related current research to inform policies.

Chapter 1 provides the conceptual framework for bank regulation and supervision and presents the latest update of the World Bank's Bank Regulation and Supervision Survey (BRSS). Using these data, the chapter analyzes the developments in capital regulation, market discipline, and supervisory monitoring since the global financial crisis.

Chapter 2 focuses on market discipline. It first defines market discipline and then analyzes the impact of the global financial crisis on long-term incentives to monitor and discipline banks. The chapter also describes recent regulatory reforms and identifies open issues in financial policy making. It concludes with policy recommendations for maximizing the benefits of monitoring by market participants.

Chapter 3 examines bank capital regulation. It discusses the role and functions of bank capital and different policy approaches. It summarizes the evidence on the effect of bank capital on access to finance, economic growth, and financial stability. The chapter also describes the trends in capital regulations and capital holdings after the global financial crisis and draws out policy implications.

Two statistical appendixes follow. Appendix A presents basic country-by-country data on financial system characteristics. It also reports averages of the same indicators for peer groups of countries, together with summary maps. It is an update of information from the 2017/2018 *Global Financial Development Report.* Appendix B provides additional country-by-country information on selected indicators of market discipline, bank capital regulation, and supervision using information from the latest wave of the BRSS.

The accompanying website (http://www.worldbank.org/financialdevelopment) contains a wealth of underlying research, additional evidence including country examples, and extensive databases on financial development, providing users with interactive access to information on financial systems. Users can provide feedback on the report, participate in an online version of the Financial Development Barometer, and submit their suggestions for topics for future issues of the report. The website also presents an updated and expanded version of the Global Financial Development Database, a data set of over 70 financial system characteristics for 203 countries compiled since 1960; and the updated Bank Regulation and Supervision Survey, a unique source of comparable country-level data on how banks worldwide are regulated and supervised.

MARKET DISCIPLINE AFTER THE GLOBAL FINANCIAL CRISIS

The global financial crisis led to unprecedented interventions by governments to stabilize their economic and financial systems. Significant government support was extended in the form of capital and liquidity injections, guarantees on bank liabilities, and repurchases of impaired bank assets (Laeven and Valencia 2018). Figure O.1 shows the percentage of countries with explicit insurance in 2016 as well as the increase compared with 2013, which is indicated by the dark blue sections of the graph. Over 80 percent of countries in the high-income group now have some form of explicit deposit insurance in place. The percentage of other countries with explicit deposit insurance has also increased since 2013, especially the percentage of those in the low-income group. Using the latest wave of the BRSS, Anginer and Demirguc-Kunt (forthcoming) show that there was also a significant expansion in deposit insurance—both coverage and scope—during the crisis, with a number of countries offering blanket guarantees. These trends we observe in the data are worrisome since research suggests that good design of deposit insurance schemes, including limited coverage, is particularly important in weak institutional settings to ensure that deposit insurance actually functions as a useful part of a country's overall system of bank regulation (Demirgüç-Kunt, Kane, and Laeven 2008).

FIGURE O.1 Deposit Insurance Systems Expanded since the Global Financial Crisis, by Country Income Group

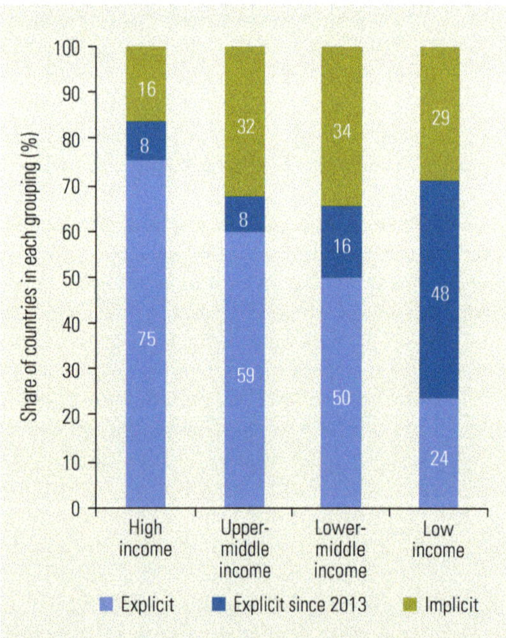

Source: Bank Regulation and Supervision Survey (BRSS), waves 4 and 5, https://www.worldbank.org/en/research/brief/BRSS.
Note: The figure shows the percentage of countries in each income group that have explicit deposit insurance. The dark blue sections show the increase in percentage since 2013. The green sections show the percentage of countries with no explicit (implicit) insurance scheme. It is assumed that any country that lacks an explicit deposit insurance scheme has implicit deposit insurance.

These widespread interventions and the significant expansion of the safety net effectively socialized private losses, distorting the incentives of bank owners, managers, and depositors, and further reinforcing expectations that they would be "bailed out" in case of trouble. Such expectations generally led financial institutions to become more connected and larger in order to maximize their "too-big-to-fail" subsidies. These trends then continued after the crisis. As a result of mergers and acquisitions (some of which were forced or encouraged by supervisors), large banks have grown even larger, and the global banking system has become more concentrated. Moreover, after the crisis, there was a further increase in the organizational complexity of large banks (Lagarde 2018). This growing size and complexity make transparency and information even more important if market discipline is to be effective.

In the postcrisis period, there was a recognition that market discipline was undermined by government intervention in the banking sector. Market discipline was first introduced as the third pillar of the Basel II capital accord as a way to complement and support official oversight of financial institutions. Following the crisis, insolvency resolution schemes were redesigned to incentivize banks' shareholders and managers to encourage the prudent management of banks. Complementing increased capital requirements, resolution schemes are intended to make it easier to protect essential functions and retail customer needs while "bailing in" the uninsured creditors of a failing bank. Such schemes are expected to increase the incentives for prudent management and investment and to reduce moral hazard. For example, progress was made in introducing both a new resolution process for bank-holding companies, implemented through a single point of entry framework, and new requirements for systemically important bank creditors to bear some of the burden of bank default by having a portion of their debt written off (also known as bail-in regulations). Large banks were required to submit plans that detailed a strategy for rapid and orderly resolution in the event of financial distress (living wills). Efforts were initiated to achieve more coordinated cross-border resolution systems, although implementation remains uncertain. Enhanced supervision of risk management and risk-reporting processes were also introduced for banks, including periodic stress tests. According to BRSS data, over one-third of developing countries introduced creditor bail-in initiatives, and close to two-fifths had requirements for bank resolution plans. However, very few developing countries have put in place a formal regulatory framework to deal with the resolution of international banks—confirming the concerns that this is an area of reform that remains weak in general (Lagarde 2018). Also, despite the greater complexity of bank regulation, the supervisory capacity in developing countries did not improve significantly since the crisis. Moreover, BRSS data do not show significant improvements in the quality and availability of information for market participants or to the broader public either, especially in developing countries.

Whether the recent reforms can dampen investor expectations of government support going forward is as yet unknown. Some aspects of these new regulatory reforms, such as higher capital surcharges and requirements to hold bail-in debt and the implementation of procedures to resolve or orderly liquidate large financial institutions, can reinforce incentives for market discipline. Overall, despite the regulatory efforts after the crisis, these newly introduced measures have yet to be tested under distress. It remains to be seen if they will be adequate to offset the long-term effects on market discipline of the widespread bailouts and blanket guarantees of the last crisis.

The financial crisis also prompted reforms of bank governance, but these may not be effective or may even backfire if risk-taking incentives are distorted and market discipline is weak. Many countries undertook bank governance reforms after the crisis, implementing changes to boards, executive compensation, and risk management processes. However, improving the corporate governance of banks while generous financial safety nets continue to distort market discipline and risk-taking incentives can backfire. Indeed, recent research suggests that in such circumstances, better-governed banks will simply better exploit the financial safety net, lowering their levels of capital and taking on more risk (Anginer et al. 2018). For example, using data for an international sample of publicly traded banks, Anginer et al. (2018) show that better bank governance—as measured by the size and independence of bank boards—is associated with higher systemic risk measures for large banks, which are more likely to benefit from too-big-to-fail guarantees (figure O.2). Moreover, they show that better governance varies more positively with individual bank and systemic risks in countries with more generous financial safety nets. Shareholder-friendly corporate governance is also associated with lower bank capitalization (Anginer et al. 2016).

BANK CAPITAL REGULATION AFTER THE GLOBAL FINANCIAL CRISIS

An important element of the postcrisis reform effort was the introduction of higher capital and liquidity requirements. Higher bank capital requirements are one way of ensuring market discipline because shareholders that have more "skin in the game" are likely to avoid excessive risk-taking. Sufficient capital also provides a cushion for absorbing losses during a crisis or other times of bank distress and

FIGURE O.2 Better Bank Governance Is Associated with Higher Levels of Systemic Risk for Large Banks

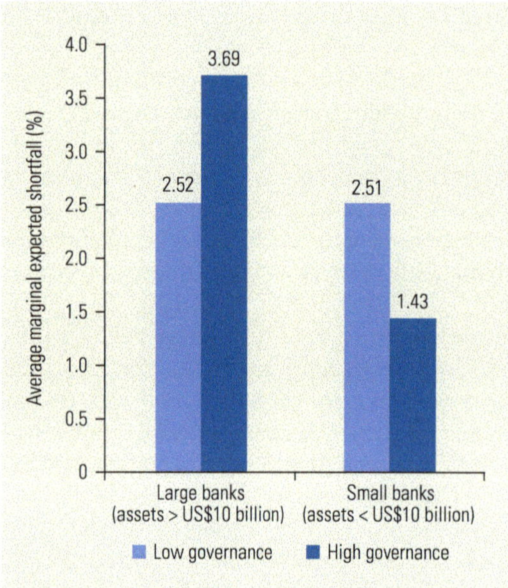

Source: World Bank staff calculations, based on Anginer et al. (2018).
Note: The average marginal expected shortfall (MES) is a measure of systemic fragility, computed as the average stock return of a firm when the market return is in the bottom fifth percentile in a given year. MES is multiplied by −1 so that higher values indicate higher risk. Bank size is based on the book value of total assets. The governance measure draws from 44 individual governance attributes related to board size and composition, compensation and ownership, external auditing, and anti-takeover measures. The sample includes international publicly traded banks over the period 2004–08.

FIGURE O.3 The Relationship between Bank Capital and Systemic Stability Is Stronger in Countries with Weaker Supervision

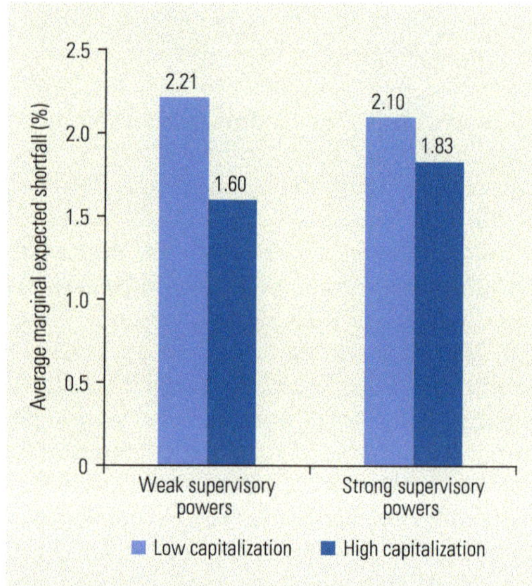

Source: World Bank staff calculations based on Anginer, Demirgüç-Kunt, and Mare (2018).
Note: For a definition of marginal expected shortfall, see the note to figure O.2. Banks are grouped by "low capitalization" (the bank's capital is in the first quartile of the regulatory capital distribution) or "high capitalization" (bank's capital is in the fourth quartile of the regulatory capital distribution). Countries are also grouped by those with "weak supervisory powers" (the supervisory power index in the first quartile of the supervisory power index distribution) and "strong supervisory powers" (the supervisory power index in the fourth quartile of the supervisory power index distribution). Supervisory power is an index measuring supervisory authorities' power to take specific preventive and corrective actions. The sample includes publicly traded banks in 61 countries over the period 1997–2012.

may improve screening and monitoring by banks (Calomiris 2012; World Bank 2012).

Higher capital requirements may also compensate for weaknesses in private monitoring and weak supervisory capacity, particularly in developing countries. Recent research using data from an international sample of publicly traded banks finds that the relationship between bank capital and systemic risk varies, depending on the institutional environment, information availability, and monitoring efficiency of bank regulators (Anginer, Demirgüç-Kunt, and Mare 2018). These results suggest that in countries with weaker market monitoring and supervisory capacity, having well-capitalized banks is even more important for systemic stability. For example, figure O.3 illustrates that in countries with weaker supervision, an increase in bank capital is associated with a significantly greater reduction in systemic risk, compared with countries with stronger supervisory capacity. These findings suggest that enhancing the quality and quantity of bank capital is likely to be even more important for mitigating the adverse effects of a lack of supervisory capacity and information availability. In countries where regulating and supervising banks can be prohibitively costly, higher capital regulations may compensate for weaker official oversight.

The Basel III capital framework, proposed in 2009 and currently being implemented, aims to increase the quality and quantity of capital. Data suggest that in high-income countries, reforms have indeed led regulatory capital (capital to risk-weighted assets) to increase and catch up with that of developing countries since the crisis—but the ratio of capital to total assets has increased much less (figure O.4).[2] Therefore, the increases in regulatory capital are mostly driven by a shift toward asset categories with lower risk weights.

We observe similar patterns when we investigate these ratios for banks of different sizes. The largest European banks—and, to a lesser extent, the largest American banks—have increased their capital ratios by at least partially reducing their risk-weighted assets, consistent with the findings of Gropp et al. (2019) and BCBS (2018c). For small banks in high-income countries, and for large and small banks in developing countries, changes over time in these ratios are more muted, resulting in the above-noted aggregate patterns.[3]

Studies of bank capital during the global financial crisis suggest that investors paid much less attention to risk-weighted capital ratios. Using Bankscope data for an international sample of publicly listed banks, Demirgüç-Kunt, Detragiache, and Merrouche (2013) examine the relationship between bank capital and stock market returns around the time of the global financial crisis. They examine different measures of capital to determine which measure shows the strongest correlation with stock returns. Their results reveal that higher capital was linked with higher stock returns during the crisis and that this relationship is stronger when capital is measured as a simple leverage ratio rather than a risk-weighted ratio, particularly for large banks (figure O.5). This finding may reflect the fact that market participants viewed the risk adjustment under Basel rules as subject to manipulation or at least as not reflective of true risk for large banks. These results also suggest that authorities should be cautious of improvements in capital that hinge on the assumption that risk weights reflect actual risk across different asset classes.

Quality matters. Another finding of this research is that higher-quality capital—Tier 1 capital and common equity—displays a stronger correlation with subsequent stock market returns than lower-quality Tier 2 capital, especially for larger banks. Overall, these findings support the view that a stronger capital position is an important asset during a crisis,

FIGURE O.4 Regulatory Capital-to-Asset Ratios over Time, 2004–18

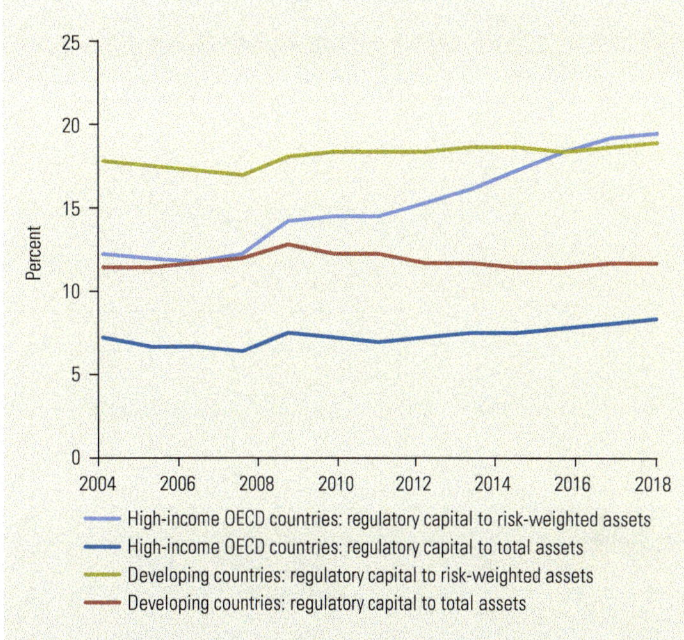

Source: World Bank staff calculations, based on data from Financial Soundness Indicators (FSI), an IMF database: http://data.imf.org/?sk=51B096FA-2CD2-40C2-8D09-0699CC1764DA.
Note: The Financial Soundness Indicators (FSI) provide country-level data on total capital and asset holdings of the banking sector, as reported by participating countries to the IMF. All ratios used in the figure are calculated based on the underlying totals. For example, regulatory capital to total assets is calculated as total regulatory capital divided by total assets of the banking sector. Country-level ratios are then averaged across high-income OECD countries and developing countries using a simple average. Weighting FSI data by GDP when averaging across countries leads to comparable trends. Developing countries are those classified as such in the World Bank developing regions. OECD = Organisation for Economic Co-operation and Development.

suggesting that the postcrisis emphasis on strengthening capital requirements is appropriate. Introduction of a minimum leverage ratio to supplement minimum risk-weighted capital requirements is advisable (and is part of the Basel III regulation), because properly measuring risk exposure is very difficult, especially for large and complex financial organizations. Furthermore, a greater emphasis on higher-quality capital in the form of Tier 1 capital or common equity is justified.

Indeed, the ratio of Tier 1 capital to total regulatory capital has increased since the crisis, likely reflecting the regulatory changes. From 2005 to 2017, the ratio of Tier 1 capital to total regulatory capital increased from 75 percent to about 90 percent in high-income Organisation for Economic Co-operation and Development (OECD) countries and from 80

FIGURE O.5 **Response of Bank Stock Returns to Lagged Bank Capital, 2006–08**

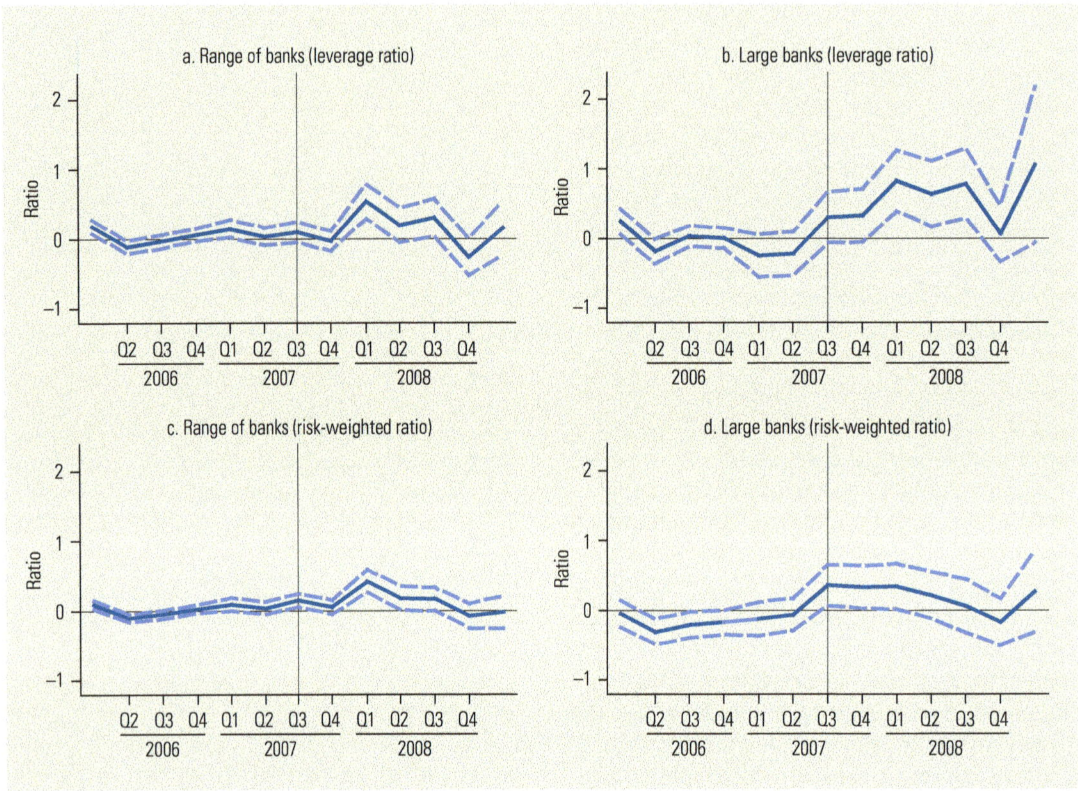

Source: Demirgüç-Kunt, Detragiache, and Merrouche 2013.
Note: The leverage ratio is measured as Tier 1 + Tier 2 capital to total assets; the risk-weighted ratio is defined as Tier 1 + Tier 2 capital to risk-weighted assets.

percent to 90 percent in developing countries (figure O.6). However, BRSS data also suggest that the definition of Tier 1 capital was broadened in many countries, and now includes hybrid debt capital instruments, asset valuation gains, and subordinated debt. This potentially reduces the quality of Tier 1 capital and its loss absorption capacity in times of distress. There is no evidence that institutions are currently relying on these laxer forms of capital in their composition of Tier 1 capital. However, going forward, this is an issue that also bears watching.

Increases in the quantity and quality of capital can foster financial stability, but there are concerns that increased capital requirements can also reduce access to credit, at least in the short run. There is limited evidence on this relationship, but available research suggests that banks prefer to reduce their lending rather than raise capital because issuing equity is costly (Aiyar, Calomiris, and Wieladek 2015; Gropp et al. 2019). Several studies point out that the regulation-tightening in high-income OECD countries has led banks in those countries to lend less in developing countries. The effects on lending may be mitigated by allowing banks to use contingent convertible bonds (CoCos), which is less costly than equity capital. However, experience with this instrument remains limited, and it is not clear how well it will perform in distress. It is also not a viable option for countries without developed capital markets. Other studies dismiss the cost reasons and argue that substantially higher equity capital requirements in the long run will not affect the loan supply adversely, but curb excessive risk-taking (Admati and Helwig 2013). How long banks take to adjust to higher capital requirements, the long-term impact of these changes on loan supply, and whether increasing the capital requirements significantly would change these relationships, are still open questions.

ADOPTION OF REFORMS IN DEVELOPING COUNTRIES AND AN INTEGRATED FRAMEWORK FOR BANK REGULATION AND SUPERVISION

High-income countries have adopted Basel III more quickly than middle- and low-income countries. In the BRSS, all countries reported using one of the Basel regimes, but many were still using Basel I or II. Basel III's adoption is related to country income level, with higher-income countries often having moved to Basel III. More than 80 percent of high-income countries have already adopted Basel III, followed by about half of upper-middle-income countries and one-third of lower-middle-income countries (figure O.7). Only five low-income countries reported using Basel III.

One size does not fit all. The "principle of proportionality" suggests that the level of public intervention should not exceed what is appropriate to achieve the social objectives. Thus, regulation and supervision need to be appropriate to the institutional environment, strength of market discipline, supervisory capacity, and business models of banks in a given country. Both Basel II and III were designed to fit the needs of the more sophisticated banking sectors of Basel Committee members. As such, the rules proposed under these agreements may be overly complex for banking sectors in many developing countries. The reliance of Basel II and III on market discipline and strong supervisory capacity can even have an adverse effect on the banking sectors of countries with weaker institutional environments where market discipline and supervisory capacity are thin. The fact that developing countries are taking a more cautious approach is consistent with proportionality.

Selective adoption of more complex frameworks and higher capitalization are appropriate in settings with limited market discipline and supervisory capacity. Investigating the adoption process and bank capital ratios using the BRSS data, Anginer et al. (2019) confirm this cautious approach, though they show that the ratio of bank equity to total assets also tends to be higher for developing country banks of comparable size. They find that countries at higher levels of economic development, and those that had a banking crisis, are more likely to adopt more advanced levels of regulation. Also influential in this decision are external factors such as FSB membership or widespread adoption by other countries, suggesting that emulating best practice lessons also plays an important role. Furthermore, complementarities matter: countries with more developed institutions, stronger market discipline, and regulatory and supervisory capacity are more likely to adopt more complex frameworks. Finally, research supports the higher capitalization

FIGURE O.6 Tier 1 Capital to Total Regulatory Capital, 2005–17

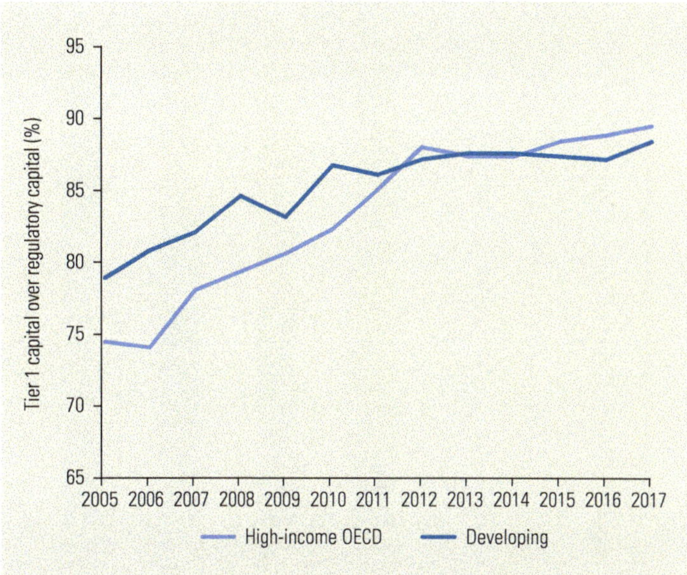

Source: World Bank staff calculations, based on data from Financial Soundness Indicators (FSI), an IMF database, http://data.imf.org/?sk=51B096FA-2CD2-40C2-8D09-0699CC1764DA.
Note: The Financial Soundness Indicators (FSI) provide country-level data on total capital and asset holdings of the banking sector, as reported by participating countries to the IMF. All ratios used in the figure are calculated based on the underlying totals. For example, Tier 1 capital to regulatory capital is calculated as total Tier 1 capital divided by regulatory capital of the banking sector. Country-level ratios are then averaged across high-income OECD countries and developing countries using a simple average. Weighting FSI data by GDP when averaging across countries leads to comparable trends. Developing countries are those classified as such in the World Bank developing regions. OECD = Organisation for Economic Co-operation and Development.

FIGURE 0.7 Share of Countries Following Each Basel Regime, by Country Income Group

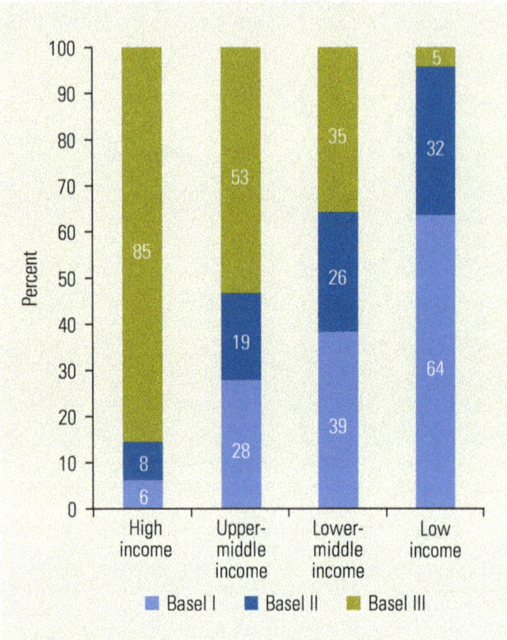

Source: Bank Regulation and Supervision Survey (BRSS), wave 5, https://www.worldbank.org/en/research/brief/BRSS.
Note: The figure is based on data from 133 countries.

of banks in developing countries as prudent policy because capital can compensate for weaker private monitoring and supervisory capacity.

Less can be more. After the global financial crisis, bank regulations became more complex, potentially reducing transparency, increasing regulatory arbitrage, and taxing supervisory resources and capacity. Simpler regulations may be more appropriate, particularly in underdeveloped institutional environments with limited information, weak private monitoring, and supervisory capacity. Complex regulatory approaches also generate arbitrage opportunities and are more difficult to enforce. Overall, research supports the view that the emphasis on strengthening capital requirements and introducing leverage ratios was appropriate. But properly measuring risk exposure is very difficult, particularly for large and complex organizations, which calls into question the usefulness of emphasizing risk-weighted concepts of bank capital. For example, a simple capital ratio—such as the leverage ratio—may be easier to observe and enforce, despite not being able to differentiate for risk. Basel III recognizes this, and introduced a 3 percent leverage ratio (as a complement to the risk-weighted ratio). Whether the minimum value is high enough is a topic for more research—some studies advocate much higher levels (see, for example, Admati 2016).

However, regulations also need to be incentive-compatible. Designing regulations in a way that reduces the incentives of institutions and markets to circumvent them is key to making them effective and breaking the vicious cycle of "regulation–innovation–re-regulation." Making regulations incentive-compatible is also how regulators can align private incentives with the social good. For example, an alternative approach to risk-based capital regulation would be to have a simple leverage ratio, adjusted upward by the loan spreads banks charge their customers (Calomiris 2011). Using loan spreads to measure loan risk is desirable because these spreads are accurate forecasters of the probability that a loan will become nonperforming and would be an improvement over a simple leverage ratio. This is an example not only of a simple regulation but also of an incentive-compatible one. Banks clearly would not have the incentive to lower their interest rates just to reduce their capital budgeting against a loan, because doing so would reduce their income and defeat the purpose of circumventing the regulation. An added advantage of this approach is that monitoring interest rates is fairly uncomplicated, even in the least developed emerging markets.

An integrated framework for bank regulation and supervision can build on its strengths and compensate for weaknesses. Bank regulations, official supervision, and market discipline are all interrelated. When they work well, the different elements can reinforce and complement each other, strengthening the overall impact. However, with poor design and implementation, regulators and market participants may find themselves at odds, undermining the overall effectiveness of regulation. Therefore, a key challenge for bank regulators is to design policies that align private incentives with the public interest without taxing or subsidizing private risk-taking.

As memories of the global financial crisis fade away, the determination of regulators and reform momentum tend to decline. Globalization and technological change are also important trends that make it even more challenging to provide effective oversight of banks. Globalization leads to more competition, intensifying the industry pressures on authorities to reduce transparency and accountability. It also contributes to the problem through regulatory arbitrage—since financial institutions are generally able to negotiate less oversight by threatening to move to jurisdictions with lighter regulation. The technological revolution since the crisis has already greatly increased the pace of financial innovation, making it ever more difficult for regulators to catch up with the industry. Fintech, high-frequency trading, and digital currencies all present opportunities but also stability challenges. Furthermore, despite the recent reforms, the crisis experience may have increased the confidence of large banks in their ability to socialize their future losses, leading them to be more creative in seeking new risks. Although it is not possible to predict when and how the next financial crisis will strike, finance is a risky business and crises will continue to happen. The ultimate goal of public policy is to minimize the frequency and severity of crises. Effective bank regulation and supervision will become more and more challenging in the years to come.

NOTES

1. For an early analysis of the causes of the global financial crisis, see, for example, Caprio, Demirgüç-Kunt, and Kane (2010); French et al. (2010); Rajan (2010); and World Bank (2012) and the references therein.
2. Multiple sources of data—aggregate, country-level Financial Soundness Indicators of the International Monetary Fund (IMF), BRSS data, and bank-level data from 20,000 banks and 158 jurisdictions—reveal consistent patterns in bank capital. These are more comprehensive data sets than those used in earlier investigations (see, for example, FSB's fourth annual report (FSB 2018b), which focuses on approximately 110 large international banks in its 27 member countries, plus those in the European Union).
3. While analyzing 36 large banks in 9 developing and high-income countries in their "rest of the world" sample, BCBS (2018c) also finds increases in regulatory capital ratios as well as increases in risk-weighted assets. These results are still in line with those reported in figure O.4, however, because the BCBS sample is dominated by developing countries such as China and India.

CHAPTER 1: KEY MESSAGES

- *Bank regulation* refers to the rules that regulate the establishment and operations of banks. *Bank supervision* refers to the implementation of those rules and regulations.
- The goals of bank regulation and supervision are to provide for the stability of the overall financial system, protect consumers and investors, and ensure adequate competition in the provision of banking services.
- The banking sector is particularly subject to negative externalities and information asymmetries, which make the simultaneous achievement of these goals challenging.
- A key purpose of regulation and supervision is therefore to limit excessive risk-taking by financial institutions to avoid the negative externalities of financial fragility. Authorities can regulate the disclosure of information to facilitate sound decisions, and even regulate financial products. But designing and enforcing the appropriate policies can be problematic. Safety net policies and interventions need to be designed so they do not undermine the incentives of the private sector to exert strong corporate control over financial institutions and defeat the original purpose of regulation and supervision.
- The 2007–09 global financial crisis was a good example of the difficulties encountered in getting this balance right, and its aftermath ushered in a period of intense regulation, with several initiatives put in motion to address the flaws revealed during the crisis.
- Analysis of the World Bank's 2019 Bank Regulation and Supervision Survey reveals that reforms after the crisis led to an increase in capital requirements and implementation of new resolution processes for systemically important banks. However, even though regulatory capital ratios are at their highest levels since the crisis, that development has been accompanied by a shift toward asset categories with lower risk weights. Thus, improvements in capital hinge on the extent to which risk weights reflect the actual risk across different asset classes. In addition, most authorities now allow a wider array of instruments to satisfy Tier 1 capital requirements—the regulatory capital component intended to have the greatest capacity for loss absorption. This issue is important since it may lead to deterioration of the quality of regulatory capital in the future. In a similar vein, noncash assets, including borrowed funds, are increasingly allowed to serve as initial bank capital in developing countries, probably weakening the loss-absorbing capacity of bank capital.
- The global financial crisis led to widespread government interventions to rescue distressed banks. Deposit insurance systems around the world expanded and became more generous. The availability and quality of information disclosed as part of bank supervision have not improved significantly. Such factors may have undermined market discipline, reducing the incentives and ability of the private sector to monitor financial institutions. Although, since the crisis, new regulations have been put in place to improve the resolution of systemically important banks, cross-border resolution systems remain underdeveloped, and many of these mechanisms are untested.
- After the crisis, bank supervision became stricter and more complex. But supervisory capacity did not improve proportionally to match the greater complexity of bank regulations. Capacity constraints for bank supervisors may limit the monitoring and enforcement of the rules.
- Overall, since the crisis a growing number of countries have adopted components of Basel II and III. Developing countries have been shifting out of Basel I, and nearly 40 percent have adopted some aspects of Basel III. Many, however, have also been selective in their adoption, eschewing some of the more complicated aspects, such as using internal models to assess bank risk. Having undergone a systemic banking crisis is an important factor in explaining a country's increase in regulatory capital ratios, but it is not significantly associated with the leverage ratios of banks in those countries. Countries are also influenced by neighbors in adopting capital regulation.

1

Banking Regulation and Supervision: Conceptual Framework and Stylized Facts

BANK REGULATION AND SUPERVISION: FOUNDATIONS AND RATIONALES

Bank regulation refers to the rules that regulate the establishment and operations of banks. *Bank supervision* refers to the implementation of those rules and regulations.[1] Bank regulations cover entry into banking, ownership, the definition and holding of capital, types of permitted activities, information disclosure, corporate governance, the financial safety net, accounting, bank failure, bank resolution, and consumer protection. Supervisory or counterparty discipline is needed to create the incentives for regulated parties to obey the rules. Without oversight and penalties, rules have no teeth. Supervision also entails monitoring the overall banking system, including identifying potential issues outside the current regulatory perimeter. This supervisory monitoring can also be beneficial for the regulatory process (for example, it may inform policy makers), and it provides information that enables market participants to monitor banks. The more skilled and informed the supervisory workforce, the more effective this monitoring can be.

The goals of bank regulation and supervision are to provide for the stability of the overall financial system, protect consumers and investors, and ensure adequate competition in the provision of banking services. Financial stability is indispensable to having a banking sector that funds a variety of risks, allocates capital efficiently, protects consumers and investors from being victims of fraud and of their own limited understanding of financial products, and provides broad access to financial services. The banking sector is particularly subject to negative externalities (costs borne by a third party for economic activities carried out by banks) and information asymmetries (different information sets for counterparties to financial transactions), which make the simultaneous achievement of these objectives challenging.

Information frictions can induce shocks that propagate through the banking system by contagion. Banks are in the business of asset transformation and liquidity creation because they transform short-term liquid deposits into long-term illiquid assets. Reliance on short-term funding, combined with high leverage, creates an inherently unstable system prone to runs. In their seminal paper, Diamond and Dybvig (1983) model bank runs using demand deposit contracts and depositors' incentives to withdraw their funds at a bank, depending on the observed withdrawal behavior of other depositors. If depositors in the banking system cannot distinguish between healthy and distressed banks, problems at one bank quickly spread throughout the banking system.[2] Banks are thus subject to negative externalities that can have a significant impact on the wider economy. Moreover, when banks' stakeholders find it difficult to fully understand complex investments or do not factor in the possibility of rare but extreme events, they can make systematic mistakes that can jeopardize the stability of the banking sector. This situation can have adverse implications for people who neither made those investments nor had any influence over those who made the investments. Greater information asymmetry resulting from the growing opacity, complexity, and interconnectedness of financial institutions and the limited abilities of market participants to process information only exacerbate the tendency of market participants to display common behaviors (so-called herding).

Having outside parties capable of and incentivized to monitor bank operations is therefore critical to banking stability. However, many bank creditors are unsophisticated investors with a limited capacity to monitor bank operations. Incentives to monitor bank risk-taking can also be weakened by the financial safety nets that guarantee repayment to bank creditors. These safety nets, coupled with the fact that shareholders' losses are capped to a fixed multiple of their capital holdings because of limited liability, can give banks incentives to take on excessive risk.[3]

Implicit and explicit government guarantees intended to instill confidence and provide stability can also distort the incentives of bank managers and bank liability holders. The incentive distortions are twofold. First, government guarantees incentivize banks to take on riskier investments because economic profits from excessive risk-taking are privately captured by the bank, but losses are socialized through the deposit insurance fund or other guarantees. Second, because depositors and other bank liability holders are protected when a bank fails, their incentives to monitor the financial condition of their bank are significantly reduced.

Negative externalities associated with excessive risk-taking are especially a concern for large financial institutions. They often do not bear the full risks of and the potential losses associated with their portfolios, and risk exposures at one institution can endanger the survival of other institutions or lead to greater systemic risk for a banking sector because of herding behavior. When a large bank makes risky investments that pay off, it stands to benefit from the profits. But when those investments fail, experience has shown that the bank may not bear the full costs. As described later in this chapter, bailouts of distressed banks during recent financial crises entailed costs that were shouldered by society as a whole, meaning taxpayers who had no connection to the original risky investment decisions. This potential for cascading effects is an important reason to regulate the banking sector by imposing "limits" on risk-taking by banks.

Government regulation and supervision can improve welfare by providing the monitoring functions that dispersed stakeholders (depositors, shareholders, and bondholders) are unable or unwilling to perform.[4] Banks raise funds with retail deposits held mostly by unsophisticated depositors who do not have the incentives, information, or means to perform effective monitoring. Therefore, regulation should mimic the control and monitoring that depositors are unable to provide because of a lack of appropriate information, financial knowledge, and coordination (Santos 2001). For example, Dewatripont and Tirole (1994) developed a model of banks' capital structure that shows how optimal regulation can be achieved using a combination of basic capital adequacy requirements (with external intervention when those are violated) and elements of market discipline as an important complement to (though not a substitute for) this regulation.

Regulatory reform is a slow-moving process that does not match the speed at which the private sector innovates and evolves. The financial sector is dynamic—changing as information, technology, competition, and regulation change—and therefore its supervision and regulation necessarily must be dynamic as well. The different dynamism in the private sector and prudential regulation generates capacity constraints that should be addressed with an appropriate design of incentive-based regulations. A normative approach might be of limited use because of the speed of innovation, incentives to circumvent too-detailed prescriptions by finding loopholes in financial regulation, or a limited capacity to enforce the rules on systemically important banks. This last point reflects not only regulatory capture but also the lack of options or the implicit constraints faced by bank supervisors during a financial crisis.

REGULATORY CHANGE: THE GLOBAL FINANCIAL CRISIS AS CATALYST

The decade prior to the 2007–09 global financial crisis was characterized by the deregulation of banking sectors in several countries, supervisory shortcomings, and accounting misrepresentations, especially in advanced countries. The onset of the crisis ushered in a period of intense regulation, with several initiatives put in motion to address the flaws that emerged during the crisis (see box 1.1 for a discussion of the policy lessons for developing countries). In doing so, the crisis reignited debates about the right blend of regulation, supervision, and market discipline to ensure the safety and efficient functioning of banking systems.

Whereas much has been written about the global financial crisis and associated changes in bank regulation and supervision from the perspective of advanced countries, there has been less focus on how those changes have affected banking sectors in developing regions.[5] Indeed, there is a lack of evidence on the detailed reforms undertaken by developing countries to decrease the fragility of local banking sectors, while helping to ensure that they support economic growth and financial inclusion as providers of credit.[6] An exception is the work carried out by the Basel Committee on Banking Supervision (BCBS), the Committee on Payments and Market Infrastructures (CPMI), the Financial Action Task Force (FATF), the Financial Stability Board (FSB), the International Monetary Fund, and the World Bank to address the significant decline in the number of correspondent banking relationships due also to the introduction of anti-money laundering/counter terrorism financing (AML/CFT) regimes.[7] Further, filling this gap in evidence on developing countries is a key objective of this report.

Although the global financial crisis helped focus attention on the importance of regulatory and supervisory changes to curb excessive risk-taking, it is important not to lose sight of other motivations for bank regulation and supervision. Most fundamentally, banks support economic growth by screening borrowers and allocating credit to worthy projects. In trying to curb excessive risk-taking, regulators and supervisors must recognize the potential tension between ensuring stability and promoting growth. Eliminating all risk-taking would come at a big cost in terms of growth, and thus the design and implementation of banking regulation seek to balance these potentially competing objectives. Curtailing all risk-taking could also constrain access to credit in those areas needed to achieve the sustainable development goals.

The financial crisis tilted policy makers' attention toward financial stability, but regulation and supervision are also required to protect consumers and curb anticompetitive behavior. Market misconduct regulation is needed to ensure that participants act with integrity and that sufficient information is available for consumers of financial services to make informed decisions. Greater competition constrains monopoly power and allows efficient allocation of resources and intermediation of funds.

Banking crises often come with enormous costs that exceed the private cost to individual banks.[8] Financial stability is a core objective of the microprudential and macroprudential reforms adopted as a result of the crisis. Microprudential regulation focuses on the

BOX 1.1 Root Causes of the 2007–09 Global Financial Crisis and Policy Lessons for Developing Countries

What were the root causes of the global financial crisis, and what lessons can be learned by developing countries? Caprio, Demirgüç-Kunt, and Kane (2010) highlight the role of the financial safety net in providing incentives to financial institutions to shift losses onto governments and taxpayers. The authors also discuss how several key factors in the crisis plagued both advanced and developing countries. For example, excessive bank leverage and risk-taking drove the boom and bust in the prices of financial assets (Crotty 2009). The adoption of complex financial regulations, such as some prescriptions in the Basel II capital accord, and the greater reliance on credit ratings in determining bank regulatory capital made it more difficult to hold regulatory authorities accountable. Moreover, failures in the incentives of supervised entities and regulators, as well as limitations in the information environment, were also factors relevant to the crisis. Other key elements discussed by pundits and policy makers are macroeconomic vulnerabilities, the role of nonbank financial intermediaries performing credit intermediation, resolution schemes for financial institutions, agency problems (that is, conflicts of interest), incentives for bank regulators and supervisors and their impact on enforcement, and accounting misrepresentations (see, among many others, Obstfeld and Rogoff 2009; Claessens, Dell'Ariccia, and Laeven 2010; Demirgüç-Kunt and Servén 2010; French et al. 2010; Barth, Caprio, and Levine 2012; and Calomiris and Haber 2014).

In discussing some of the root causes of the crisis, Caprio, Demirgüç-Kunt, and Kane (2010) point to specific regulatory failures that exacerbated or introduced distortions. First, structured securitization (pooling financial contracts to reap diversification benefits and allocate risk "efficiently" to "appropriate" counterparties) failed to provide the intended benefits and increased the risk of contagion in the financial system—see Ashcraft and Schuermann (2008) for an overview of the subprime mortgage securitization process. Moreover, bank capital regulation and arbitrary risk weights provided banks with incentives to move assets into off–balance sheet securitization vehicles. The complexity and opaqueness of securitization made it difficult to price these financial instruments, and the financial institutions that originated these products grew more complex and interlinked with other financial institutions, which made them more difficult to resolve in the event of a crisis and increased their potential claims to safety net subsidies.

Second, credit ratings for financial institutions were inaccurate, in part because those institutions paid the issuers for those ratings, which generated a conflict of interest for credit-rating agencies. In addition, although regulation favored the widespread use of credit ratings, it also limited the contestability of the credit-rating market.

Third, complex regulation had the double disadvantage of making the job of bank supervisors more difficult while also making them less accountable for their actions. Basel II introduced complexity both in the quantification of bank regulatory capital and in the computation of assets weighted for risk exposure. The supervisory review of banks' capital adequacy (also known as Pillar II) granted national regulators substantial discretion without differentiating across countries with different institutional environments and levels of supervisory capacity.

Finally, regulation aimed at strengthening market discipline (also known as Pillar III) ignored the role of financial deepening and economies of scale in the provisioning of public services. All of these factors contributed to more opportunities for regulatory arbitrage, reduction of transparency, and supervisory forbearance.

Caprio, Demirgüç-Kunt, and Kane (2010) conclude that complex methods for regulating risk-taking largely failed, and thus simpler (but effective) approaches to regulation and supervision are preferred, especially for developing countries. This conclusion ties in well with the concept of proportionality put forth in this report.

determinants of the stability of individual institutions. Macroprudential regulation targets factors that affect the stability of the financial system as a whole. Since the global financial crisis, macroprudential tools have been included in bank supervisors' toolkits in order to identify and curb the risks posed by individual banks to the overall financial system.

Macroprudential and microprudential tools differ in their focus and in the skill sets necessary for their effective employment. Moreover, effective use of these instruments by bank supervisory agencies involves the availability of adequate information, resources, and qualified personnel.

The measures undertaken by governments during crises to restore trust in domestic financial systems and avoid their collapse contain important lessons for developing countries. Overall, there is broad agreement that elementary regulatory features—the so-called basics—should be addressed first. This means having well-capitalized banks able to weather "normal" and "distressed" market conditions and establishing a coherent institutional and legal framework that hinges on market discipline, complemented by strong, timely, and anticipatory supervisory action. However, although the financial crisis produced some general lessons for developing countries, that does not imply that the regulation and supervisory practices adopted by advanced countries in the wake of the crisis should be adopted without modification by developing countries. Regulatory policies and supervisory approaches are likely to work differently in different country contexts.

PROPORTIONALITY: DESIGNING BANK REGULATION FOR DEVELOPING COUNTRIES

Sound economic reasons support the view that the state should play an active role in banking systems to mitigate the negative effects of market imperfections. But there are practical reasons to be wary of the state playing too active a role in banking systems. The tensions inherent in these two views capture the complexity of financial policies for the banking sector. Moreover, the same government policies that ameliorate one market imperfection could create other distortions. Regulations can be overly complex, and this complexity often entails worse outcomes because it may lead to manipulation and regulatory arbitrage. In addition, it places a burden on bank supervisors who, particularly in developing countries, may lack the capacity needed to enforce such regulations effectively.

Proportionality should therefore be a guiding principle in the design of bank regulation and supervision in developing countries. The concept of proportionality, which is deeply embedded in legal systems throughout the world, holds that the level of public intervention in the form of rules, restrictions, or sanctions should not exceed what is appropriate to achieve the desired social objectives.[9] In the context of designing bank regulation and supervision for developing countries, this report therefore defines *proportionality* as a set of regulations and supervisory tools and approaches that are appropriate to the institutional environment, supervisory capacity, and business models of banks in a given country.[10]

Proportionality can refer to differences in the appropriate regulatory/supervisory frameworks across countries or in the treatment of different banks operating within the same country.[11] Within banking sectors, proportionality can be used to justify the application of simplified prudential requirements for small or noncomplex institutions to reduce excessive compliance costs. Some observers make a distinction between proportionality in regulation, which refers to reducing the costs of compliance for banks, and proportionality in supervision, which focuses on the adjustment of supervisory intensity to the risk profile and size of individual banks. This report uses a data-driven approach to describe proportionality in both regulation and supervision. Because it focuses on differences in banking regulation and supervision across countries in the wake of the global financial crisis, most of the discussion of proportionality focuses on differences in appropriate frameworks across countries.

Proportionality implies that one-size-fits-all policies are not appropriate, especially in developing countries where the adoption of sophisticated rules designed for developed countries may not fit local circumstances. As briefly summarized in box 1.2, the Basel Committee on Banking Supervision (BCBS) is the main standard-setting body for bank regulation and supervision, and it is dominated

BOX 1.2 A Brief Historical Perspective on International Coordination and Harmonization in Banking Regulation and Supervision

The recent history of international coordination and harmonization in banking regulation and supervision dates back to 1986, when the U.S. Federal Reserve Board and the Bank of England agreed on a novel approach to regulating bank capital. Instead of simply enforcing a capital ratio computed as a bank's equity relative to the sum of its assets and off–balance sheet exposures, the U.S.–U.K. accord introduced a new denominator based on the weighting of assets according to exposure to credit risk (see chapter 3, table B3.1.1, for the key characteristics of regulatory capital instruments). This bilateral agreement influenced the first international set of capital standards issued in 1988 by the Basel Committee on Banking Supervision (BCBS), a committee of central bank representatives established by the central bank governors of the Group of 10 countries (G-10) at the end of 1974. This first accord, known as Basel I (BCBS 1988), focused on capital adequacy for internationally active banks and was intended for member countries, although most banking authorities worldwide ended up adopting its principles and enforcing the capital standards in all domestic banks. The overarching goal was to strengthen the stability of the international banking system and create a level playing field by removing a source of competitive inequality stemming from differences in national capital requirements.

Over time, the membership of the BCBS increased, reaching 45 members from 28 jurisdictions and 9 observers, including by the end of 2016 central banks, supervisory groups, international organizations, and other bodies. The BCBS also saw an increase in the number of standards covering distinct aspects of the banking business, such as a broader range of risks (for example, market and operational risk) and effective risk disclosure. In the years that followed, the BCBS agreed on two new capital frameworks. Proposed in 2004, Basel II was finalized in 2006 (BCBS 2006). And Basel III, which comprised updated standards for capital regulation, was agreed to in 2010. It was revised in June 2011 (BCBS 2011) and updated in December 2017 (BCBS 2017a). Within the Basel III framework, two new liquidity standards—the liquidity coverage ratio and the net stable funding ratio—were revised in 2013 (BCBS 2013) and 2014 (BCBS 2014), respectively. These liquidity ratios are described in more detail later in this chapter. Most "developing" countries are not signatories to the Basel Accords and have no obligation to adopt the guidelines. Nevertheless, as explained in box 3.6, developing countries often adopt international standards to signal sophistication and strong domestic regulatory standards.

The 2007–09 global financial crisis highlighted the need for further international cooperation to promote stability in the international financial system. In 2009, the Financial Stability Board (FSB) replaced the Financial Stability Forum, which was established in the wake of the 1997–98 Asian crisis, and membership was expanded from the G-7 to the G-20 countries. The FSB now includes large emerging economies (such as Brazil, China, India, and Indonesia), and it has core responsibilities in monitoring and assessing vulnerabilities affecting the global financial system. Specifically, the FSB has coordinated the main financial reforms in the G-20 countries in the following priority areas: improving the resilience of financial institutions (such as through the Basel III reform agenda); addressing the too-big-to-fail issue (such as through resolution frameworks and minimum total loss absorbency capital requirements); increasing the safety of derivatives markets (such as through central clearing); enhancing the resilience of nonbank intermediation (also known as shadow banking); proposing sound compensation practices for large financial institutions; and strengthening adherence to international financial standards (FSB 2018b). The FSB has also evaluated the effects of reforms on specific areas, such as infrastructure finance and the clearing system for over-the-counter markets of financial derivatives. The financing of infrastructure by the financial sector is especially important for developing countries to support trade and economic development. The FSB evaluation found that there are no significant negative effects on the availability and cost of infrastructure finance because of the G-20 financial regulatory reforms in emerging and developing countries (FSB 2018a).

by a handful of advanced countries. Thus, policy designed for advanced countries may not reflect the idiosyncrasies of developing countries in terms of the purposes and powers of the regulatory agencies. At the same time, regulation and supervision proportional to different banking features can be difficult to design and enforce, resulting in greater financial fragility. Correcting market imperfections is a complicated task that requires considerable information and expertise to design, implement, and enforce sound policies. Government interventions in finance need to be risk-sensitive, but measuring risk properly and enforcing risk-based regulations are also complex tasks.

Complex regulation and supervision of the banking sector can be costly for smaller and less developed countries if there are economies of scale in the provision of public sector services. For example, over the last few decades central banks have taken on a more prominent role as lenders of last resort. However, the ability of central banks to provide liquidity in times of distress is limited in developing countries, especially when public and private debts are denominated in a foreign currency. Similarly, information generation and provision of ancillary financial services, such as credit ratings, tend to have high fixed costs. These require a certain level of market development, which can be difficult to achieve in developing countries because of a lack of scale and insufficient market depth.

Although proportionality is an important guiding principle, political considerations often influence the design of bank regulation and supervision. The dynamic outcomes of banking sector regulation stem from the supply and demand of regulation. Government is often the main supplier of regulation, and consumers and the banking industry are the main demanders. The industry has a disproportionate influence on the demand for regulation because benefits for other actors are dispersed, whereas the costs and benefits for the industry are concentrated. It follows, then, that bankers and the politically well-connected will have a marked influence on interaction with the government to determine the exact shape and purpose of regulation. Politicians and regulators are often subject to intense pressure from regulated firms to modify regulations, which can result in suboptimal regulation and supervision (Laffont and Tirole 1993). Accordingly, the political/regulatory capture view advocates a greater reliance on market discipline, information disclosure, loose regulation, and significant oversight of the regulatory process itself (Stigler 1971; Shleifer 2005). A country's banking system and its regulatory framework can therefore be characterized by the degree to which they are consistent with the institutions that govern the distribution of political power (Calomiris and Haber 2014). This report recognizes the importance of political economy in the design and adoption of bank regulation and supervision and attempts to identify the factors that drove regulatory and supervisory change in the wake of the global financial crisis.

Regardless of the level of development of a country and its banking sector, or the complexity of its approach to regulation and supervision, the independence of supervisors is crucial to achieving a banking system that functions well. This independence provides credibility, helps avoid political pressures, and limits regulatory forbearance. Bank supervisors assess who is appropriate and qualified to enter the banking industry, help banks exit when they fail to comply with the various rules, and verify the accuracy of the information that banks publish. In general, the incentives and accountability of bank supervisors for their decisions and actions will have an important bearing on the effectiveness of regulation and supervision.

NARROWING THE FOCUS: CAPITAL, PRIVATE MONITORING, AND SUPERVISION

The global financial crisis called into question the role of financial policy in banking, revealing major shortcomings in market discipline, regulation, and supervision. The immediate reaction was to fix alleged deficiencies and weaknesses in bank regulation and supervisory monitoring to contain the crisis and to prevent repetition of those events. The postcrisis reforms called for more and better-quality bank capital and higher bank liquidity. Nevertheless, as revealed by previous crises, the regulatory reform cycle eventually runs its course, reaching a point at which the distant memory of the crisis and confidence in the measures introduced to avoid a financial crisis can generate a false sense of safety and accomplishment. The focus should, however, always remain on the implications of the regulatory changes for incentives and competition.

Bank capital regulation, market discipline, and bank supervision are interrelated and may complement or substitute for each other in different contexts. Bank capital regulation curbs the adverse incentives created by deposit insurance. Market discipline may complement bank capital regulation by identifying undercapitalized credit institutions relative to risk exposure and exerting pressure on a bank's risk-taking behavior. Supervision of bank leverage and asset quality can also influence a bank's risk-taking behavior, and it may substitute for stricter capital regulation and greater scrutiny by market participants. Along the same lines, continuous scrutiny by market participants adds a shorter time horizon to the medium- to long-term perspective often adopted by bank supervisors. For example, market discipline may work as a restraining device and substitute for government regulatory oversight of banks.[12]

A key purpose of bank capital regulation is to internalize the social costs of potential bank failures. The imposition of capital requirements can have a stabilizing effect on banks because such requirements give bank owners ex ante incentives to improve risk management and curb excessive risk-taking. As noted, because of limited liability, shareholders of a defaulted bank can lose up to their initial investment. This upper bound for potential losses prods bank shareholders to take on more risk than is socially optimal. If shareholders were liable for all the unpaid debts of a failed bank, their risk-taking behavior would be sharply curtailed. Consistent with this argument that identifies bank capital as a key "incentive" mechanism, several theories emphasize that higher capitalization improves the borrower screening and risk monitoring functions of banks, thereby reducing individual bank risk-taking (Holmstrom and Tirole 1997; Coval and Thakor 2005; Allen, Carletti, and Marquez 2011; Mehran and Thakor 2011).

Depositors and creditors also influence banks' risk-taking behavior. Binding capital requirements affect the liability composition of banks, and, depending on the heterogeneity of bank debtholders, debt can be an effective disciplining device for banks' excessive risk-taking behavior. According to Diamond and Rajan (2000, 2001), optimally banks would have a fragile capital structure, relying on demand deposits to force them to behave well, thereby avoiding a bank run. Nevertheless, in the presence of uncertainty, an all-debt capital structure could be too fragile, and bankers must invest some equity to trade the disciplining role of debt off against the fragility it creates. Moreover, and as noted earlier, monitoring by debtholders has its own limitations. Aside from hurdles related to the lack of information and expertise, asset risk is not priced fairly by banks' creditors (such as depositors and bondholders) because of the implicit or explicit financial safety net, and thus banks do not fully internalize asset losses in their risk-taking behavior. The state of the world therefore matters in choosing the appropriate combination of debt and equity, leading to efficient transfers of control to creditors and encouraging portfolio diversification and truthful revelation of investment outcomes, all of which can reduce funding costs.[13] In short, important context-specific trade-offs must be considered in designing the right blend of capital requirements and monitoring by banks' creditors.

Bank supervision can enable bank monitoring by depositors and market participants by increasing the information available for monitoring. In this regard, it is important to build up supervisory capacity to enforce existing rules and, as a by-product, produce information useful for a risk assessment of banks. New challenges are constantly emerging in the private sector that regulators and supervisors have to address, such as the regulation and supervision of new services and products using financial innovations and the risks associated with financial technology (see box 1.3 for an illustration of the challenges in regulating and supervising fintech and cybersecurity). By the same token, accounting standards should enable a faithful representation of bank operations and provide useful information to facilitate banking supervisors'

BOX 1.3 Regulation and Supervision of Fintech Companies and Cybersecurity

Fintech companies and challenges related to cybersecurity have recently been on the minds of regulators. *Fintech* can be defined as technologically enabled innovation in financial services that could result in new business models, applications, processes, or products affecting financial markets, institutions, and the provision of financial services (FSB 2017a; BCBS 2018b). Fintech covers a large number of technologies (cryptography, cloud computing, and data analytics, among others), products, and services. However, a specific current challenge for bank regulators is the outsourcing of functions and processes to entities not subject to bank regulation and supervision. Examples are cloud computing and multiple entry points for the payment system (such as mobile and Internet payment providers).

The challenge for prudential regulation and supervision is how to define the regulatory perimeter and supervise the outsourced activities of regulated financial intermediaries. Fintech is transforming the way in which traditional financial institutions run their back offices and front-line procedures. Often, regulated financial intermediaries enter into partnerships with third-party providers for services. These providers assume specialized roles that can vary widely, from credit scoring to prepaid account management or data storage. Third-party providers are often unregulated, or they are regulated by national regulators other than the financial sector regulator, or regulated in home countries. In such instances, a large segment of the "financial production chain" is outside of the regulatory perimeter, and questions about system safety, data ownership, and access remain unresolved. If third-party providers are regulated by a nonfinancial sector regulator or a home supervisor, challenges of coordination between supervisors can emerge. Reliance on a large body of data and technology also makes financial institutions vulnerable to cyberattacks.

Fintech has led to the emergence of new players, primarily technology firms, that have started providing financial services, from payments to loans and investment opportunities. Examples are Apple, Tencent, and Ant Financial. Because the authority of most regulators is defined by the type of firms they oversee, these new entrants fall outside of the existing regulatory perimeters. Such providers could become systemically important, especially in the payment system, because they can create critical interdependencies for other institutions. To allow for experimentation and yet limit the emergence of systemic risk, several regulators have decided to create test environments for fintech, including sandboxes. For example, the Financial Conduct Authority in the United Kingdom launched a regulatory sandbox in June 2016 to test new products and services in a customized regulatory environment, and Mexico established a sandbox for fintech companies in 2018 through the Law Regulating the Financial Technology Institutions (the Fintech Law).

Cybersecurity is a very different kind of operational risk that recently became a top priority for banks and bank regulatory agencies. As defined in the Basel II capital framework, *operational risk* is the "risk of loss resulting from inadequate or failed internal processes, people and systems or from external events" (BCBS 2006). In 2016 and 2017, financial services was the sector most frequently attacked, experiencing 27 percent of total security incidents and 17 percent of attacks respectively (IBM 2018). In 2016, for example, 4 of 35 fake instructions sent via the Swift network were enough to steal US$81 million from the account of Bangladesh Bank at the New York Federal Reserve Bank (*New York Times* 2018). In 2017 the massive exfiltration of data from a major U.S. credit reporting firm affected more than 145 million persons (*Register* 2018). As the reliance of the financial services sector on information technology increases, including in the management of customer relationships, its information security challenges are likely to become even more prominent. In view of the spread of highly contagious malware, such as the

(box continued next page)

BOX 1.3 Regulation and Supervision of Fintech Companies and Cybersecurity *(continued)*

waves of ransomware that temporarily paralyzed the world's leading shipping company (ZDNet 2018) and a major U.S. city in 2018 (CNN 2018), it is not difficult to imagine a similar incident eventually crippling an entire national financial system.

Because cybersecurity is related to disruptions in information technology (IT), perhaps it is not surprising that too many bank senior managers still believe that the solution, if it exists at all, must also be technological. In 2015, for example, a World Bank survey of Eastern European central banks on cyber preparedness found that, although the strongest self-assessments corresponded to technical issues under the charge of IT departments, the weakest ones were related to areas typically in the hands of senior management, the governor, or the board (Almansi 2018a). At about the same time, Accenture found a similar gap among the CEOs and board members of the largest banks in the world (Lumb, Macchi, and Moreno 2016). Inadequate managerial attention to information security issues may not only result in a suboptimal allocation of resources but also hamper the response to cyber incidents. After all, top decision makers cannot delegate to their IT staff critical business continuity decisions, such as assuming the cost of immediately shutting down an infected system or taking the risk of keeping it going while cybersecurity specialists search for a solution.

Although cyber risk is a type of operational risk, the old prescriptions for confronting operational risks may no longer apply. The World Bank has compiled and regularly updates a digest of the growing body of cybersecurity guidance and regulations that national jurisdictions, multilateral agencies, and other organizations have been publishing (Financial Sector Advisory Center 2017). Particularly challenging for old approaches is dealing with the evergrowing outsourcing of information technology services, including the processing of transactions and the storing of data by third-party "cloud" providers. Connectivity among financial sector institutions, and between them and everybody else, necessitates coordination between financial sector authorities and other state agencies, both in the regulation of minimum cybersecurity standards and in the response to cyber incidents (Almansi 2018b).

assessments of bank risk exposures. The overall message is that capital, monitoring, and supervision all influence each other and must work in concert to ensure efficient credit allocation while preserving banking sector stability. The remainder of this chapter therefore describes developments on these three fronts in the wake of the global financial crisis.

LATEST TRENDS IN BANK REGULATION AND SUPERVISION IN DEVELOPING AND HIGH-INCOME COUNTRIES

Using the latest data released from the World Bank's Bank Regulation and Supervision Survey (BRSS), this report investigates the regulatory reforms undertaken in the 10 years since the onset of the global financial crisis. As summarized in box O.1 in the overview, five waves of the BRSS are available, and the latest wave summarizes regulatory developments that characterized the period 2011–16. The fourth wave of the BRSS covered the reforms in the immediate aftermath of the crisis, but most of those changes were marginal (Čihák et al. 2012) and did not fully reflect the regulatory reforms subsequently undertaken by countries. However, the fifth wave of the BRSS allows a full assessment of the regulatory reforms enacted in high-income and developing countries in core areas such as capital regulation, regulations enhancing market discipline, and supervisory monitoring. Although financial regulatory reforms undertaken since the financial crisis have touched on different areas, such as cross-border cooperation and the resolution of systemically important banks (SIBs), the analysis in this section focuses on the core aspects of reform that are central to financial regulation (Anginer et al. 2019).

BANK REGULATORY CAPITAL

The level of bank regulatory capital has increased over time; however, some elements of capital regulations have become more lax. The global financial crisis highlighted the risk of having thin capital buffers to cover unexpected losses. Banks were also found to have low-quality capital in terms of loss absorbency. As explained in chapter 3, bank capital can be defined as accounting capital, regulatory capital, or economic capital. From a financial stability perspective, a key role of bank capital is to increase the resilience of banks to cope with unexpected losses in their asset portfolios. Basic questions are then how to quantify the amount of capital relative to risk exposures and how to define the items counted as regulatory capital.

Worldwide, there has been a trend toward increasing minimum regulatory capital requirements to improve banking system resilience, although, on average, the trend has been more marked for developing countries than high-income ones. The mean value for high-income countries has changed little (figure 1.1, panel a), but these countries are also more apt to have in place additional capital

FIGURE 1.1 Banks' Capital Requirements, 2008–16

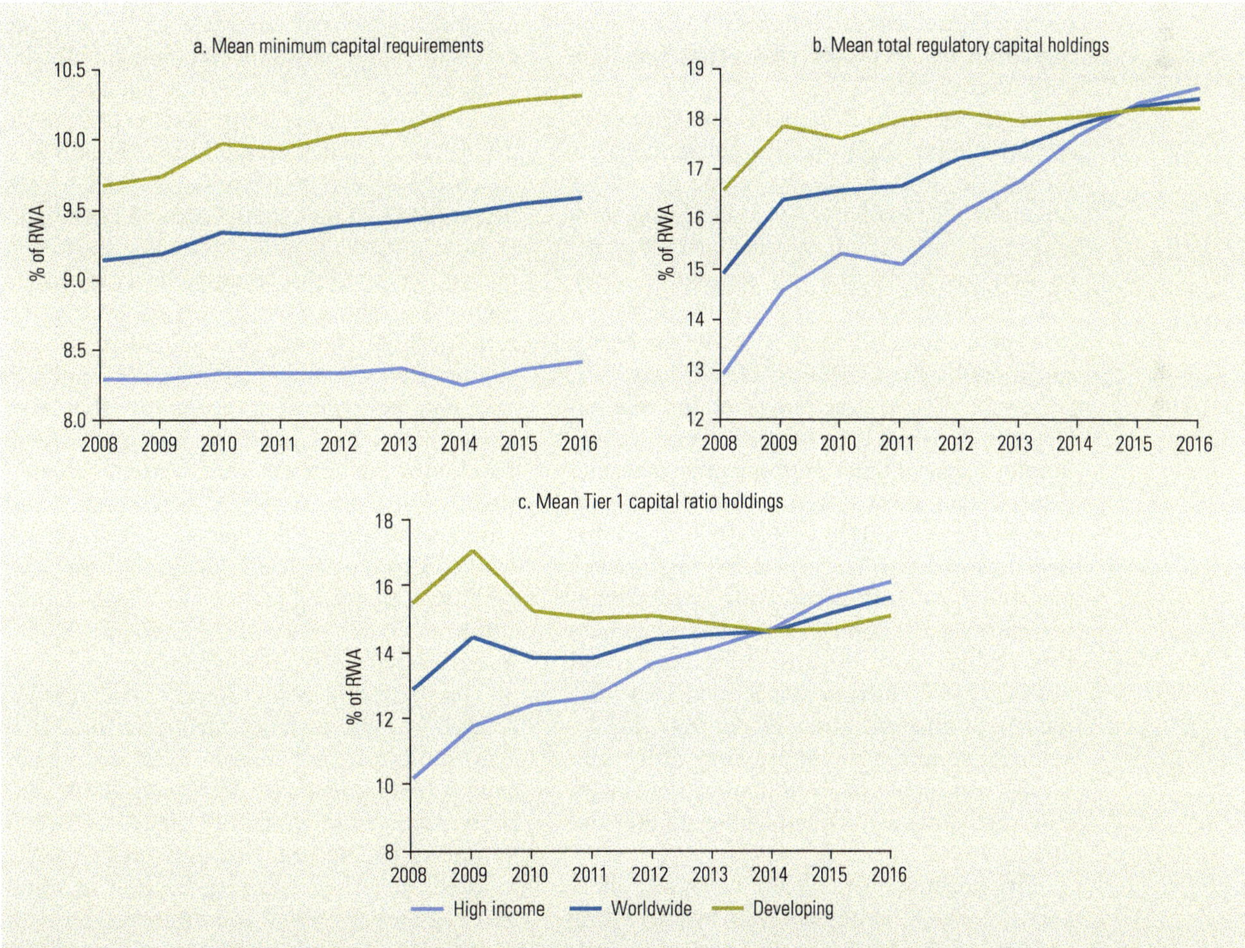

Source: Bank Regulation and Supervision Survey (BRSS), waves 4 and 5, https://www.worldbank.org/en/research/brief/BRSS.

Note: In this figure and subsequent figures, offshore financial centers are excluded from the computations. In panel a, 99 countries for which information is available over 2008–16 are included; in panel b, 82 countries; and in panel c, 65 countries. RWA = risk-weighted assets.

surcharges, meaning that the minimum regulatory capital set for banks is, in practice, higher than before the financial crisis. The increase in the minimum regulatory capital requirement has translated into higher levels of actual holdings of regulatory capital (figure 1.1, panel b). This is particularly true for high-income countries, where capital holdings increased from a mean value of 12.9 percent of risk-weighted assets (RWA) in 2008 to 18.6 percent of RWA in 2016. Developing countries, which began from a higher average level of regulatory capital holdings early in the period, saw an increase in capital through 2011, reaching roughly 18 percent of RWA. Since then, increases in regulatory capital among developing countries have been slower, and in 2016 the mean value of regulatory capital holdings for developing countries was lower than that for high-income countries.

Levels of Tier 1 capital, the regulatory capital component with the greatest capacity for loss absorption, also increased over time, driven by the new Basel III capital framework and regulatory capital reforms enacted at the country level. For the full sample of countries, the mean value of the Tier 1 capital ratio (Tier 1 capital divided by RWA), increased substantially from 2008 to 2016 (figure 1.1, panel c).[14] There were, however, notable differences between high-income countries and developing countries. High-income countries displayed an upward trend in the Tier 1 capital ratio between 2008 and 2016, a trend that began as early as 2005 (earlier years are not pictured in panel c). Because this trend continued through 2016, it indicates that the regulatory push to shore up bank capitalization was not exhausted in the period immediately after the global financial crisis. By contrast, for developing countries the mean value of the Tier 1 ratio was higher in 2008 than in 2016, with a marked downward trend between 2009 and 2014.

The adequacy of capital to cover unexpected losses can be achieved by increasing the level and quality of regulatory capital or by decreasing the regulatory measures factored into calculating total risk exposure. For the quality of bank capital, the global financial crisis highlighted the crucial importance of defining bank capital narrowly to improve bank performance in times of crisis. For example, the regulatory treatment of sovereign exposures has been the subject of heated debate, especially in Europe following the 2012 sovereign debt crisis because of the zero risk weight attributed to the sovereign bonds of fiscally distressed countries.[15]

Post–financial crisis increases in the Tier 1 capital ratio in high-income countries were accompanied by declines in RWA; improvements in simple leverage ratios were more limited. Large banks in high-income countries showed a modest increase in their leverage ratios (calculated as capital to total banking assets) from around 8 percent in 2008 to around 10 percent in 2014–15.[16] Leverage ratios for large banks in developing countries were generally flat, but with a small upward trend that took the ratio to 11 percent in 2014–15.[17] Their leverage ratios are still at a much lower level than those of small banks, despite the fact that small banks in both high-income and developing countries showed a marked decline in their simple leverage ratios (figure 1.2, panel a).[18] At the same time, the ratio of RWA to total banking assets was declining after the financial crisis for banks in high-income countries, especially for large banks (figure 1.2, panel b). For banks from developing countries, that ratio increased slightly after the crisis for large banks and remained relatively flat but volatile for small banks. Although figure 1.1 suggests that capital buffers increased for banks in high-income countries in the wake of the crisis, figure 1.2 indicates that this conclusion partly hinges on the decline in RWA. Recent academic literature (see for instance Gropp et al. 2019) also indicates that banks react to higher capital requirements by decreasing RWA proportionally more than they increase capital holdings. The accuracy of measures of RWA is therefore a key concern, bearing in mind that regulatory capital requirements set as a proportion of risk exposure were mostly dismissed by market participants at the time of the crisis because those risk exposures did not

FIGURE 1.2 Leverage and Risk Weights of Large Banks versus Rest of National Banking Systems, 2005–15

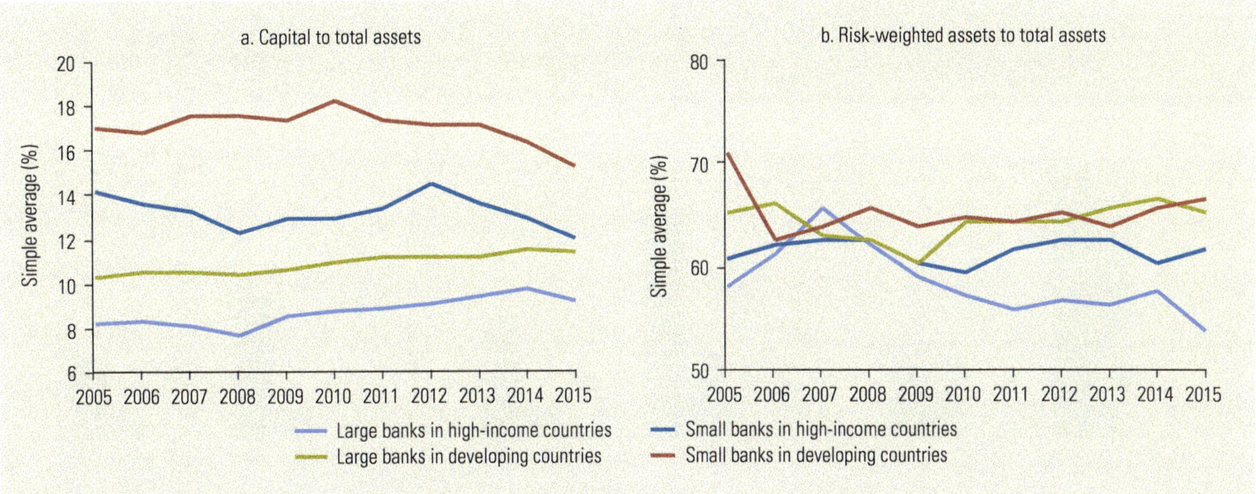

Sources: Archived data from Bankscope (Bureau van Dijk) and World Bank staff calculations.
Note: Large banks are defined as those at or above the 80th percentile of banks within each country, in each year, in terms of assets, whereas small banks constitute the rest of the banking system (that is, below the 80th percentile). Country-year observations are dropped if there are data for fewer than five banks. Simple averages are taken across banks to calculate country-level values and across country averages to compute values for income group levels.

adequately reflect actual risk (Demirgüç-Kunt, Detragiache, and Merrouche 2013).[19]

The fourth annual report of the Financial Stability Board (FSB 2018b) on the implementation and effects of the G-20 financial regulatory reforms indicates that large banks have almost doubled their risk-based capital ratios and halved their total assets over Tier 1 capital ratio, in line with findings reported in the 2018 Basel III monitoring report (BCBS 2018c). These results are not directly comparable with the data presented in figure 1.2 because of country coverage, type of banks considered in the analyses, and methodology. We offer an additional perspective because we report results for a larger number of banks and a larger number of developing countries and, among them, countries that are not current signatories to the Basel accords. The analyses in FSB (2108b) and BCBS (2018c) focus on the very largest banks (globally systemically important banks or top internationally active banks) in BIS-member countries, whereas the trends reported in figure 1.2 are computed using bank-level data for approximately 20,000 banks from a larger number of countries at all income levels.[20]

Because minimum regulatory thresholds for bank capital are set as a percentage of RWA, the "weighting" of bank assets to accurately reflect risk exposures is crucial. If banks reshuffle their portfolios toward assets that are truly risky but carry low risk weights (a form of regulatory arbitrage), the meaning of RWA can become distorted. Probing asset quality reviews (AQRs) have been used successfully, particularly in Europe, to dispel doubts about the valuations of bank assets.[21] A supplementary limit on a simple leverage measure has also been introduced in the Basel III international capital agreement (BCBS 2011). Nevertheless, because bank capital is a scarcer and costlier source of funding because of information (Majluf and Myers 1984) and managerial problems (Kashyap, Rajan, and Stein 2008), banks may prefer to meet the regulatory requirements using "hybrid" or "loophole" items or instruments whose capacity to absorb losses is less than that of straightforward shareholder-contributed capital.

Beyond the levels of the Tier 1 capital ratio, another element for appraising the quality of bank capital is the balance sheet items allowed in the computation of Tier 1 regulatory

FIGURE 1.3 Quality and Definition of Regulatory Bank Capital

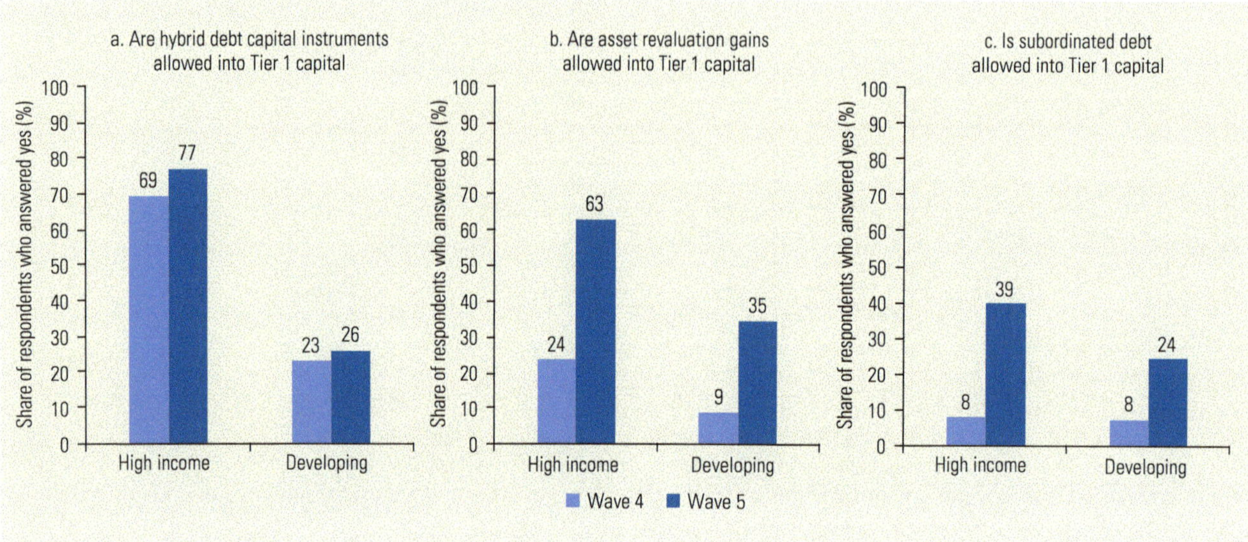

Source: Bank Regulation and Supervision Survey (BRSS), waves 4 and 5, https://www.worldbank.org/en/research/brief/BRSS.
Note: In this figure and in subsequent figures, the sample of countries is balanced over time. For example, a country that has information in wave 5 but not in wave 4 is excluded from the computations.

capital. As shown in figure 1.3, between BRSS waves 4 and 5 the number of countries allowing hybrid debt capital instruments, asset revaluation gains, and subordinated debt to be used in the computation of Tier 1 capital rose. Broadening the definition of Tier 1 capital in this way raises at least three concerns, especially for developing countries. First, a broader definition of bank capital may increase opacity for private monitors in assessing bank risk—an issue highlighted by the global financial crisis (see, for example, Haldane 2011). Second, there may be much less liquidity for debt contracts in developing countries where financial markets are less developed. And, third, the valuation of hybrid debt capital instruments, asset revaluation gains, and subordinated debt is inherently complex, placing a greater burden on supervisory authorities, which may lack the information, knowledge, and skills needed to review banks' capital calculations. According to an analysis of archived bank-level data from Bankscope (not presented here), hybrid debt capital instruments, asset revaluation gains, and subordinated debt comprised a small share of Tier 1 capital through 2015 (less than 5 percent). Concerns about these forms of capital may not therefore be pressing in the near term, although this is an issue that bears watching going forward.

Data from wave 5 reveal that since wave 4, some elements used to define the quality of bank capital have been relaxed, especially for developing countries. For example, 62 percent of developing countries answered that the initial disbursement or subsequent injections of capital cannot be carried out with assets other than cash or government securities—a lower percentage than in wave 4, indicating less stringency in initial capital provision from bank owners (figure 1.4, panel a). In addition, 60 percent of developing countries indicated that initial capital contributions by prospective shareholders cannot be in the form of borrowed funds—a lower percentage than that recorded in wave 4. For high-income countries, those ratios were very similar in BRSS waves 4 and 5. They were, however, substantially lower than for developing countries, indicating that advanced markets continue

FIGURE 1.4 Definition of Regulatory Capital

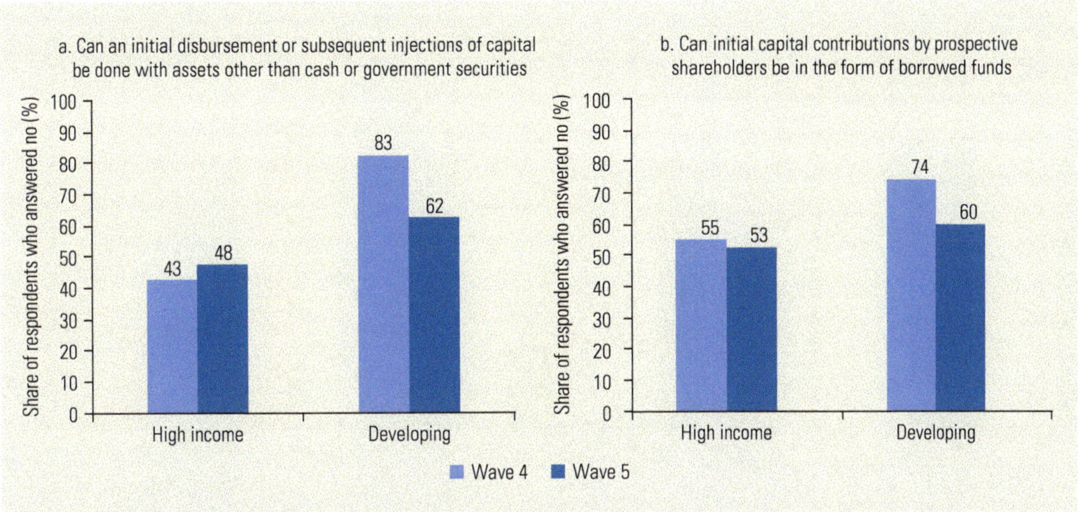

Source: Bank Regulation and Supervision Survey (BRSS), waves 4 and 5, https://www.worldbank.org/en/research/brief/BRSS.
Note: In panels a and b, a higher number entails greater stringency in the definition of capital.

to permit a wider set of options for satisfying initial capital requirements.

In the wake of the global financial crisis, bank capital regulations were complemented with macroprudential tools aimed at increasing systemic stability. Examples of the tools introduced since the crisis are countercyclical capital buffers, stress testing, and liquidity requirements.[22] Countercyclical capital buffers provide banks with additional capital cushions at times of distress. During "good times," banks can save capital for use during periods of financial distress instead of shrinking their assets or trying to raise new capital under distress. Stress-testing gives bank supervisors a means of forcing individual banks to hold more capital. Capital ratios are projected at the end of one or more periods under a stress scenario (for example, a prolonged fall in housing prices). Bank supervisors can force a bank to hold more capital if the projected capital ratio drops under a predetermined regulatory threshold (Wall 2014). Liquidity requirements address situations in which distress is caused by financial losses that make it difficult for banks to raise funds (funding illiquidity) or to sell assets at non–fire sale prices (market illiquidity). Liquidity crises can affect all banks indiscriminately rather than being specific to certain institutions (Brunnermeier et al. 2009). By imposing regulatory thresholds that limit maturity mismatches between assets and liabilities, regulators could reduce the risk of bank runs and the freezing of interbank markets because of illiquidity.

According to BRSS data, the percentage of countries where stress-testing is conducted as part of their systemic stability assessment decreased between waves 4 and 5. For both high-income and developing countries, slight decreases were observed between the waves in the percentage of countries that employ this tool to assess the macro stability of the banking sector, although the vast majority still reported that they use this tool. In countries that no longer conduct stress-testing, supervisors may have less leverage to compel banks with risky exposures to raise more capital. At the same time, the credibility of the stress-testing approach and the ability of bank supervisors to address potential revealed weakness are crucial factors for the successful use of this tool (Wall 2014). For example, in the European Union in 2010 and 2011, stress-testing undermined the credibility of the supervisory agency in the eyes of market participants

FIGURE 1.5 Capital Regulations: Complementary Tools

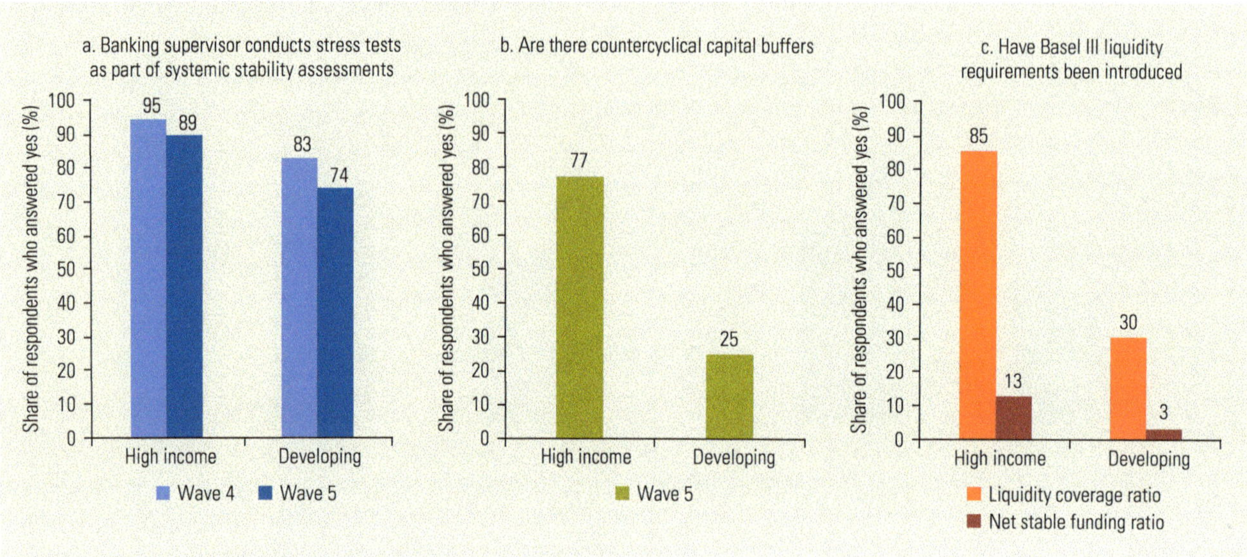

Source: Bank Regulation and Supervision Survey (BRSS), wave 5, https://www.worldbank.org/en/research/brief/BRSS.
Note: The questions reported in panels b and c were introduced in wave 5 of the BRSS.

because the scenarios used were not realistic. For lower-income countries, it may be wise to learn from the experience of high-income countries before fully implementing this supervisory approach.

A higher percentage of high-income countries than developing countries have introduced countercyclical capital buffers. Only one in four developing countries has added this measure to its bank supervisory toolkit, compared with 77 percent of high-income countries (figure 1.5, panel b). Because adoption of this tool implies the development of sound dynamic analyses to assess whether bank credit growth implies excessive risks, developing country authorities should first consider the implementation challenges in terms of availability of resources and supervisory powers (such as the power to restrict profit distributions) to adapt the use of countercyclical capital buffers to the specificities of their domestic credit cycles.

Basel III liquidity requirements also have been adopted more by high-income countries than by developing countries. A lower percentage of developing countries have adopted both the liquidity coverage ratio (LCR), which refers to the ratio of unencumbered, high-quality liquid assets to net cash outflows under an acute 30-day stress scenario (BCBS 2011), and the net stable funding ratio (NSFR), which is the minimum amount of available stable funding relative to the required amount of regulatory stable funding over one year. The adoption rate is higher for the LCR because the NSFR was introduced only toward the end of 2014 and the BCBS agreed-on implementation date was January 2018 (figure 1.5, panel c). Moreover, implementing liquidity standards in developing countries could be more difficult because of concentration risk (such as higher holdings of sovereign debt), dependence on wholesale funding, low availability of high-quality domestic securities, and high loan-to-deposit ratios (Basel Consultative Group 2014; Jones and Zeitz 2017).

Overall, although capital ratios are at their highest levels since the financial crisis, supervisors would be wise to interpret them with caution. The increase in the Tier 1 capital ratio for banks in high-income countries has been accompanied by a decline in RWA (as a share of total banking assets). A deeper understanding of whether and how banks have shifted assets to categories with lower risk weights is likely needed in many country contexts. It may also be wise to question whether lower risk weights are an accurate reflection of actual risk across asset types. Looking forward, BRSS wave 5 responses indicate that a wider array of instruments is permitted to satisfy Tier 1 capital requirements and that noncash assets, including borrowed funds, are increasingly permitted in banks' initial capital formation in developing countries. Even though few banks have relied heavily on the new instruments and noncash options to date, that, too, is an issue worth monitoring. So far, macroprudential tools related to capital and liquidity have not been widely adopted by developing countries, a situation that is likely attributable to the difficulties faced in adapting those approaches to local contexts.

MARKET DISCIPLINE

Market discipline may have deteriorated because of bank bailouts that undermind long-term incentives for private monitoring. Based on the latest BRSS responses, market discipline may have waned because of weaker incentives to monitor bank risk-taking. Deposit insurance coverage has increased, and government interventions in the banking sector to rescue ailing banks have likely weakened the incentives of market participants to monitor banks' risk-taking behavior. This outcome has likely encouraged banks—especially large banks—to take on excessive risk. Moreover, according to the BRSS wave 5 responses, the information available to assess the risk profile of banks is now less expansive than it was in 2008–10, the years covered by wave 4.

Bank monitoring by market participants is influenced by the presence of an explicit deposit insurance scheme, which can reduce the incentives of depositors to monitor banks. Today, many more countries have explicit deposit insurance than before the financial crisis (104 in wave 5 versus 88 in wave 4).[23] Furthermore, the existing schemes have become more generous in some countries because deposit insurance funds can be used for purposes other than depositor protection (meaning that uninsured liability holders might be covered),[24] coverage has been expanded, and the amount insured has been increased.

Expansions of deposit insurance coverage and scope may have helped to restore confidence in banking sectors across the globe, but these expansions have likely come at a cost in terms of market discipline. With only

FIGURE 1.6 Deposit Insurance Protection Scheme

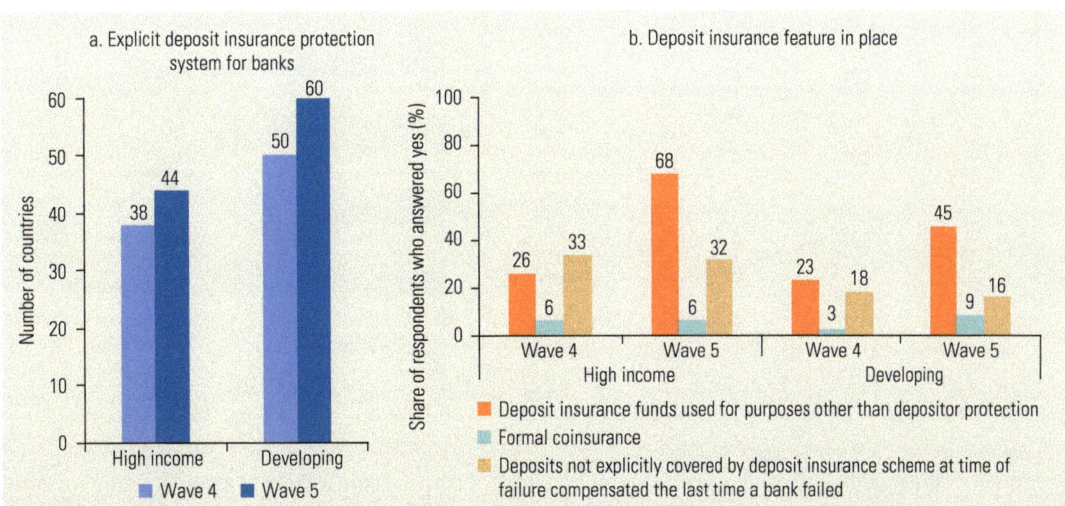

Source: Bank Regulation and Supervision Survey (BRSS), waves 4 and 5, https://www.worldbank.org/en/research/brief/BRSS.

a few exceptions, there have been no contagious runs by retail depositors in recent years (Hasan et al. 2017). Although adequate funding of the financial safety net is crucial for deposit insurance to be credible, an overreaction to restore public confidence in the banking system in the short term can ultimately be destabilizing over the longer term. Limited (but credible) ex ante funding commitments are therefore crucial in three important respects. First, they limit excessive risk-taking incentives by banks. Second, they limit the amount of taxpayer funds potentially at risk. Finally, they help to harmonize insurance schemes in common banking areas to limit regulatory arbitrage.

Government intervention to avoid or curtail a banking crisis can undermine market discipline. Although governments are expected to intervene in a systemic crisis, the approach and the actions taken have a clear link to future moral hazard if banks perceive that they will be bailed out during future crises, thereby increasing their willingness to risk insolvency. By increasing expectations of future rescues, some types of government interventions (such as blanket guarantees and extensive liquidity support to insolvent institutions) may also undermine incentives for monitoring by market participants (Demirgüç-Kunt and Servén 2010).

The response to the global financial crisis by governments and central banks was quite extensive. Although crisis response policies smoothed the impact of the financial crisis on the real economy,[25] they also extended the safety net to banks' shareholders, executives, and debtholders to an unprecedented degree. Those actions may therefore have intensified moral hazard for banks' decision makers going forward. As reported in figure 1.7, panel a, the contingent liabilities to support financial institutions in the 28 countries making up the European Union (EU) peaked in 2009 at around 11 percent of their gross domestic product (GDP).[26] Government assets and liabilities for crisis support reached around 5 percent and 6 percent of GDP, respectively. Even though the aggregate government support had fallen by 2017, it was still more than 6 percent of the EU-28's GDP. Furthermore, figure 1.7, panel b, documents that bank liability guarantees and recapitalizations were more prevalent during and after

FIGURE 1.7 Government Interventions to Rescue Banking Sectors

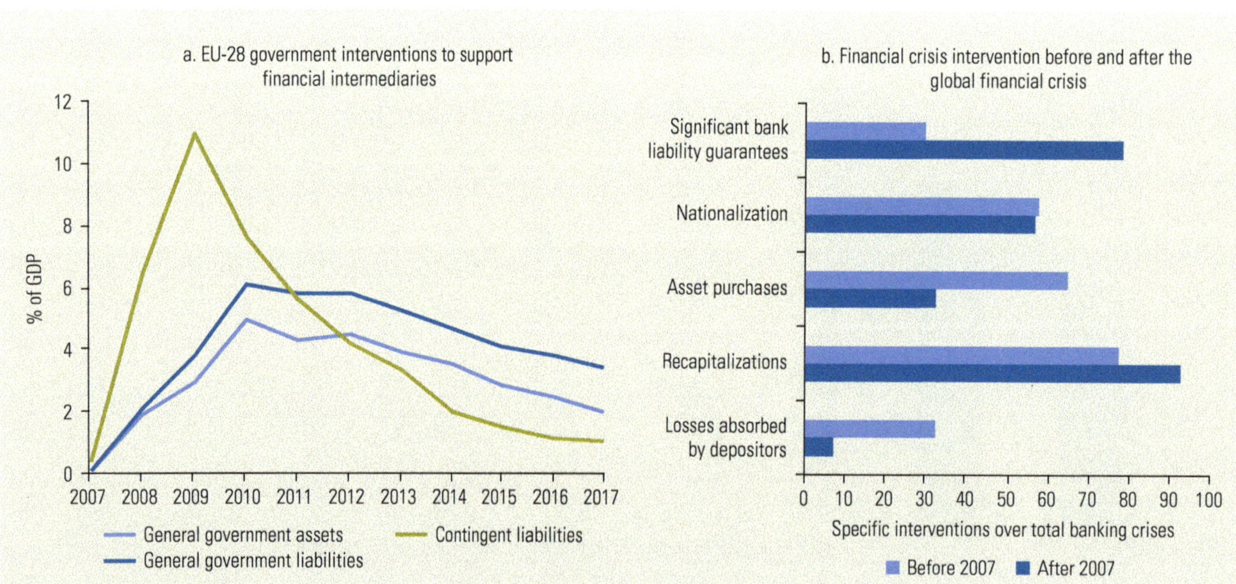

Sources: Panel a: Eurostat (database, European Commission); panel b: Laeven and Valencia 2018.

the recent crisis than during banking crises before 2007. Losses imposed on depositors were very rare, occurring in less than 10 percent of the banking crises after 2007, whereas depositors suffered losses in more than 30 percent of the banking crises before the global crisis. These government interventions imply that at least part of the real costs of the crisis was not shouldered by the responsible parties.

Although the global financial crisis was a developed country crisis, policy makers and supervisors in countries at other levels of economic development can gain insights from the experience. According to Laeven and Valencia (2018), of the 24 countries that experienced either a systemic banking crisis or a borderline systemic crisis during 2007–09, just two were lower-middle-income countries—Ukraine (box 1.4) and Nigeria—and two were upper-middle-income countries—Kazakhstan and the Russian Federation. One insight was that as economies grow and

BOX 1.4 Bank Resolution Cases: The Ukrainian Banking Crises

The Ukrainian banking crises are a clear illustration of the issues associated with resolving distressed banks in developing countries. In the 15 years leading up to the global financial crisis, Ukraine's boom-and-bust cycles were reflected in its banking sector performance. The sector enjoyed very high growth rates in the mid-2000s under a favorable financial and economic outlook. Private sector credit increased exponentially in the run-up to the crisis, from 33 percent of GDP in 2005 to 80 percent in 2008. Foreign lenders financed most of this credit boom, and at the end of 2008, foreign currency loans constituted about half of lending to nonfinancial firms and almost 65 percent of lending to households. Nontransparent ownership structures, pocket banks (banks run by business owners as a vehicle to fund nonfinancial undertakings), ineffective corporate governance arrangements, distorted financial statements, and ineffective bank supervision were also defining characteristics of the Ukrainian banking system.

The first systemic crisis struck Ukraine in 2009. The combination of a sudden stop in capital inflows, the rapid depreciation of the hryvnia, and a precipitous economic slowdown hit the banking sector hard. Banks felt the immediate effects of the drying up of foreign financing in 2009, and the devaluation of the hryvnia and a crisis in the country's sixth-largest bank triggered a deposit run. Amplified by the drastic deterioration of economic conditions—the country contracted by 15 percent in 2009—acute asset quality pressures emerged, with nonperforming loan (NPL) shares increasing from 17 percent to 40 percent. The central bank embarked on a series of emergency measures such as large-scale liquidity support, controls on early withdrawals of time deposits, restrictions on foreign currency lending, an increase in deposit insurance coverage, and state-funded recapitalization of five banks, while more than 20 banks were liquidated. However, these crisis containment measures were temporary fixes that did little to address the vulnerabilities that had built up in the sector.

Ukraine experienced a short-lived recovery but relapsed into a financial crisis, with the backdrop of a domestic political crisis and external security threats. In 2014 the government began to revoke the licenses of more than half of Ukraine's 180 banks. As of October 2018, 88 banks had been liquidated by the Deposit Guarantee Fund (which in 2012 became the resolution authority), with losses exceeding US$20 billion incurred by the state and by uninsured depositors. Affected shareholders have on occasion successfully challenged the authorities' decision to take action against banks that are considering failing or otherwise not compliant with regulatory requirements. Meanwhile, the political consensus necessary to bring the owners and management to justice for causing banks to fail was lacking.

Today, together with the International Monetary Fund and the World Bank, Ukrainian authorities are undertaking a sustained effort to restore the long-term health of the banking sector. And yet the aftermath of a cumulative 16 percent decline in real GDP in 2014–15, lingering national security tensions, and downward pressure on the currency continue to stress the Ukrainian financial system, as illustrated by further increases in the NPL ratio, which reached 55 percent of gross loans at the end of 2017. A framework for the resolution and recapitalization of banks

(box continued next page)

BOX 1.4 Bank Resolution Cases: The Ukrainian Banking Crises *(continued)*

has been established in an effort to curb the excessive bank risk-taking. Banks have also been forced to provide a more realistic representation of credit risk, and work has continued to reduce related party exposures and enforce transparency in ownership structures. Bank recapitalization plans and timely enforcement actions have helped to strengthen solvency in the sector, although the resolution of problem banks in a manner that maximizes asset recovery while minimizing costs to the state continues to present a considerable challenge.

The Ukrainian experience provides a sobering illustration of the importance of establishing the basics of effective prudential supervision. These include issues related to concealed and underreported related party exposures, shareholder transparency, deficient frameworks for licensing and transfer of ownership of banks, regulatory and supervisory gaps in the recognition of and provisioning for problem assets, and the lack of independence and resources for bank regulatory agencies. Going forward, bank bailouts and a generous deposit insurance system may have the unintended consequences of both undermining the incentives of market participants and encouraging excessive risk-taking behavior by banks.

develop their debt and tax capacity, implicit deposit insurance guarantees are likely to reduce the incentives of market participants to discipline bank behavior.

In the post–financial crisis period, there was recognition that market discipline could be undermined by government intervention in the banking sector. An effort to design clear rules to wind down distressed institutions was undertaken by many countries while recognizing the key role of banks for well-functioning economies. Furthermore, there was explicit recognition by the Financial Stability Board and other international bodies that larger and more interconnected banks presented a critical challenge because of the economic and political ramifications of their failure. This effort led governments to shore up resolution frameworks by, for example, creating separate procedures for banks and nonfinancial firms. It remains to be seen how much those frameworks will influence the expectations of market participants that governments will step in to rescue ailing banks, especially considering the frequency and size of recapitalizations and liquidity support during recent crises.

Insolvency resolution schemes were redesigned to give banks' shareholders and managers incentives to encourage the prudent management of banks. For example, some governments introduced regulation that forces banks' creditors to bear some of the burden of banks' defaults by having a portion of their debt written off (also known as "bail-in" regulations). Calomiris and Herring (2013) argue that the effective design of convertible contingent capital (a type of bail-in instrument) can provide banks with ex ante incentives to measure risk accurately and ex post incentives to raise additional capital in a timely fashion when it is depleted. An important distinction was also made in terms of the size of individual institutions and the potential domestic and international impact of distressed institutions. The Financial Stability Board has been publishing the list of globally systemically important banks (G-SIBs) since 2014. Since 2012, there has also been discussion of adapting the policy framework for G-SIBs to domestic systemically important banks (D-SIBs). Both G-SIBs and D-SIBs are discussed in greater detail in chapter 2.

Also in the postcrisis period, more than three-quarters of high-income countries and nearly one-third of developing countries introduced creditor bail-in initiatives, which should have enhanced market discipline (figure 1.8, panel a). Moreover, to limit disruptions after bank defaults, banks were required to submit plans that detailed a strategy for rapid and orderly resolution in the event of material financial distress or failure (resolution plans

FIGURE 1.8 New Resolution Rules and Bail-In Debt Requirements

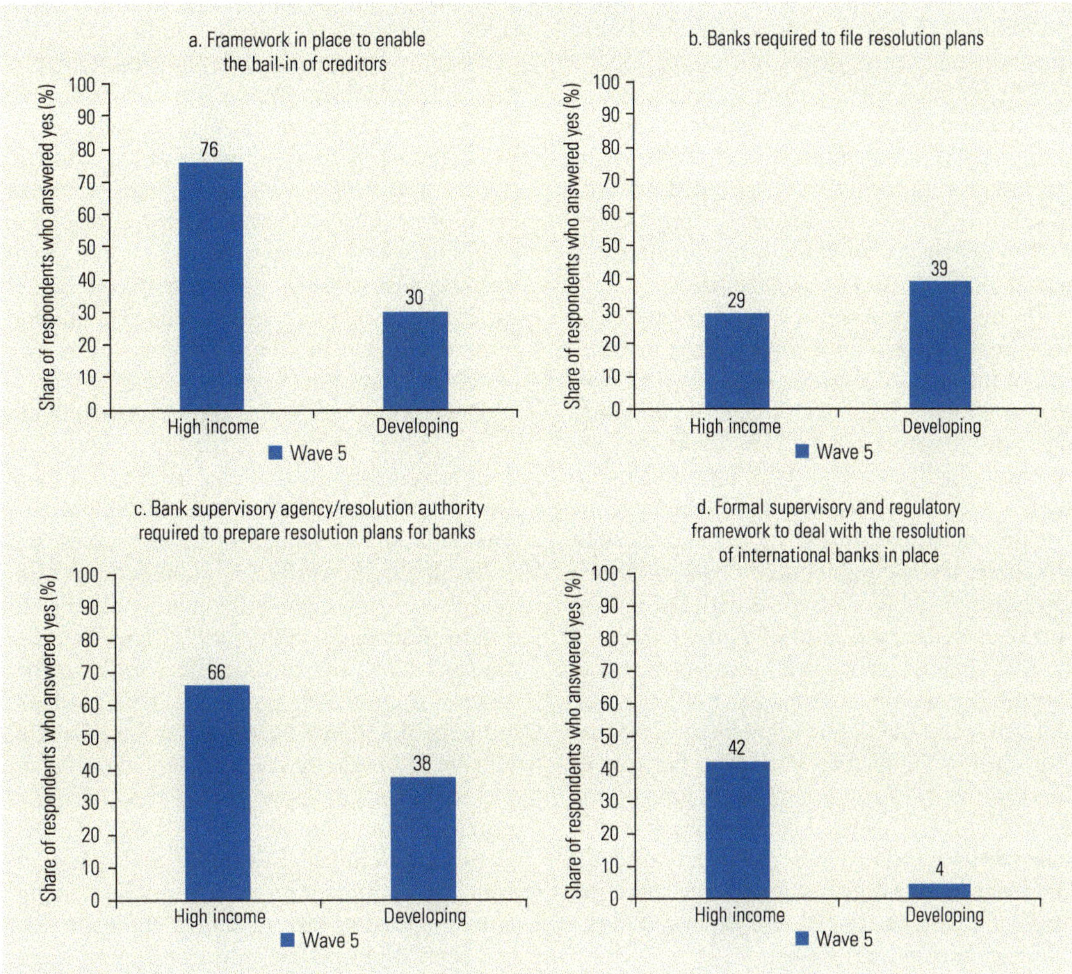

Source: Bank Regulation and Supervision Survey (BRSS), wave 5, https://www.worldbank.org/en/research/brief/BRSS.
Note: The questions reported in this figure were introduced in wave 5 of the BRSS.

also known as "living wills"). As reported in figure 1.8, panel b, almost two-fifths of developing countries had this requirement in place by the end of 2016. Resolution plans could also be prepared by the bank supervisory agency or the resolution authority. As shown in figure 1.8, panel c, two out of three high-income countries opted for this arrangement, whereas the relative take-up by developing countries has been lower. To be sure, until the next crisis bail-ins and "living wills" are untested, and many observers are skeptical that they will work as advertised because of authorities' reluctance to allow large-scale losses on their watch.

After the crisis, new rules were also put in place to resolve systemically important financial institutions (SIFIs). SIFIs are invariably holding companies that can own both bank and nonbank subsidiaries. This effort addressed concerns that disorderly liquidation of SIFIs could cause significant disruptions in financial systems. Because their failure can cause substantial economic damage, they are viewed by market participants as being too big to fail (TBTF). To strengthen market discipline and to reduce the likelihood that taxpayer funds will be at risk, several countries implemented single point of entry resolution processes for bank holding companies and added new requirements for systemically important banks to hold bail-in debt following guidelines set by the Financial Stability Board (discussed in greater detail in chapter 2). But new regulations for the orderly resolution of SIFIs are still untested, and because of changes in the way SIFIs are monitored by supervisors and the presumption that those entities would be safe or "saved" in case of distress, investors' incentives to monitor large or interconnected entities could be undermined.

Domestic regulations and cooperation with host countries for cross-border resolution of international banks are crucial in markets in which a high percentage of the banking system's assets are held by banks that are foreign-controlled. The banking sectors in many developing countries are dominated by foreign-owned banks, but by the end of 2016 just three developing countries had in place a regulatory framework to deal with the resolution of international banks (figure 1.8, panel d). Although there has been some progress in adopting measures to enhance market discipline, many of the newly implemented mechanisms are still untested. Moreover, because of the complexity of foreign banks in developing countries, there is also a case for greater reliance on leverage ratios because it is difficult for local authorities to determine whether banks are gaming the risk weights used in the calculation of capital ratios.

For effective monitoring, market participants must have access to reliable and timely data relevant to the economic condition of a bank. The adequacy of a country's accounting standards is paramount for the reliable provision and analysis of such data. For instance, the use of International Accounting Standard 39 (IAS 39—Financial Instruments: Recognition and Measurement) may have exacerbated the declines in the value of collateralized debt obligations (CDOs).[27] The latest International Financial Reporting Standards 9 (IFRS 9 Financial Instruments) was introduced as a regulatory response to the unsatisfactory performance of the previous accounting standards. Nonetheless, using the fair value approach to appraise financial assets in many developing countries is problematic because of illiquid markets and, often, the lack of an observable yield curve. Moreover, stringent disclosure rules, independent outside audits, and the availability of public and private credit rating agencies all increase transparency and allow greater discipline by market participants. In countries with shallow financial systems, the information environment may be weak because of a lack of scale in the production of public sector services. In those countries, it may be wise to rely more heavily on higher capital requirements rather than on market monitoring to increase systemic resilience (Anginer, Demirgüç-Kunt, and Mare 2018).

Developing countries have shortfalls in some aspects of the availability and quality of information. Knowledge of the ultimate owner and controller of a bank facilitates a consolidated assessment of its exposures. But in developing countries, bank supervisors frequently do not have information on the ultimate (beneficial) owner of a bank because the institution sits outside the regulatory perimeter (figure 1.9, panel a). This problem has been noted, for example, by the Financial Market Supervisory Authority of Azerbaijan, and it was a key issue during the Ukrainian banking crises summarized in box 1.4. Disclosure of a bank's governance and risk management frameworks to the public enables assessment of its risk management approach. For both high-income and developing countries, however, this information was disclosed less frequently in wave 5 of the BRSS than in wave 4 (figure 1.9, panel b).

Credit ratings are an important source of information when evaluating the creditworthiness of counterparts, though it should not be the sole source of information to appraise a bank's risk exposure, as highlighted in the discussion in box 1.1. The BRSS data show a modest increase in the share of countries that require banks to have external credit ratings (figure 1.10, panel a). Although large banks are more likely to demand and be able to afford the cost of external credit ratings, on average less than half the top 10 banks in a developing country have credit-ratings from an international credit-rating agency (figure 1.10, panel b).

FIGURE 1.9 Banks' Disclosure of Risk Information

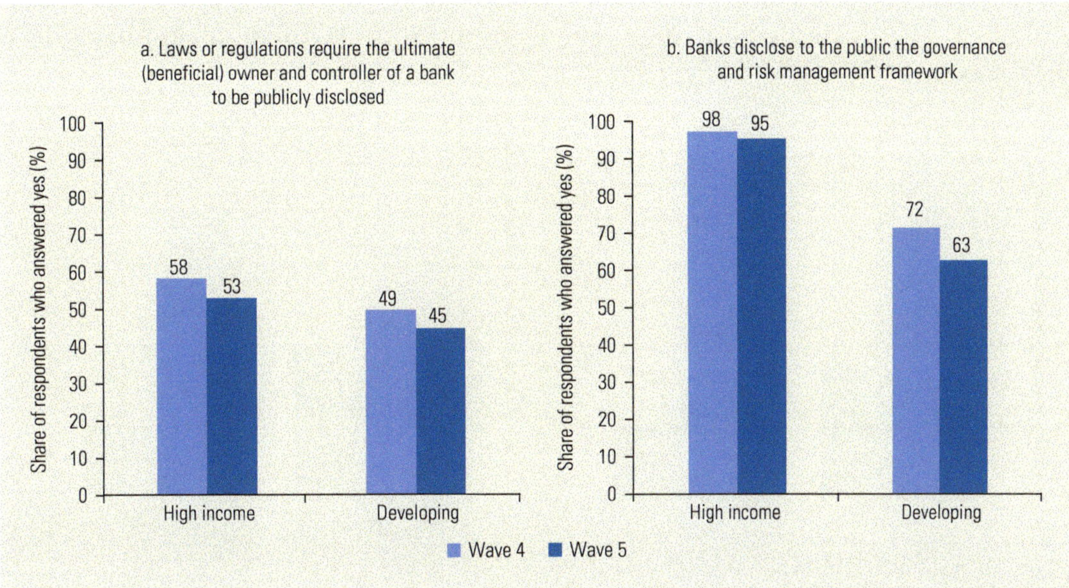

Source: Bank Regulation and Supervision Survey (BRSS), waves 4 and 5, https://www.worldbank.org/en/research/brief/BRSS.

FIGURE 1.10 Information on Credit Ratings

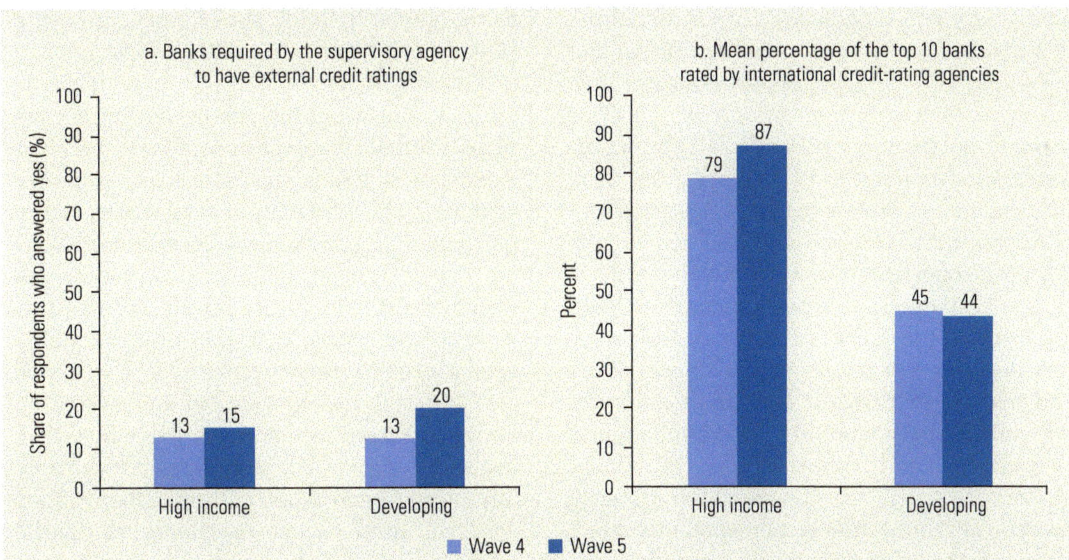

Source: Bank Regulation and Supervision Survey (BRSS), waves 4 and 5, https://www.worldbank.org/en/research/brief/BRSS.

Bank supervisory reporting is also important for market discipline because it has an indirect influence on banks' behavior and increases the information available to market participants when it is publicly available. For example, disclosure of enforcement actions has been associated with a decline in the cost of borrowing firms due to the lower reputation of punished banks after enforcement and potential competition from other incumbents (Deli et al. 2019). Information on enforcement actions and on the fines and settlements

FIGURE 1.11 Public Availability of Supervisory Reporting

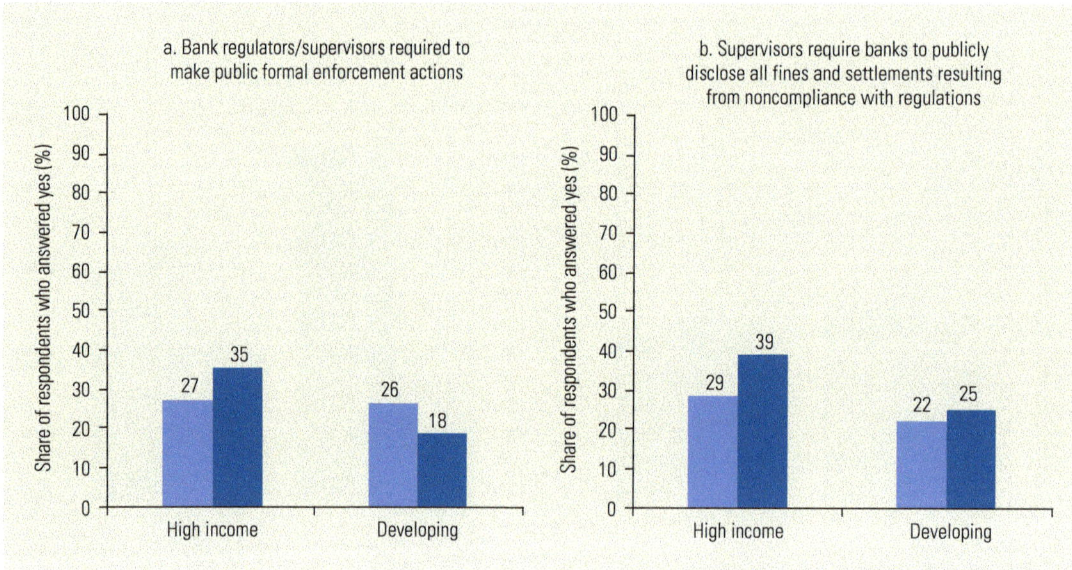

Source: Bank Regulation and Supervision Survey (BRSS), waves 4 and 5, https://www.worldbank.org/en/research/brief/BRSS.

resulting from noncompliance with regulations indicates the compliance of individual banks with regulations, the corporate culture of frequently or severely penalized firms, and the extent of bank supervisory agency forbearance. Information on enforcement actions is made public in 35 percent of high-income countries, according to BRSS wave 5, up from 27 percent in wave 4 (figure 1.11, panel a). However, that ratio actually declined for developing countries from wave 4 to wave 5.

It is also an effective best practice for bank supervision to assure the regular and accurate disclosure of financial data to regulators and market participants because it enhances individual bank stability (Demirgüc-Kunt, Detragiache, and Tressel 2008). The share of countries that require banks to publicly disclose all fines and settlements increased, although the gains were greater among high-income countries (figure 1.11, panel b). Overall, however, the data from wave 5 show no strong improvement in the quality of information and its availability to market participants and the broader public, especially for developing countries. These findings are in line with recommendations of recent Financial Sector Assessment Programs (FSAPs) in developing countries to improve poor financial reporting standards (Vietnam 2014 FSA) and enhance the quality of financial statements disclosed to the public by bank supervisory authorities (Bosnia and Herzegovina 2015 FSA).

Overall, market discipline may have decreased since the global financial crisis because of government interventions during the crisis, expansion of deposit insurance, and some limitations in the information available to market participants. Government interventions during the crisis were large and unprecedented, which could have future ramifications. In the wake of the crisis, deposit insurance frameworks became more expansive. There were also efforts to incorporate bail-in features and improve resolution frameworks, but these measures are a work in progress, and resolving international bank failures remains a key concern. Information disclosure to market participants has not improved, which hampers monitoring. Banks are required to have credit ratings in only a few countries, and even the top 10 banks in developing countries are typically not required to have a rating from an international credit-rating agency. Supervisory actions tend not to be made public, but the availability of this information could be useful for monitoring the behavior of banks and bank supervisory agencies.

BANK SUPERVISION

Bank supervision has become stricter, and also more complex. Supervisory capacity has not improved proportionally to match the greater complexity of bank regulations. Although there have been increases in the number and complexity of regulations since the crisis, there has not been a corresponding increase in supervisory powers and supervisory capacity. As banks become larger and more complex, there is a growing need for supervisory resources and talent to monitor the risks and the financial soundness of these institutions. New rules requiring disclosure and stress-testing put additional strain on supervisory resources to generate, process, and disseminate information. Tailored tools, methodologies, and capabilities are also needed to meet the increased focus of bank supervisors on climate-related risks as a source of financial risk and the implications for the stability of the financial system.[28] Finally, new regulations (especially regarding resolution) allow for a significant amount of discretion by supervisors, and thus they require highly experienced and specialized personnel. By the same token, capacity constraints are likely to limit the ability of supervisory agencies in developing countries to take advantage of the latest technological developments, as described in box 1.5.

In many developing countries, a lack of regulatory independence is also a major

BOX 1.5 Use of Financial Technology in Banking Regulation and Supervision

Rapid advances in financial technology are transforming the provision of banking services. Policy makers are keen to harness the potential benefits of financial innovation while assessing and managing the inherent potential risks. In this regard, the Bali Fintech Agenda developed by the IMF and the World Bank offers insight into key issues that should inform policy discussions.[a] The Agenda provides a high-level framework and comprises 12 elements that policy makers should consider as individual countries formulate their policy approaches.

One of the elements in the Bali Fintech Agenda is the modification and adaptation of the regulatory framework and supervisory practices to facilitate the development of the new products, services, and intermediaries while ensuring the stability of the financial system. Recent technological developments in the collection and processing of information may enhance compliance with bank regulation (regtech) and improve bank supervision (suptech). One definition of regtech (short for regulatory technology) is technology-enabled solutions that enhance compliance with regulations while minimizing associated time and costs (Institute of International Finance 2016). Regtech can be applied to regulatory reporting, risk management, identity management and control, compliance, transaction monitoring, and trading in financial markets. Suptech (short for supervisory technology) can facilitate and enhance supervisory monitoring and internal processes. Suptech applications have been developed in the areas of market conduct[b] and in general for data collection and data analytics.[c] Both regtech and suptech pose challenges in developing or using the relevant software solutions and computer applications related to data gathering, processing, and management; information technology infrastructure; specialized human resources; and standardized reporting.

Many regtech and suptech solutions are still at the concept or pilot stage, where budget and resource constraints are more severe (Toronto Centre 2017). At this point, the best approach for developing countries could be to build on the experiences of early users to harness the benefits of the new technology-enabled solutions and to understand the challenges and risks posed by the implementation of regtech and suptech in their jurisdictions (for example, operational, legal, and reputational risks; data privacy concerns; and the required supervisory expertise).

a. For more detail, see https://www.worldbank.org/en/news/press-release/2018/10/11/bali-fintech-agenda-a-blueprint-for-successfully-harnessing-fintechs-opportunities.

b. See Boeddu et al. (2018) for examples of suptech applications in the United States, Lithuania, and Brazil.

c. See Broeders and Prenio (2018) for an overview of the existing tools.

impediment to performing effective banking supervision. The assessments performed during recent FSAPs in several developing countries identified gaps in the legal protection of the senior management and supervisory board members, availability of sufficient independent financial resources, and supervisory powers vis-à-vis state-owned banks. For instance, the 2016 FSAP for Turkey identified issues with the board appointments process of the Banking Regulation and Supervision Agency (BRSA) and the power of the relevant minister to take action against the BRSA. In the same vein, the 2017 FSA for Bulgaria pinpointed a lack of legal protection for staff of all financial oversight authorities.

To undertake effective monitoring and supervision, authorities must have the power to take timely corrective action. Some elements of supervisory powers have improved, but other elements have deteriorated since the last BRSS wave. Figure 1.12, panel a, shows that a higher percentage of both high-income and developing countries had the power to require banks to reduce or suspend bonuses and other remuneration to bank directors and managers in wave 5 than in wave 4. A higher percentage of developing countries now have the power to force a bank to change its internal organizational structure. Although from wave 4 to wave 5 the power to require banks to reduce or suspend dividends to shareholders grew more prevalent in high-income countries, it declined in developing countries. Finally, a lower percentage of countries in wave 5 than in wave 4 stated that the supervisory agency has the power to require banks to constitute provisions to cover actual or potential losses in both high-income and developing countries. Thus, figure 1.12, panel a suggests that recent changes in the extent of supervisory powers have been mixed.

In addition to facilitating monitoring by market participants, external audits are an integral part of effective supervision. An external auditor performs audits of a bank's

FIGURE 1.12 Supervisory Powers

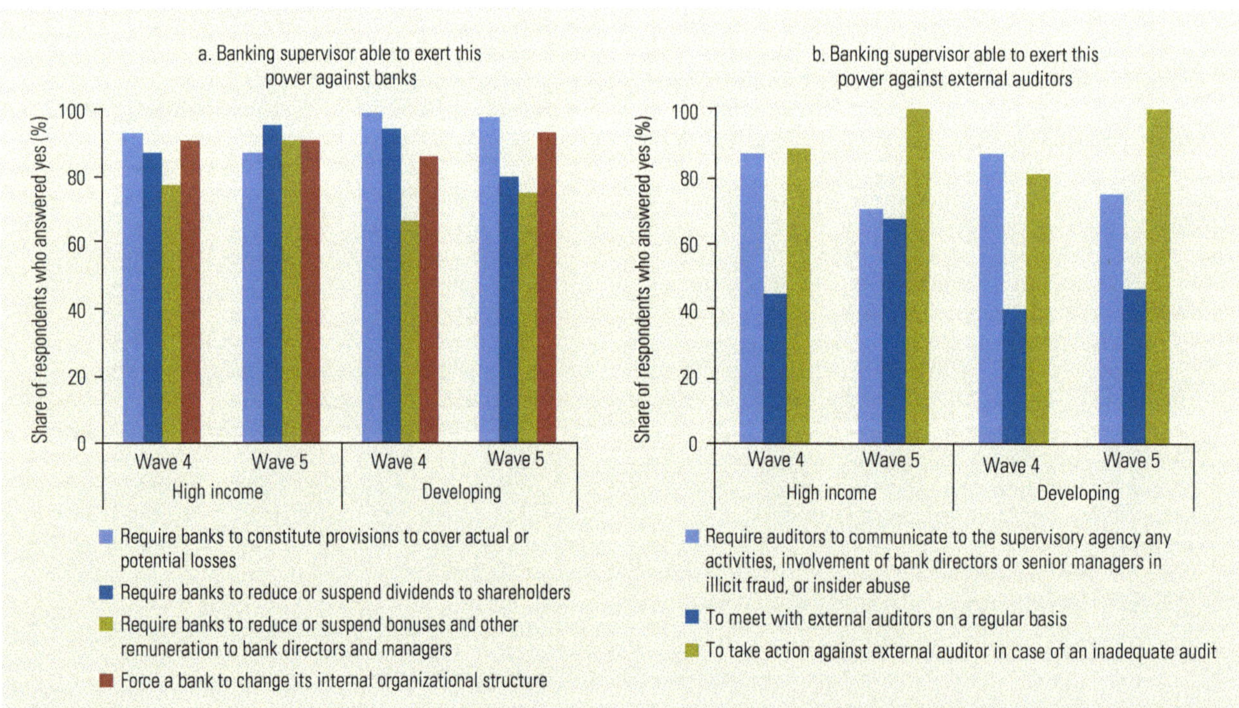

Source: Bank Regulation and Supervision Survey (BRSS), waves 4 and 5, https://www.worldbank.org/en/research/brief/BRSS.

financial statements to ensure that financial statements do not contain misrepresentations of the bank's financial condition and are in compliance with internationally accepted accounting standards. Building effective relationships with external auditors can enhance banking supervision by ensuring that the risks and balance sheet information reported by banks is accurate. The audits may also uncover weaknesses in internal controls related to financial reporting at a bank. Figure 1.12, panel b, shows that the percentage of both high-income and developing countries that require auditors to communicate directly with the supervisory agency about any presumed involvement of bank directors or senior managers in illicit activities, fraud, or insider abuse has declined since the last survey. This suggests that an important source of information is now not available for supervisory purposes in a number of countries. Communication between the supervisor and the external auditor enhances the effectiveness of supervision of the banking sector. Regular meetings with the external auditor and an ability to take disciplinary action against auditors who perform inadequately also contribute to audit quality. A higher percentage of both groups of countries now provide the banking supervisory agency with the right to meet with external auditors on a regular basis and to take action against external auditors for inadequate auditing.

Supervisory capacity has not kept pace with the growing regulations, bank size, and complexity of bank operations. As noted, there was a substantial increase in the number and complexity of regulations in the aftermath of the global financial crisis. With Basel III, greater emphasis has been placed on systemic stability and macroprudential regulation, which requires looking not at the risk of individual financial institutions but at an individual bank's contribution to the risk of the financial system as a whole. Following FSB guidelines, new rules have been proposed and implemented for the resolution of systemically important financial institutions. The new resolution schemes in many countries give supervisors a significant amount of discretion and flexibility. At the same time, new macroprudential rules require continuous monitoring and stress testing of large financial institutions (see chapter 2). These new capital and macroprudential regulations require a sizable investment in supervisory infrastructure and personnel. Figure 1.13, panel a, shows the log change in the number of supervisory personnel reported in BRSS waves 4 and 5 plotted against the log change in total bank assets for each country, distinguishing by color high-income and developing countries.[29] Although there has been a steep increase in the quantity and complexity of regulations, the figure suggests that there is not even a positive, let alone significant, relationship between growth in bank assets and growth in the number of supervisors who oversee these banks.[30]

The sophistication and complexity of new regulations and bank operations require highly specialized, trained, and experienced supervisors to oversee banks. As reported in panel b of figure 1.13, there has been some improvement in the education levels of supervisory personnel because BRSS wave 5 indicates that a greater percentage now hold advanced degrees than in wave 4. However, on-the-job training appears to be less prevalent than in wave 4 (figure 1.13, panel c), and the mean percentage of bank supervisors with more than 10 years of experience in bank supervision declined in high-income countries between waves 4 and 5, whereas it increased slightly in developing countries (figure 1.13, panel d). Overall, despite some increases in supervisory powers and indications that supervisory personnel are better educated, the BRSS wave 5 survey data indicate that regulatory complexity has advanced more quickly than supervisory capacity.

Greater supervisory resources are required as more developing countries fully implement Basel II and some incorporate elements of Basel III. According to figure 1.14, panel a, a growing number of countries have adopted or implemented components of Basel II and III in the last two surveys. For high-income countries, the shift has been from Basel II to Basel III. Meanwhile, developing countries

FIGURE 1.13 Supervisory Capacity

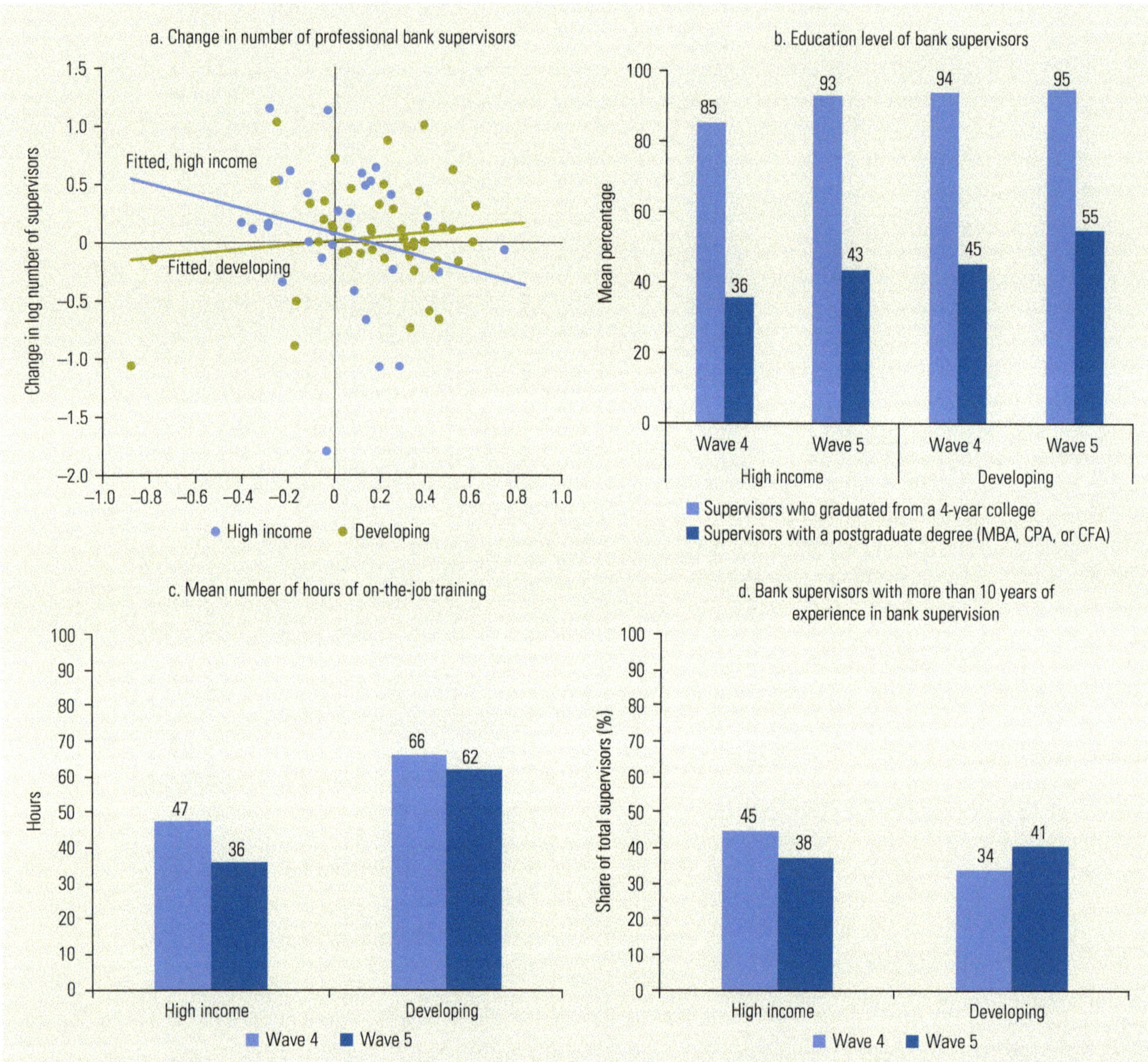

Source: Bank Regulation and Supervision Survey (BRSS), waves 4 and 5, https://www.worldbank.org/en/research/brief/BRSS.
Note: The two linear fitted lines in panel a represent the prediction line for high-income countries and developing countries. CFA = chartered financial analyst; CPA = certified public accountant; MBA = master's in business administration.

have been shifting out of Basel I, and nearly 40 percent have adopted some aspects of Basel III. This is not necessarily a bad thing. Most developing countries have been selective in adopting Basel II/III provisions, eschewing some of the more complicated ones, such as using internal models to calculate banks' credit risk (figure 1.14, panel b). And under Basel II, many developing countries still use the simple standardized approach to computing risk weights. In general, developing countries should focus on establishing a basic robust framework that reflects the characteristics of their local financial systems and refrain from incorporating unnecessarily complex elements. Again, recent empirical studies suggest that during crisis periods, market participants tend to ignore regulatory capital

FIGURE 1.14 **Basel Capital Framework Adoption and Basel II Implementation**

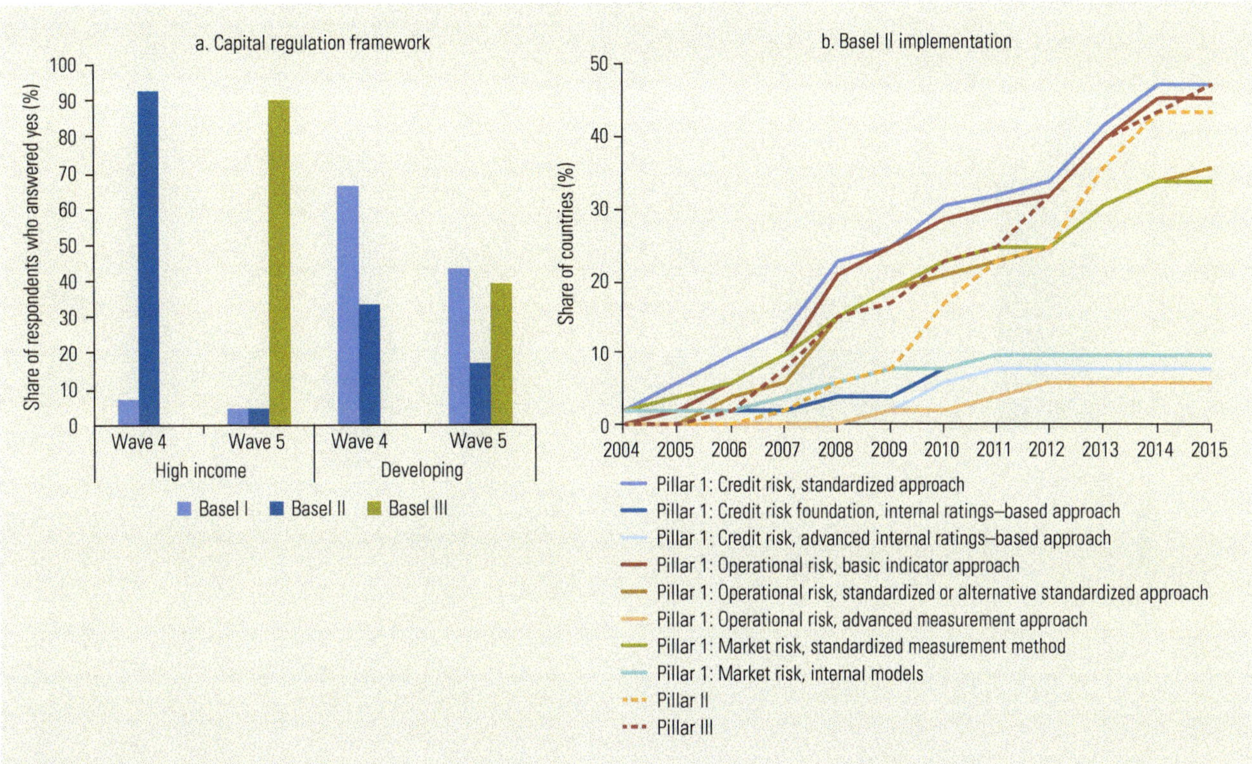

Sources: Panel a: new questions introduced in Bank Regulation and Supervision Survey (BRSS), wave 5, https://www.worldbank.org/en/research/brief/BRSS; panel b: Financial Stability Institute survey (FSI 2015).
Note: Panel b reports on 53 developing countries, using information from the FSI survey. Adoption of a pillar is defined as whether a country has a final rule in force. The percentage of countries that have adopted a specific Basel II component is then computed.

and focus on simple leverage ratios, presumably because they suspect risk weights may be manipulated to inflate the reported ability of institutions to absorb losses (Demirgüç-Kunt, Detragiache, and Merrouche 2013). There are also arguments against complex regulations that are cumbersome to implement, make crisis control suboptimal (see, for example, Haldane and Madouros 2012), and increase the level of opacity, making it difficult to assess regulatory authorities and hold them accountable (Barth, Caprio, and Levine 2012).

In the wake of the global financial crisis, there has been a growing consensus that capital requirements should be adjusted to better reflect a bank's idiosyncratic risk and its contribution to system-wide risk. Panel a of figure 1.15 shows that a high percentage of high-income countries are applying capital conservation requirements and additional surcharges for systemically important banks consistent with the principles of Basel III.[31] Those requirements have been adopted to a significant degree by developing countries as well. But again, as for Basel II, developing countries have been selective in their adoption of Basel III principles. For example, changes in the definition of capital have been much more prevalent than adoption of capital conservation buffers (figure 1.15, panel b).

The adoption of capital regulations is associated with a set of macroeconomic determinants and country characteristics. The likelihood of adopting the Basel III capital framework is higher for countries with higher GDP per capita and larger population. The likelihood of moving from Basel I to a more recent capital framework (in other words, Basel II or Basel III capital frameworks) is negatively related to GDP per capita and to

FIGURE 1.15 Basel III Adoption and Implementation

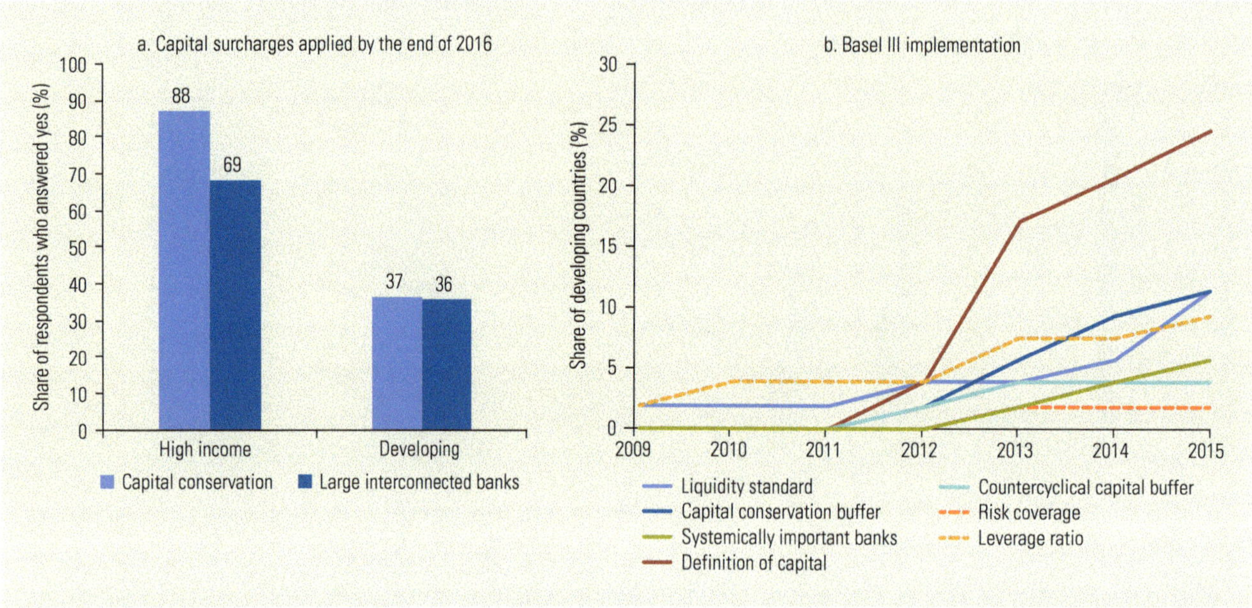

Sources: Panel a, new questions introduced in Bank Regulation and Supervision Survey (BRSS), wave 5, https://www.worldbank.org/en/research/brief/BRSS; panel b, Financial Stability Institute survey (FSI 2015).

Note: Panel b reports on 53 developing countries, using information from the FSI survey. Adoption of a pillar is defined as whether a country has a final rule in force. The percentage of countries that have adopted a specific Basel III component is then computed. "Systematically important banks" refers to additional capital buffers for either domestic systemically important banks or global systemically important banks.

the presence of undercapitalized banks. These results therefore reflect that large high-income countries have been moving to the Basel III framework, while developing countries have been moving out of Basel I. It is interesting, however, that developing countries with undercapitalized banks have been more reluctant to move away from Basel I than others. Anginer et al. (2019) also show that countries that experienced a banking crisis in 2007–09 increased their regulatory capital holdings more than those in noncrisis countries and were also more likely to relax their definition of Tier 1 capital (see box 1.6). Crisis countries were not, however, more likely to increase capital holdings when measured by a simple leverage ratio (banks' total equity divided by total assets).

In conclusion, analysis of new global survey data on the regulation and supervision of banks suggests that important interventions and regulatory changes have had significant implications for market discipline and bank capitalization. Overall, a growing number of countries have adopted components of Basel II and III since the crisis. But many developing countries have been selective in their adoption, eschewing some of the more complicated aspects of regulation. Chapters 2 and 3 of this report investigate in greater depth the implications of these regulatory reforms for market discipline and bank capitalization.

BOX 1.6 Bank Regulation and Supervision 10 Years after the Global Financial Crisis

Anginer et al. (2019) summarize recent developments in bank regulation and supervision across regions using information from the 2019 Bank Regulation and Supervision Survey (BRSS). The analyses identify bank capital regulation, market discipline, and supervisory monitoring as key areas where financial regulation has undergone significant changes between BRSS waves 4 and 5.

Minimum regulatory capital requirements and Tier 1 capital holdings (both expressed as a percentage of banks' risk-weighted assets) were higher in wave 5 than in wave 4 for all regions except the Middle East and North Africa and Europe and Central Asia. The increase in Tier 1 capital ratios was much more pronounced for banks in high-income OECD countries and was accompanied by declines in banks' reported risk-weighted assets. Whether those weights are an accurate reflection of the riskiness of banks' portfolios is, therefore, a fundamental concern.

In terms of market discipline, deposit insurance coverage has expanded in all regions and government interventions in the banking sector to rescue ailing banks have likely weakened the incentives of market participants to monitor banks' risk-taking behavior, especially in high-income OECD countries. Moreover, the information available to both private market participants and public regulators to assess the risk profile of banks did not improve significantly compared to round 4.

At the same time, banking supervision has become more complex because of increases in the number and complexity of regulations after the crisis. There was not, however, a corresponding increase in supervisory powers or supervisory capacity.

Anginer et al. (2019) also investigate the determinants of changes in bank capital defined as holdings of total regulatory capital (as a percentage of risk-weighted assets), holdings of Tier 1 regulatory capital (also expressed as a percentage of risk-weighted assets), simple leverage ratios (banks' total equity divided by total assets), and an index capturing the stringency of a country's Tier 1 capital definition, with lower values indicating that a wider variety of balance sheet items can be used to satisfy Tier 1 capital requirements. The authors find that banks in countries that experienced a banking crisis in 2007–09 increased their holdings of total regulatory

FIGURE B1.6.1 Relation between Banking Crises and Bank Capital

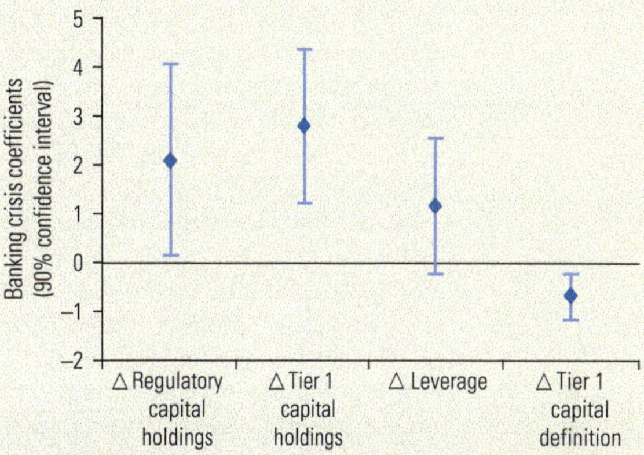

Source: Anginer et al. (2019).
Note: The figure shows coefficients (marked with a diamond) for a dummy variable indicating whether a country experienced a banking crisis between 2007 and 2009, and confidence intervals for those coefficients computed at the 10 percent significance level. The cross-country regressions relate changes in the four measures of bank capital described in this box to a set of explanatory variables, including the banking crisis dummy.

capital and Tier 1 capital more than those in noncrisis countries, but crisis countries were also more likely to relax their definition of Tier 1 capital (figure B1.6.1). There is no statistically significant relationship between banking crises and the leverage ratios of banks in those countries. The results indicate that despite the increase in Tier 1 capital ratios in countries that experienced a crisis, there has not been a significant increase in capital holdings, as measured by simple leverage.

Anginer et al. (2019) also analyze the relationship between bank risk and the quality of bank capital using bank-level financial information. They find that defining bank regulatory capital narrowly significantly reduces stand-alone bank risk. This is particularly true for large banks that have greater discretion in assigning risk weights to their assets and are better able to issue a variety of capital instruments (such as hybrid or subordinated debt). Anginer et al. (2019) also find that the decision to adopt the latest capital regulations (for example, Basel III) is associated with adoption by neighbor countries, calling for increased scrutiny to ensure that the regulations that are adopted fit the local charactersitics of a country's financial system.

NOTES

1. In general, a bank is a service institution that receives deposits or close substitutes for deposits, grants credit, and makes investments in securities. In most countries, a law defines what constitutes a bank. A bank's corporate charter contains its legal authorization for banking activity. The commercial bank is the dominant bank type across jurisdictions. It represented on average over 90 percent of domestic banking assets in 2016, according to the latest data from the World Bank's Bank Regulation and Supervision Survey (BRSS). Nevertheless, in each jurisdiction the term *bank* can refer to a wide variety of institutions, depending on the business model (such as retail versus wholesale banks), scope (such as mutual banks), organizational structure (bank holding companies versus unit banks), and ownership type (private versus state).
2. See Brunnermeier et al. (2009). Several papers have used a constrained information asymmetry framework to explain contagion risk and crises (see, for example, Gennotte and Leland 1990; Kodres and Pritsker 2002; Hong and Stein 2003; Barlevy and Veronesi 2003; Yuan 2005).
3. Excessive risk-taking can be defined as misallocation of capital. For example, an investment with a very low risk-adjusted return could be considered excessive risk-taking. A bank decision maker might be incentivized to pursue this investment to increase the volume of transactions, eventually benefiting from a larger business (such as through larger bonuses).
4. See, for example, Barth, Caprio, and Levine (2008).
5. In this chapter, developing countries are defined as upper-middle, middle-, and low-income countries following the 2018 classification used in the World Bank's World Development Indicators database. We exclude from this group the countries classified as offshore financial centers (OFCs) in groups II and III by the Financial Stability Forum (2000), which are also classified as such in the latest assessment by the International Monetary Fund (see https://www.imf.org/external/np/ofca/ofca.aspx). For the complete list of OFCs, see appendix I in Anginer et al. (2019).
6. A few studies offer limited evidence on the potential impact of the latest regulatory reforms on developing countries. Examples are Briault et al. (2018) on seven developing countries and the Financial Stability Board on the effects of reforms on infrastructure finance (FSB 2018a) and the clearing system for over-the-counter markets of financial derivatives (FSB 2017b).
7. The *Global Financial Development Report 2017/2018* discusses the retrenchment of global banks from providing financial services (for example, clearing of foreign currency transactions), leaving those services and transactions to other financial institutions. It highlights how the unavailability of these financial services poses challenges in terms of business control and bank supervision, threatening financial stability and inclusive growth, especially in developing countries (see box 3.5 of the *Global Financial Development Report 2017/2018* for an in-depth discussion). One factor associated with the reduction in the number of correspondent banking relationships in developing countries is the compliance with regulatory requirements imposed by national/local regulators of cross-border correspondent banks (Stames et al. 2017).
8. See, for example, Boyd, Kwak, and Smith (2005) and Laeven and Valencia (2018). The costs of a crisis can be especially high in developing countries, where the alternatives to bank financing are limited (Dell'Ariccia, Detragiache, and Rajan 2008).
9. See, for example, the remarks made by Fernando Restoy, chairman, Financial Stability Institute, Bank for International Settlements, in London in July 2018 (Restoy 2018).
10. This definition of proportionality is in line with recent policy work. For instance, Ferreira, Jenkinson, and Wilson (2019) posit that developing countries should consider their specific characteristics while adopting international standards, such as the complexity and size of financial institutions, the level of development of financial market infrastructure, the granularity and quality of the available information, and the capacity of bank supervisors.
11. A recent survey by the Basel Committee on Banking Supervision (BCBS 2019) documents that both those countries that are members of the BCBS, as well as those that are not

members, adopt minimum regulatory standards and supervisory practices to reflect the risk profiles of different types of banks (for example, business models and size).

12. See, for example, Calomiris and Kahn (1991) for the role of demandable debt; Flannery (2001) for how subordinated debt may prompt corrective action by bank owners or managers; and Francis et al. (2019) for the effect of senior bank loans on bank risk-taking.
13. At the same time, higher bank capital requirements may also entail higher funding costs, which can be transmitted to borrowers through an increase in lending rates (Schliephake 2016).
14. According to the definition of the Basel Committee on Banking Supervision, Tier 1 capital comprises Common Equity Tier 1 (CET1)—essentially common shares and retained earnings—or additional Tier 1 instruments (AT1)—other regulatory capital instruments that meet the criteria for inclusion in the Tier 1 capital (BCBS 2011). Under the Basel III capital accord, banks need to comply with a minimum CET1 ratio of 4.5 percent of RWAs and minimum Tier 1 ratio of 6 percent of RWAs. Basel III also introduced additional capital buffers, defined in terms of CET1 capital as a percentage of RWAs, namely, a capital conservation buffer, a countercyclical capital buffer, and surcharges for domestically and internationally systemically important banks.
15. For an in-depth discussion of the issue, see BCBS (2017b). The Basel Consultative Group (2014) also recommends a careful approach to the treatment of sovereign exposures for developing countries that have dollarized economies (meaning a foreign currency is used as payment for transaction purposes, or assets and liabilities are denominated in a foreign currency) or issue a significant amount of sovereign bonds denominated in a foreign currency.
16. The Basel Committee on Banking Supervision (BCBS 2011) defines the leverage ratio as Tier 1 capital divided by the sum of total assets and off–balance sheet items. We follow that approach here, although we recognize that other financial policy makers and researchers often define the leverage ratio as total bank assets divided by Tier 1 capital.
17. Within each country, large banks are defined as those in the 80th percentile or above of banks in terms of total assets, whereas small banks are the rest of banks in a national banking system—that is, those below the 80th percentile in terms of assets.
18. Admittedly, in the wake of the crisis the regulatory focus was on the largest banks. Nevertheless, the capitalization of smaller banks may also be important because they could impose systemic problems if they fail together—that is, the too-many-to-fail problem described by Acharya and Yorulmazer (2007) and analyzed empirically for developing countries by Brown and Dinç (2011).
19. Le Leslé and Avramova (2012) document unwarranted variation in the computation of RWA across banks and jurisdictions. Acharya, Engle, and Pierret (2014) show that average regulatory risk weights in stress tests are not correlated with market measures of risk, leading to underestimation of portfolio risk and excess leverage. Mariathasan and Merrouche (2014) find that banks allowed to employ internal ratings–based (IRB) approaches to compute assets' risk weights underreport risk because of risk weight manipulation. The decline in risk weights is larger for weakly capitalized banks and in countries where banking supervisor powers compared with those of external auditors are weaker and where many IRB-approved banks are found. Behn, Haselmann, and Vig (2016) quantify the extent of RWA "gaming," concluding that where the challenges accompanying complex regulation are too demanding, simpler rules may enhance the efficacy of financial regulation.
20. However, when we restrict the sample of banks to the largest banks in terms of total assets and to countries that are members of the BCBS, for banks in Europe and in the Americas (that is, Argentina, Brazil, Canada, Mexico, and the United States), we reach findings consistent with FSB (and BCBS analyses), meaning that we observe increases in regulatory capital holdings accompanied by decreases in risk-weighted assets between 2011 and 2017. FSB's rest of-the-world sample mixes banks from high-income and developing countries, blurring differences between these two groups, but the results for this group of banks are broadly consistent with our developing-country findings.
21. Asset quality reviews involve assessment of the value of bank assets, collateral

valuation, and related provisions. AQRs are costly in terms of setting up the information system recording bank processes, policies, and accounting practices, and acquiring the methodological framework for the assessment of the value of banking assets. Examples of AQRs can be retrieved from the European Central Bank website: https://www.bankingsupervision.europa.eu/banking/tasks/comprehensive_assessment/html/index.en.html.

22. For a detailed overview of macroprudential policy tools, see Claessens (2014).
23. China is not included among the countries that adopted a formal deposit insurance scheme in wave 5 because it did not complete section 8—Deposit (Savings) Protection Schemes—of its survey. Nevertheless, since May 2015 a formal deposit insurance system has been in place in China for all deposit-taking institutions.
24. For example, in wave 5, 11 countries answered that these funds can be used to recapitalize weak banks, clearly undermining the incentives of market participants to monitor bank risk-taking (figure 1.6, panel b).
25. See, for example, Laeven and Valencia (2013) on the effects of recapitalization measures.
26. As of the end of 2018, the European Union (EU-28) comprised the following countries: Austria, Belgium, Bulgaria, Croatia, Cyprus, the Czech Republic, Denmark, Estonia, Finland, France, Germany, Greece, Hungary, Ireland, Italy, Latvia, Lithuania, Luxembourg, Malta, the Netherlands, Poland, Portugal, Romania, the Slovak Republic, Slovenia, Spain, Sweden, and the United Kingdom.
27. See, for example, Laux and Leuz (2009) for the advantages and disadvantages of fair value accounting.
28. The Network of Central Banks and Supervisors for Greening the Financial System (NGFS) was established in December 2017 to address the challenges brought by climate change for the resilience and stability of the financial system. This forum allows central banks, bank supervisors, and international institutions—such as the BIS, the OECD, and the World Bank—to exchange experiences and identify best practices in the supervision of climate-related risks and explore options to scale up green financing. For more information, see https://www.banque-france.fr/en/financial-stability/international-role/network-greening-financial-system.
29. In 2014 the European Central Bank (ECB) assumed its role as single supervisory entity in the euro area (which at that time comprised 18 countries—and 19 countries by the end of 2016). This entailed a transfer of bank supervisors from the national central banks to the ECB. All 19 euro area countries are high-income countries, according to the 2018 classification of the World Bank's World Development Indicators database. Therefore, figures for high-income countries may underestimate the real manpower of bank supervisory agencies in high-income countries.
30. Although not reported here, there is also no relationship between the growth in the number of banks and the growth in the number of supervisory personnel.
31. Capital conservation buffers provide a mechanism for rebuilding depleted capital by either reducing discretionary distributions of earnings (such as dividend payments, shares buybacks, and staff bonus payments) or raising new capital from the private sector (see chapter 3 for an in-depth discussion). Additional loss absorbency requirements are imposed on global systemically important banks and domestic systemically important banks to account for the "negative externalities" created by large interconnected banks, as discussed earlier in this chapter (see chapter 2 for an in-depth discussion).

CHAPTER 2: KEY MESSAGES

- Market discipline is the process by which market participants—such as uninsured lenders, shareholders, and rating agencies—monitor the risks and financial positions of banks and take action to guide, limit, and price banks' risk-taking.
- For market discipline to work effectively, market participants must have the information, the means, and, most important, the incentives to monitor and influence banks to limit excessive risk-taking.
- The global financial crisis led to unprecedented interventions by governments to stabilize their economic and financial systems. There has been significant expansion of deposit insurance (both in coverage and scope), with some countries offering blanket guarantees on deposits. There has also been additional government support in the form of capital and liquidity injections, guarantees on bank liabilities, and repurchases of impaired bank assets.
- These interventions have reinforced investors' expectations of government support for large financial institutions, significantly reducing the long-term incentives to monitor and discipline these banks.
- In response, following policy goals set by the Basel Committee on Banking Supervision and the Financial Stability Board, some countries have introduced legislation and regulatory reforms to limit the economic damage posed by large financial institutions and to strengthen market discipline.
- The main regulatory reforms include:
    - Higher capital and liquidity requirements overall and additional surcharges for institutions deemed systemically important, both domestically and globally.
    - New resolution processes for bank holding companies and new requirements for systemically important banks to hold bail-in debt.
    - Enhanced supervision of risk management and risk reporting processes at banks, including periodic stress tests to determine whether banks have sufficient capital to absorb losses.
- Although these reforms have been widely adopted and have been successful, many issues remain. In particular, it is not clear whether bail-in funds will be enough to capitalize bridge banks during resolution in order for taxpayers' funds to not be put at risk. It also remains uncertain how cross-border resolution will be implemented and how bail-in funds will be shared between host and home country supervisors. It is difficult to quantify the long-term effects of widespread bailouts and blanket guarantees on moral hazard and on market discipline.
- Finally, for developing countries, the principle of proportionality must be kept in mind when implementing policies designed to enhance market discipline in order to maximize social objectives, given capacity constraints.

2

Market Discipline

MARKET DISCIPLINE

The global financial crisis highlighted the weaknesses in regulatory regimes to supervise and resolve large financial institutions. These systemically important financial institutions (SIFIs) have been deemed as too big, too interconnected, and too complex to fail by domestic authorities.[1] Because their failure would significantly disrupt the financial system and economic activity, governments worldwide have made unprecedented interventions in the markets to rescue these large financial institutions using public resources. As a result of these measures, shareholders and borrowers have been able to shift bank losses to taxpayers.

These interventions rekindled the debate on the impact of government interventions on market discipline and on the incentives of owners, borrowers, and shareholders to monitor large financial institutions. The focus of the regulatory reform agenda has also been shifting from supervision to resolution. A strong resolution regime, in which bank creditors bear the brunt of losses, is considered to be important to reinforce market discipline.

Market discipline refers to the notion that market participants—such as uninsured lenders, shareholders, and rating agencies—can influence a financial institution's behavior through monitoring its risk profile and financial position. By making risk-taking costlier, market discipline has been recognized by regulators as an important mechanism for curbing banks' incentives to take excessive risks. Market discipline was introduced as the third pillar of the Basel capital regulations as a way to complement and support official oversight of financial institutions through new public disclosure requirements.[2]

For market discipline to be effective, market participants should have not only the means to monitor the activities of financial institutions but also the ability to influence and impose discipline on these institutions. Bliss and Flannery (2002) identify two main components of market discipline: monitoring and influence. Monitoring is the process by which shareholders, depositors, and other market participants can systematically review the business activities, financial condition, and risk-taking behavior of banks. Influence can be both direct and indirect. Market participants, based on their monitoring, can take direct corrective action. This action can be in the form of refusing to roll over short-term debt, charging higher interest rates on new debt, or exercising covenants on debt contracts. Indirect influence occurs when a third party, responding to the information provided by market monitoring, engages in corrective action. For example, wholesale funding may be withheld based on external assessments by rating agencies, or, if the financial institution has publicly traded securities, the market's risk assessments can be inferred from the observed security prices, and funding may be withheld based on security prices.

Effective market discipline requires two important conditions. First and most important, market participants must have incentives to monitor banks. Large depositors, shareholders, and other unsecured creditors naturally have incentives to monitor banks because they have money at stake. Empirical evidence indicates that the amount of uninsured and subordinated debt banks carry on their balance sheets is associated with greater market discipline (Flannery and Sorescu 1996; Sironi 2003). Moreover, because uninsured depositors can lose money when a bank fails, they will demand higher rates when a bank takes on more risk. Higher market prices are a valuable signal of greater risk-taking by banks, which can be used by regulators to discipline those banks.

Second, market participants must have access to relevant and timely information. It is difficult for uninsured debtholders or shareholders to effectively monitor their investments unless they receive reliable financial information about the banks in which they are investing. Stringent disclosure rules, independent outside audits, and the availability of public and private credit ratings all increase transparency and allow for greater discipline by market participants. Anginer, Demirgüç-Kunt and Zhu (2014) show that information availability and information asymmetry in the banking sectors are important drivers of systemic risk. The importance of information in market discipline has also been recognized by the Basel Committee on Banking Supervision (BCBS).[3]

The growing complexity of the organizational structures and operations of large financial institutions make it difficult for market participants to process information. The rapid development of new financial instruments over the last two decades has increased the complexity and opacity of bank balance sheets. At the same time, financial institutions are now structured as intricate ownership hierarchies, involving hundreds or even thousands of legal entities that span multiple sovereign nations. Their multiple business lines range from insurance to investment management, and they receive a substantial portion of their income from noninterest activities. Meanwhile, growing interconnections across large banks make it difficult to assess fault lines (Gai, Haldane, and Kapadia 2011). Since the global financial crisis, there has been a further increase in the organizational complexity of large banks—see Carmassi and Herring (2016) for large global banks and Goldberg and Meehl (2019) for large U.S. banks—making transparency and information even more valuable for the effectiveness of market discipline.

Implicit and explicit government guarantees distort the incentives of market participants to monitor and discipline financial institutions. In particular, government intervention in the markets to provide liquidity and funding to rescue large financial institutions and the expansion of deposit insurance schemes in scope and coverage have reduced incentives for market discipline (see the section below, titled "Implicit Government Guarantees Become Explicit"). Because insured depositors are protected when a bank fails, their incentives to monitor the financial condition of their bank is significantly reduced (see Anginer and Demirgüç-Kunt, forthcoming, for a review). Large financial institutions that are deemed too big to fail may also benefit from implicit government guarantees on the uninsured debt they carry on their balance sheets. Empirical evidence indicates that the risk is not fully priced in the cost of uninsured funding for large banks that are deemed systemically important by the market (Acharya, Anginer, and Warburton 2017). The expectation of support by the market results in moral hazard problems in the form of excessive and correlated risk-taking, which is similar to moral hazard problems associated with deposit insurance. Thus, larger banks may lack market discipline, regardless of whether an explicit insurance scheme protects depositors. Some aspects of the new regulatory reforms such as higher capital surcharges and requirements to hold bail-in debt and the implementation of procedures to resolve or

FIGURE 2.1 **Elements of Market Discipline**

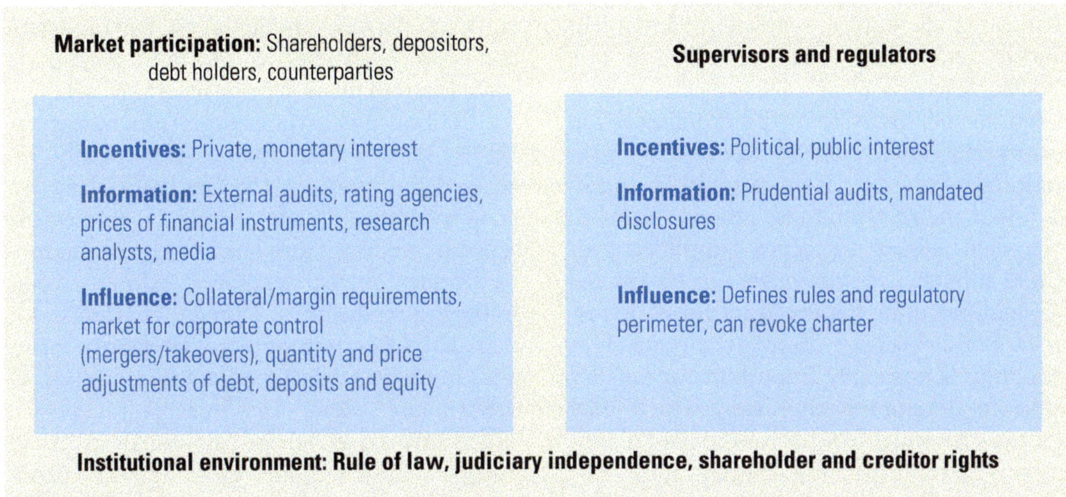

liquidate large financial institutions in an orderly fashion can reinforce incentives for market discipline. Whether the recent reforms will dampen investor expectations of government support going forward is yet unknown.

Market discipline works within the larger institutional environment in conjunction with the discipline provided by regulators and supervisors (see figure 2.1). Bank regulators and supervisors have their own set of incentives. As discussed in chapter 1, governments face political and social demands to provide financial safety nets. Although the goal of regulators and supervisors is to maximize public welfare, political considerations can also play a role. Meanwhile, an interplay is at work between the discipline provided by the private market and that provided by regulators and supervisors, and at times they can complement or substitute for each other. For example, information is critical for effective public monitoring of banks. Regulators and supervisors generate information through prudential audits and mandated disclosures, which are also used by market participants to monitor and influence risk-taking by banks. Similarly, regulators and supervisors can use data on security prices and other information generated by the private market to monitor and discipline banks. The form of influence by regulators and supervisors tends to be more direct—they define the rules and the regulatory perimeter and can impose extreme discipline in the form of shutting down banks and revoking bank charters. Specific regulations and, more important, the actions taken by supervisors can affect the incentives of private market participants and can enhance or hinder market discipline. For example, increasing the cost of bank failure by redesigning safety nets, credibly committing to not bailing out failing banks, or increasing the incentives for bank managers to respond to market signals can all affect the incentives of private market participants.

There must be institutions in place and mechanisms available for market participants to exercise market discipline. Information generation and provision of ancillary financial services, such as credit ratings, tend to have high fixed costs. These require a certain level of market development, which can be curtailed by the lack of scale and insufficient market depth—important hindrances in developing countries. Enabling a competitive environment that makes it easier for depositors and other investors to shift their investments between banks according to their assessments of relative risk is also important. Effective private monitoring also requires strong adherence to the rule of law. In particular, enforcing debt contracts and covenants, holding directors and managers accountable for fraud, and protecting minority shareholders from self-dealing all require a strong, independent judiciary and laws protecting shareholder and creditor rights.

Significant cross-country differences in institutional environments imply that proportionality must be kept in mind in thinking about the rules and regulations meant to strengthen market discipline. Simplified prudential rules and requirements can be applied for small or noncomplex institutions in order to avoid excessive compliance costs. This possibility is especially important for smaller banks in developing countries, which may lack the economies of scale for the compliance function. Proportionality should apply not only to regulations but also to supervision. Smaller developing countries may lack informational and operational infrastructure and face steep scale curves in the supervision and enforcement functions. Proportionality must be kept in mind to use supervisors' scarce resources effectively, thereby maximizing the desired social objectives. This need may in some cases imply a lower degree of stringency and simplified enforcement processes for smaller and less complex institutions.

IMPACT OF THE GLOBAL FINANCIAL CRISIS ON INCENTIVES AND MORAL HAZARD

The global financial crisis led to unprecedented interventions by governments to stabilize their economic and financial systems. Deposit insurance was significantly expanded (in both coverage and scope) during the crisis, with a number of countries offering blanket guarantees on deposits. Government support was also extended in the form of capital and liquidity injections, guarantees on bank liabilities, and repurchases of impaired bank assets.

Expansion of Explicit Guarantees

During the global financial crisis, a number of countries introduced new deposit insurance schemes or extended the scope and coverage of existing schemes to restore confidence in their banking systems and to avert runs. Several countries, such as Australia and Singapore, introduced explicit deposit insurance schemes for the first time. Many others, including the United States and Spain, substantially increased the limit on deposits covered by deposit insurance. Other countries increased the scope of securities and bank liabilities guaranteed under deposit insurance. Most notably, Ireland introduced a blanket guarantee for most liabilities of its banks. The deposit insurance in Ireland was expanded to cover bonds, subordinated debt, and interbank deposits. The increased coverage amounted to about 200 percent of Ireland's gross domestic product (GDP). Figure 2.2 shows the percentage and number of high-income and developing countries that implemented changes in their deposit insurance systems in response to the crisis. Most countries, especially those in the high-income group, significantly increased both the limit and the type of accounts covered under deposit insurance. Since the crisis,

FIGURE 2.2 Increase in Deposit Insurance Coverage in Response to the Global Financial Crisis

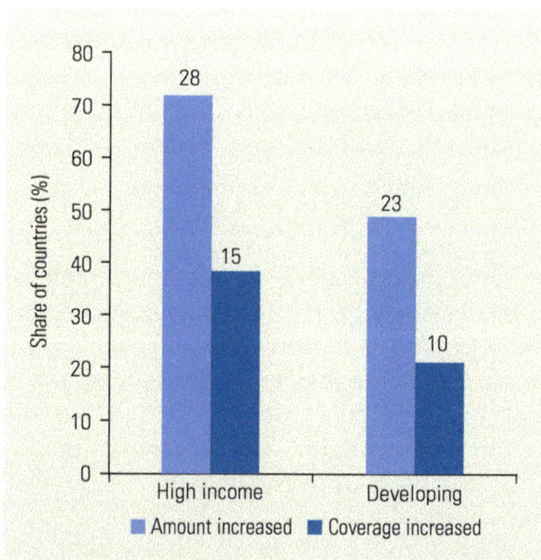

Source: Bank Regulation and Supervision Survey (BRSS), wave 5, https://www.worldbank.org/en/research/brief/BRSS.
Note: This figure shows the number and the percentage of countries implementing changes to their bank deposit systems as a result of the 2007–09 global financial crisis.

there has been further expansion of explicit insurance coverage. Currently, over 110 countries have some form of explicit deposit insurance, up from 93 in 2013, according to the most recent Bank Regulation and Supervision Survey (BRSS). Over 80 percent of countries in the high-income group have some form of explicit deposit insurance in place.

Expansions of deposit insurance coverage and scope have helped to restore confidence in banking sectors across the globe. Except for a few exceptions, there have been no contagious runs by retail depositors (Hasan et al. 2017). However, these expansions may come at a significant cost to market discipline. Although adequate funding of insurance schemes is crucial for deposit insurance to be credible, governments have ended up doing far more to avoid crises and restore stability. Limited commitment ex ante by governments is crucial in three important respects for deposit insurance schemes to work effectively. First, it limits risk-taking incentives by banks. Second, it limits the amount of taxpayer funds that could be at risk. And, third, it helps to harmonize insurance schemes in common banking areas to limit regulatory arbitrage.

Expanding coverage beyond what was promised to depositors during the crisis may have reinforced market expectations of blanket government support, potentially distorting the incentives of both bank managers and depositors. A number of papers have shown that more generous deposit insurance coverage and scope lead to greater moral hazard (Honohan and Klingebiel 2000; Demirgüç-Kunt, and Detragiache 2002). Although deposit insurance can enhance depositor confidence and reduce the likelihood of contagious bank runs during crisis periods, it also increases incentives for banks to take on more risks in normal times. The net effect of deposit insurance on bank risk and stability depends on whether the benefits of deposit insurance outweigh its costs. Much of the empirical research suggests that the overall effect of deposit insurance on stability is negative (see box 2.1). It is not surprising, then, that expansions during the financial crisis may have reduced market discipline. Although

BOX 2.1 How Does Deposit Insurance Affect Stability?

Deposit insurance can increase moral hazard and make financial systems more vulnerable to crises during good times, but it can also enhance depositor confidence and reduce the likelihood of bank runs during crises. The net effect of deposit insurance on bank risk and stability depends on whether the benefits of deposit insurance outweigh its costs.

Anginer, Demirgüç-Kunt, and Zhu (2014) examine the effect of deposit insurance on banks' standalone and systemic risk before and after the global financial crisis. They find that more generous deposit insurance schemes increase bank risk and reduce systemic stability in noncrisis years. During the global financial crisis, bank risk was lower and systemic stability was greater in countries with more generous deposit insurance coverage. The authors also examine the level of risk across countries over the full sample period. They find that the overall effect of deposit insurance over the full sample remains negative because the destabilizing effect during normal times is greater in magnitude than the stabilizing effect during global turbulence.

The study sample consists of 4,109 publicly traded banks in 96 countries, and the study period includes the crisis years 2007–09 and the three years, 2004–06, leading up to the crisis. The authors use the *Z*-score and stock return volatility to measure the stand-alone risk of an individual bank and the marginal expected shortfall (MES) of Acharya, Engle, and Richardson (2012) to measure systemic risk. The authors use two variables to measure the generosity of deposit insurance coverage. The first indicator—from Barth, Caprio, and Levine (2008)—is a dummy variable that takes on a value of 1 if a country has

(box continued next page)

BOX 2.1 How Does Deposit Insurance Affect Stability? *(continued)*

TABLE B2.1.1 Stand-Alone and Systemic Risk before and after the Global Financial Crisis

	Risk variable	Has no deposit insurance	Has deposit insurance	Difference	*p*-value
Precrisis	Log (Z-score)	3.7611	2.4710	1.2901	*0.0000*
	Volatility	0.0184	0.0295	−0.0111	*0.0000*
	MES	−1.2617	−2.0150	0.7534	*0.0001*
Postcrisis	Log (Z-score)	3.3148	3.1170	0.1978	*0.0218*
	Volatility	0.0369	0.0303	0.0067	*0.0020*
	MES	−3.3644	−3.0699	−0.2945	*0.0000*

Note: This table reports univariate analyses of the impact of deposit insurance during crisis and noncrisis periods for the sample of 4,109 banks in 96 countries over the period 2004–09. MES = marginal expected shortfall (from Acharya, Engle, and Richardson 2012).

explicit deposit insurance and depositors were fully compensated the last time a bank failed. The second indicator—from Demirgüç-Kunt, Kane, and Laeven (2008)—takes on a value of 1 if a country offers full coverage of deposits.

Table B2.1.1 shows the key results of the study using the second deposit insurance measure. It presents averages for the risk measures, which are partitioned based on whether a country offers deposit insurance and whether the country is in a crisis period. In the noncrisis period, banks in countries without deposit insurance experience 0.7 percent lower daily volatility, 0.3 percent higher stock returns during a market decline, and half a standard deviation higher Z-score. During the crisis period, banks in countries with deposit insurance show more favorable figures. However, the net effect of deposit insurance on risk over the full sample period is still negative.

The authors also examine how the quality of regulation and supervision affects the impact of deposit insurance on stabilization and moral hazard. A bank supervisory quality index measures whether the supervisory authorities have the power and authority to take specific preventive and corrective actions such as replacing the management team. They find that good bank regulation and supervision enhances the stabilization effects during crisis periods, while dampening the negative effects associated with moral hazard during normal times. These results are consistent with the literature, which shows that a well-designed deposit insurance scheme combined with effective regulation and supervision can provide stability while minimizing some of the distortions introduced by deposit insurance (Demirgüç-Kunt, Kane, and Laeven 2008). For example, limiting coverage and scope and implementing risk-based pricing can help alleviate moral hazard problems and help internalize banks' risk-taking. Similarly, better bank supervision may limit the extent to which banks can engage in correlated risk-taking activities in the presence of deposit insurance. Overall, the results highlight the importance of the underlying regulatory and institutional framework and support the view that the appropriate incentive framework is important for ensuring that deposit insurance works effectively.

these expansions have been temporary and were scaled back after the crisis, they reinforce investor expectations that the government will step in and expand coverage when a new crisis arises. In other words, temporary expansions do not temporarily reduce market discipline and can result in moral hazard with potentially long-lasting effects.

A limited commitment by governments also reduces the costs of providing insurance during times of distress. In most theoretical models, bank runs result from a self-fulfilling prophecy where a lack of confidence in the banking sector causes investors to withdraw funds from otherwise solvent banks, resulting in unnecessary economic loss—see, for example, Diamond and Dybvig (1983). However, as Allen, Babus, and Carletti (2009) point out, bank runs often coincide with deteriorating economic conditions and declining asset values. Ex-post expansion of guarantees is therefore very costly for taxpayers. In some instances, as the Ireland example illustrates, guarantees can threaten the solvency of a country. Acharya et al. (2011) and Demirgüç-Kunt and Huizinga (2013) point out the increase in sovereign credit default swap (CDS) spreads after the announcement of government guarantees in the financial sector and the strong correlation in movement between bank and sovereign CDS spreads after bailouts. By limiting fiscal costs, a limited ex-ante commitment can also improve the reliability and credibility of deposit insurance schemes.

A limited commitment also ensures that deposit insurance schemes will be harmonized across countries. This approach levels the playing field and reduces regulatory arbitrage, whereby investors move funds to countries where they expect the local authorities to increase coverage during a crisis. With the growing globalization of financial systems and cross-border banking, the harmonization of deposit insurance schemes has become an important issue. The possibility that governments will intervene after a crisis to either increase coverage or provide other types of support can weaken harmonization. There can also be differences in how domestic and foreign banks are treated in home and host countries. According to Bertay, Demirgüç-Kunt, and Huizinga (2016), internationalized banks benefit less from home country financial safety nets than their domestic counterparts. The global financial crisis experience highlighted that countries may even decide to selectively honor their deposit insurance, possibly distinguishing domestic and foreign depositors or retail depositors and others.[4] The 2014 European Union directive to require member countries to have the same coverage in terms of amounts and types of deposits is a step in the right direction to ensure a harmonized level of protection for depositors.

Finally, it is important for deposit insurance schemes to incorporate features to help internalize risk-taking by banks. The empirical evidence reveals that poorly designed schemes can increase the likelihood that a country will experience a banking crisis.[5] Effective deposit insurance also requires monitoring by supervisors that have the incentives and legal authority to intervene quickly to resolve troubled institutions.[6] Since the crisis, reforms have limited the amount of taxpayer funds to be put at risk, and new rules resolve insolvent financial institutions quickly with minimal damage to the country (see the section below, titled "Regulatory and Supervisory Remedies"). Nevertheless, because many countries provided blanket guarantees with full coverage during the crisis, the empirical evidence suggests that moral hazard problems associated with full blanket guarantees may remain for a long time.

Implicit Government Guarantees Become Explicit

During the global financial crisis, policy responses went beyond the use of explicit guarantees. In many countries, losses by uninsured creditors were covered using taxpayer funds, confirming market expectations of implicit government guarantees. The financial sectors in high-income and developing countries received extended periods of liquidity, bank nationalizations, recapitalizations, and asset purchases, as well as state guarantees on bank liabilities (Laeven and Valencia 2018). For example, one of the largest Dutch banks, ABN Amro, was nationalized and subsequently merged with the already-bailed-out Dutch operations of the Belgian bank Fortis. Box 2.2 details the size of some of these policy measures and their impact on government finances during and after the global financial crisis. Although these measures were successful in reducing the severity of the recent banking crises (Rose and Wieladek 2012; Hryckiewicz 2014), along with expansions of deposit insurance, state interventions to rescue banks will have adverse effects in the long

BOX 2.2 Economic Costs of State Support during the Global Financial Crisis

Government interventions to support national banking systems were widespread during the global financial crisis. Before the crisis, systemic banking crises mostly occurred in developing countries, but the 2007–09 crisis represented a big change in this pattern. More than half of the 28 systemic banking crises documented by Laeven and Valencia (2018) since 2007 were in Europe, with only a few in developing countries. Figure B2.2.1 shows the cost of government interventions in terms of liquidity support and recapitalizations since 2008. The average peak liquidity support provided by the authorities reached 15 percent of deposits, and the average capital support provided to banks across countries was 7 percent of GDP.

FIGURE B2.2.1 Recapitalizations and Liquidity Support during Banking Crises, 2007–17

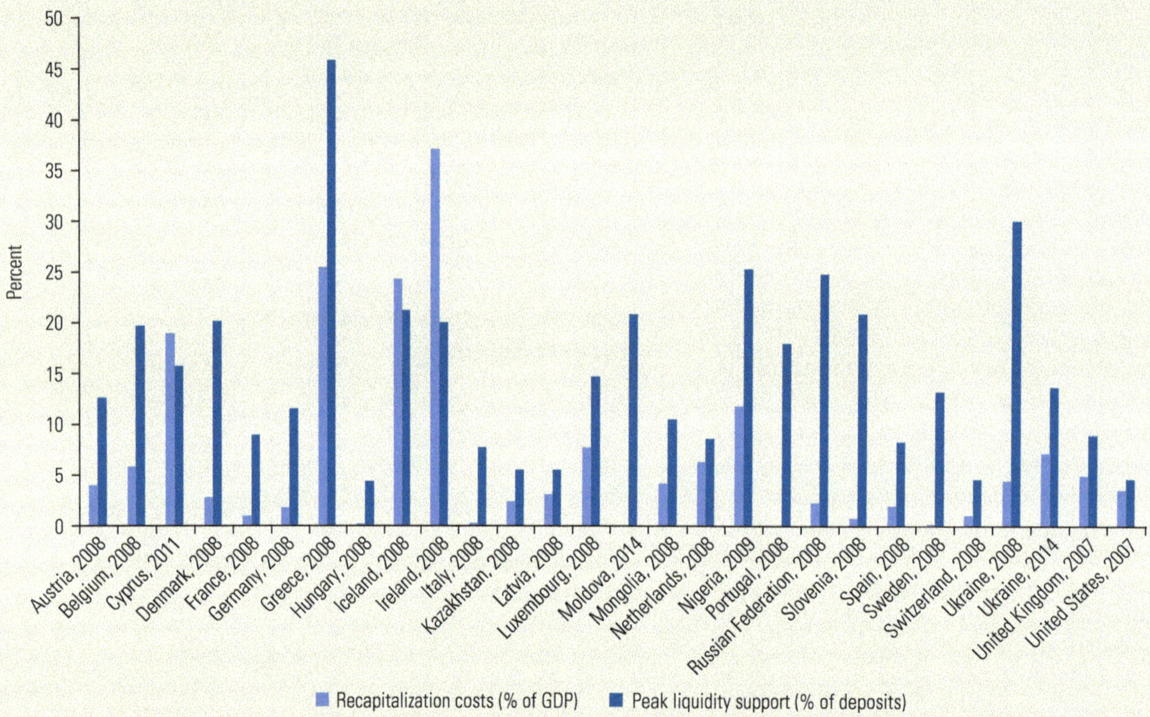

Source: Laeven and Valencia 2018.
Note: This figure shows the relative size of recapitalizations and peak liquidity support during the banking crises after 2006.

More than 100 European banks were bailed out between 2007 and 2013 through various liquidity, asset relief, and recapitalization interventions (Gerhardt and Vander Vennet 2017). Contingent liabilities, such as government guarantees, to support financial institutions reached €1.34 trillion in 2009. By 2017, this amount remained above €150 billion, which is almost as large as the budget of the European Union in that year. Figure B2.2.2 shows the impact of these interventions on government budgets. Between 2007 and 2017, EU-28 countries incurred net costs of around €241 billion. Ireland, Germany, and Spain each incurred net costs of more than €40 billion.

The literature suggests that such interventions may help the banking systems by reducing the possibility of contagious runs. The long-term adverse impact of government interventions on market discipline is more difficult to capture and may outweigh the short-term economic gains.[a]

(box continued next page)

BOX 2.2 Economic Costs of State Support during the Global Financial Crisis *(continued)*

FIGURE B2.2.2 Government Interventions in the European Union during Banking Crises, 2007–17

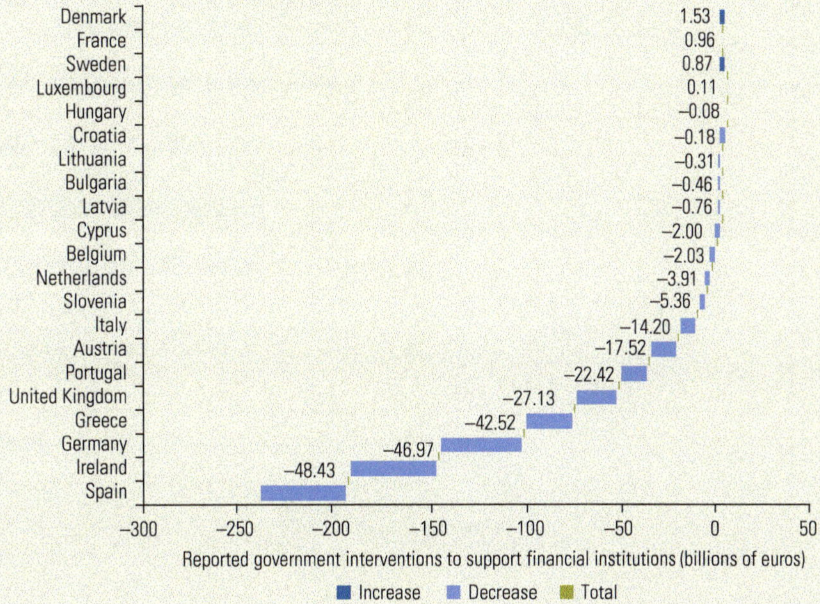

Source: Eurostat (database, European Union).
Note: This figure shows the net impact of government interventions to support financial institutions in the EU-28 countries on general government budgets.

a. According to Berger, Roman, and Sedunov (forthcoming), the U.S. Troubled Asset Relief Program (TARP) reduced the systemic risk contributions of the banks benefiting from the program during the crisis years 2009 and 2010, but increased their systemic risk contributions after the crisis.

term. Arguably, the most serious negative effect on market discipline going forward will stem from the blanket guarantees put in place in many countries during the crisis.[7]

The real economic costs of government interventions to rescue financial institutions go beyond the direct costs of capital and liquidity injections and other forms of direct support. In accounting terms, most of the programs implemented during the financial crisis have been a success, with the outlays of most programs paid back in full with interest (Webel and Labonte 2018). However, this simple accounting calculation ignores the true economic value of guarantees: the potential but not realized costs to taxpayers. Economic models that treat implicit guarantees within a contingent pricing framework come up with significantly larger estimates for the value of guarantees (Lucas 2018). An apt analogy for the economic cost of guarantees during a crisis would be the cost of providing fire insurance for a house that is on fire. More important, there are indirect economic costs that are difficult to quantify. These include distortions to incentives for risk-taking and monitoring financial institutions, distortions from adhoc bailout policies (such as those for rescuing some institutions and not others), economic distortions resulting from regulatory responses, and the growing public distrust of financial institutions. These indirect economic

FIGURE 2.3 **Bank Sizes Worldwide and Regional Bank Concentrations**

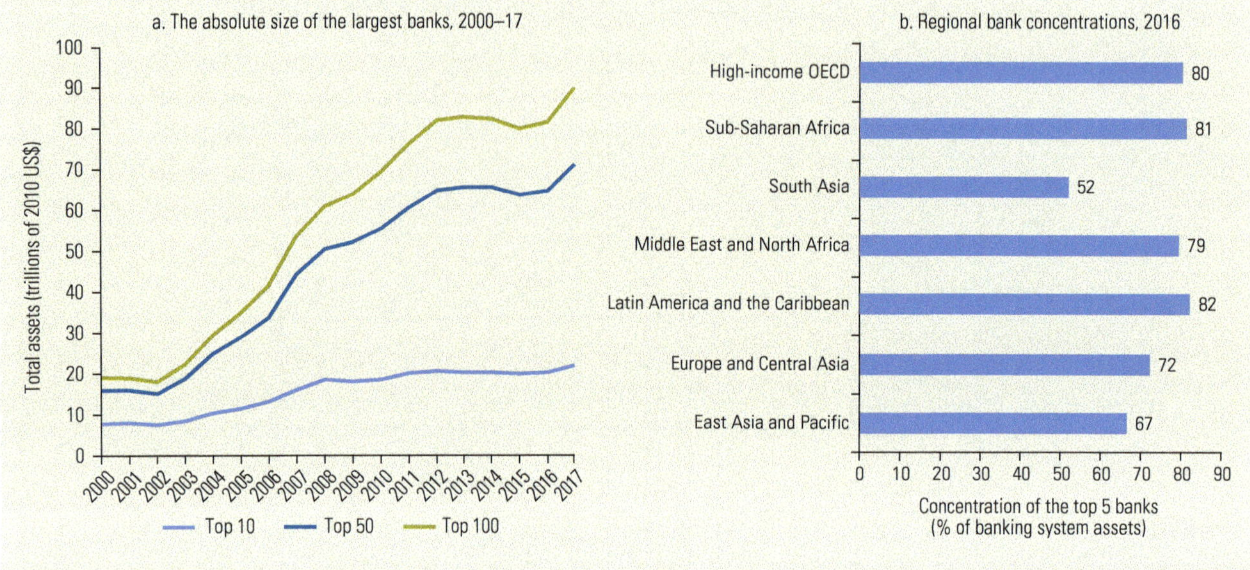

Sources: 2000–12: archived data from Bankscope (Bureau van Dijk); 2013–17: Orbis Bank Focus (Bureau van Dijk); World Bank staff calculations.
Note: This panel shows the total assets of the largest commercial banks, using unconsolidated statements on a rolling basis.

Sources: Global Finance Development Database (World Bank) and World Bank staff calculations.
Note: This panel shows the share of countries' banking system assets held by the largest five banks, averaged at the regional level. OECD = Organisation for Economic Co-operation and Development.

costs are difficult to quantify, but they can have long-lasting effects.

Banks have grown large in size in the aftermath of the global financial crisis. Figure 2.3, panel a, shows the total assets of the largest banks worldwide between 2000 and 2017. As a result of mergers and acquisitions (some of which were forced or encouraged by supervisors), the largest banks have grown even larger in many countries, and the banking systems remain highly concentrated. There has also been a decline in the number of financial institutions. In Europe, the number of banks fell, from more than 10,000 in 2005 to around 7,000 in 2018 (European Central Bank SDW 2019). There has been a similar decline in the United States, where the number of commercial banks declined from around 7,500 in 2005 to around 4,700 in 2018 (FFIEC 2019). As seen in figure 2.3, panel b, the banking systems in most regions remain highly concentrated. The top five banks on average account for around 80 percent of total banking system assets in high-income countries and in regions such as Sub-Saharan Africa, the Middle East and Northern Africa, and Latin America and the Caribbean.

Regulatory and Supervisory Remedies

The Financial Stability Board (FSB) was established by G-20 members to set up new macroprudential rules to govern bank behavior in the aftermath of the global financial crisis.[8] Working with the Basel Committee on Banking Supervision (BCBS), one of the key objectives of the FSB is to protect the public from any economic damage caused by the failure of systemically important institutions. This objective reflects the concern that SIFIs may engage in excessive and correlated risk-taking behavior resulting from market perceptions that these institutions are too big to fail (TBTF). After the crisis, the FSB adopted a policy goal of ending moral hazard and ending TBTF. The main changes to the regulatory frameworks to deal with TBTF include: (1) higher capital and liquidity requirements overall and additional surcharges for institutions deemed systemically important; (2) a new resolution process for bank holding companies and new requirements for systemically important banks to hold bail-in debt; and (3) governance reforms—specifically, enhanced supervision of risk management and risk-reporting processes at banks, including periodic stress tests.

Capital and Liquidity Requirements

The BCBS set guidelines to identify both global and domestic systemically important banks. The assessment is based on the average of 12 indicators associated with five dimensions of systemic risk identified by the BCBS: size, interconnectedness, substitutability/financial institution infrastructure, complexity, and cross-jurisdictional activity (Barth et al. 2013; BCBS 2018a). These banks are required to hold additional common equity Tier 1 capital ranging from 1 percent to 3.5 percent, depending on their importance. Most countries have applied a range of capital surcharges to their domestic SIFIs, reflecting the extent of their domestic systemic importance following the BCBS approach to global SIFIs.[9] These banks are also required to hold additional bail-in debt that can be converted to equity. Figure 2.4 shows the percentage and number of countries by income group that have implemented additional capital and liquidity requirements and other restrictions on banks deemed systemically important by local supervisors.

These additional capital requirements are intended to provide a sufficient equity cushion to make these institutions more resilient and to internalize the social impact of their failure. The capital surcharges should make bailouts less likely by reducing the default probability of these banks. The surcharges also curb the incentives to grow too much because larger banks may face higher capital requirements. Critics argue that the surcharges are too low for these banks to survive a financial crisis similar to that of 2007–09 (Passmore and von Hafften 2017).

During the global financial crisis, the high reliance on wholesale short-term funding by financial institutions caused a series of

FIGURE 2.4 New Rules for Systemically Important Banks

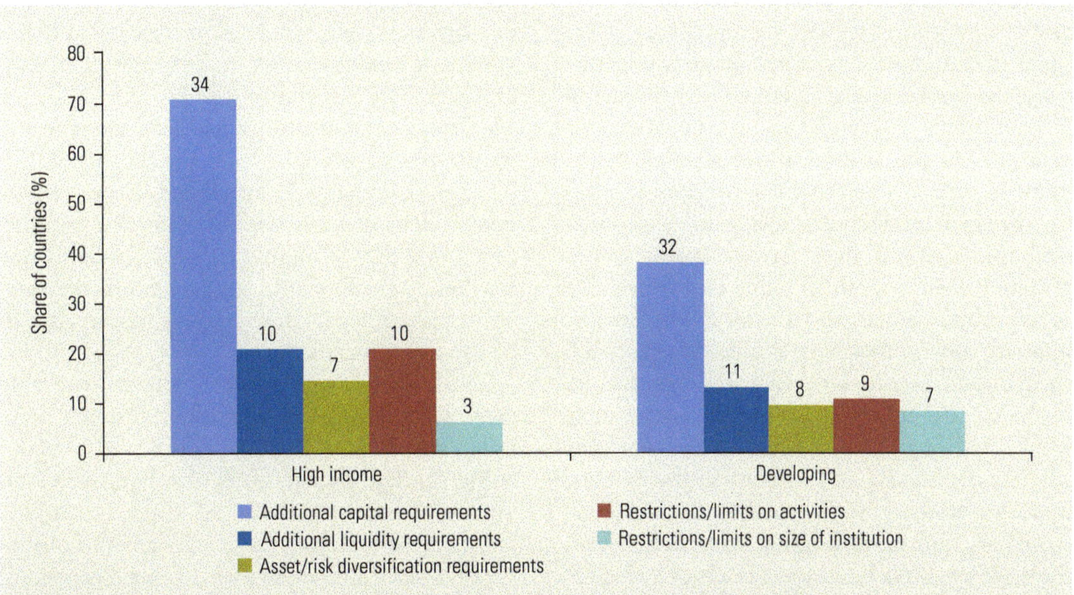

Source: Bank Regulation and Supervision Survey (BRSS), wave 5, https://www.worldbank.org/en/research/brief/BRSS.
Note: This figure shows the number of countries (over the bars) as well as the percentage of countries (height of the bars) that have implemented new rules for systemically important banks.

liquidity problems. The dominance of short-term funding over longer-term, less volatile sources of funds (such as retail deposits or equity) also resulted in cross-border contagion (De Haas and Van Lelyveld 2014). The regulatory response, which was part of the Basel III reforms, was to introduce two new minimum liquidity standards: the liquidity coverage ratio (LCR) and the net stable funding ratio (NSFR). The LCR was designed to make banks more resilient to brief but severe liquidity shocks. The NSFR was designed to ensure that banks have sufficient stable funding sources to begin with in order to reduce the possibility of system-wide liquidity shortages. Although many theoretical banking models emphasize the complementarity between capital and liquidity (see, for example, Kashyap, Tsomocos, and Vardoulakis 2017), the introduction and application of new liquidity regulations have been more limited than that of capital regulations (figure 2.4).

Resolution Rules and Bail-In Debt Requirements

The bankruptcy in 2008 of the U.S. investment bank Lehman Brothers highlighted the many difficulties in resolving banks with global operations subject to regulatory oversight in different countries. In many countries, the resolution of failed smaller financial institutions is a straightforward process. For example, in the United States a small failed bank is typically taken into conservatorship by the Federal Deposit Insurance Corporation (FDIC), and then an agreement is negotiated with a healthy bank to assume the failed bank's assets and business operations. It is not uncommon for a failed bank to be shut down over a weekend and resume its business operations as a new bank the next week. Although this process is efficient and ensures confidence and stability in the system, it does not work well for large financial institutions and bank holding companies with multiple business lines and operations in dozens of countries subject to different types of regulatory oversight. It is also difficult to find healthy banks able to assume the operations of a large financial institution in times of market distress.

An important component of new regulations aimed at improving systemic stability has therefore been to develop institutional rules and procedures to resolve large financial institutions without having a destabilizing effect on the financial system. In 2011 the FSB proposed 12 key attributes to serve as part of policy responses at the national level to resolve SIFIs (FSB 2014). The main goal has been to resolve these large financial institutions in an orderly manner without major disruptions of the financial system and the real economy, and without exposing taxpayers to a risk of loss. Most countries in which SIFIs are domiciled have introduced legislation to resolve these institutions consistent with FSB principles. Figure 2.5 shows the number and percentage of countries in each income group that have implemented new resolution schemes in response to the global financial crisis.

In the United States, the FDIC created a detailed plan to resolve SIFIs using a single point of entry (SPOE) approach. Under this scheme, the FDIC creates a bridge company and takes over a failed institution at the top bank holding company level, allowing different business lines such as insurance and investment banking arms, to continue their operations. The assets and some of the liabilities of the failed institutions are then transferred to the bridge company set up by the FDIC. The new company is capitalized by pre-issued bail-in debt. If more capital is needed and the new company is unable to raise funds in the market, then the FDIC would lend to the new company under its new powers under Title II of the Dodd-Frank Act.[10]

Under the SPOE scheme, supervisors can now assign losses to specific claimants of a failed institution, thereby significantly weakening market expectations of a bailout. Convincing bank creditors that their funds are truly at risk increases their incentives to monitor and discipline these institutions. As part of the Dodd-Frank Act, SIFIs are also required to submit resolution plans, so-called living wills, to the FDIC. These resolution plans describe the institution's strategy for orderly resolution and liquidation in the event the institution fails. The reliability of these plans in a crisis, however, has not been tested.

The resolution framework implemented in the European Union (EU) and other countries is similar to the framework in the United States. The Bank Recovery and Resolution Directive (BRRD) was adopted in the spring of 2014 by the EU to provide plans to implement the core attributes outlined by the FSB and to create cooperation arrangements to tackle cross-border banking failures. Three main institutional differences characterize the FDIC and BRRD approaches. First, because there is no treasury in the EU's banking union, fiscal resources available at the time of resolution are limited. However, the Single Resolution Fund was set up in 2014 as part of the Single Resolution Mechanism to finance the resolution and restructuring of banks supervised by the European Central Bank (ECB).[11] The second difference is that in the EU, several different regulations and laws deal with resolution at the national level, making it difficult to have a unique resolution process. And, third, the FDIC relies on an SPOE at the holding company level, whereas BRRD is more flexible and allows for multiple points of entry at the subsidiary level.

Although most market participants agree that the new resolution policies have strengthened market discipline and reduced the likelihood of taxpayer funds being put at risk, some criticisms of the new resolution rules have emerged.[12] First, some argue that the regulatory authorities, by explicitly defining systemically important institutions, are reinforcing the expectations of large financial institutions that they will receive support when they get into trouble.[13] Indeed, there is some evidence that the designation of institutions as SIFIs has produced positive stock price reactions (Bongini, Nieri, and Pelagatti 2015; Dewenter and Riddick 2018). Institutions may be incentivized to become SIFIs or large enough banks to qualify under the new resolution rules because the market would provide them with cheaper funding (Skeel 2010). However, some firms have tried to avoid the

FIGURE 2.5 New Resolution Rules for Systemically Important Banks

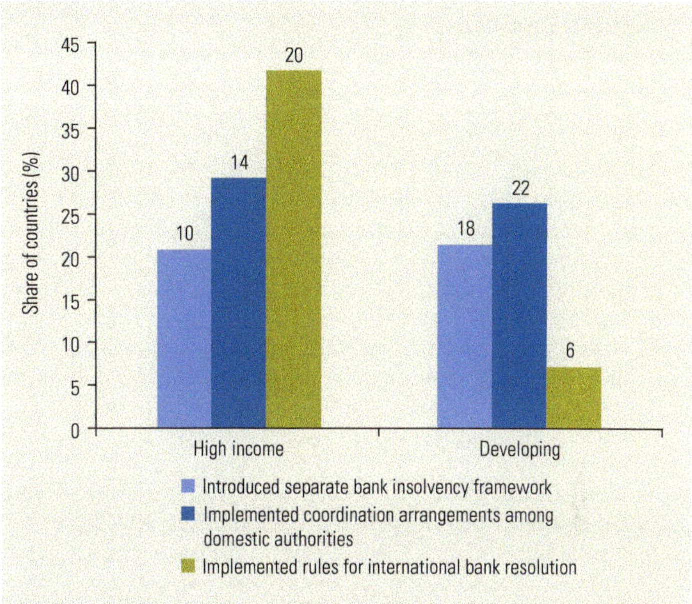

Source: Bank Regulation and Supervision Survey (BRSS), wave 5, https://www.worldbank.org/en/research/brief/BRSS.
Note: This figure shows the number of countries (over the bars) as well as the percentage of countries (height of the bars) that have implemented new resolution schemes for systemically important institutions in the aftermath of the global financial crisis.

SIFI designation. MetLife, for example, successfully sued to avoid the SIFI classification, and General Electric reorganized to become smaller in order to avoid the new resolution rules. Violon, Durant, and Toader (2017) show that a SIFI designation by the FSB has resulted in these banks expanding their balance sheets more slowly and has led to improvements in their leverage ratios.

A second criticism is that the new resolution policies give too much discretion to regulatory authorities. In the United States, for example, the FDIC could take alternative action that would unsettle creditors and put taxpayers at risk. Similarly, the ECB has considerable discretion in determining whether a bank is failing or likely to fail and whether it will be subject to resolution under the Single Resolution Mechanism (see box 2.3 for how various bank resolutions and liquidations are handled in the EU). Critics argue that a strengthened or modified bankruptcy code may work better for large, complex financial institutions.

BOX 2.3 Bank Resolution Cases: One Law with Different Applications by European Union Countries

The Bank Recovery and Resolution Directive (BRRD) is the legal framework for bank resolution in the European Union (EU), including bail-in–related directions. Since its inception, however, the BRRD has been subject to different applications, even under a common law in the EU. Although cases differ and come with important lessons, they indicate that, even with the recent reforms in the EU, it will be challenging to resolve or liquidate banks by imposing losses on shareholders and unsecured liability holders, especially because of conflicts of interest with national and political interests.

Andelskassen (2015, Denmark). The resolution of Andelskassen was the first application of the BRRD outside the euro area. Because there was not enough capital and bail-in debt to absorb the losses, uninsured depositors incurred losses (World Bank 2016).

BPE (2017, Spain). Banco Popular Español (BPE) was the first bank deemed failing or likely to fail by the European Central Bank in its role as a banking supervisor and the first resolution case under the Single Resolution Mechanism (SRM). In the resolution process, equity and other junior debt instruments (such as additional Tier 1 notes and other hybrid capital instruments) were wiped out, and the bank was sold to another Spanish bank, Santander. The process was a success, but the resolution nevertheless raised important questions. In particular, BPE had passed regulatory stress tests even under adverse scenarios in 2016 (*New York Times* 2017).

ABLV (2018, Latvia). ABLV, the third-largest bank in Latvia, was hit by a money-laundering scandal and was considered as failing or likely to fail under the BRRD (Politico 2018). Under SRM it was decided that the continued operation of the bank was not in the public interest, and that a resolution process should not be implemented. ABLV and its Luxembourg subsidiary instead went through a liquidation process. This case illustrated that the liquidation of banks remains a possibility under the SRM if the resolution and continued operations of a bank are not in the public interest.

CCB (2018, Cyprus). Cyprus Cooperative Bank (CCB) was bailed out in 2013 using taxpayer funds, and the government continued to inject capital over the years. The BRRD may choose not to resolve banks if state aid is provided. This was the case for the CCB. The good assets of the bank (its performing loan portfolio) were eventually sold, and the government took over the bad assets (its nonperforming portfolio).

Veneto Banca and Banca Popolare di Vicenza (2017, Italy). These banks were also deemed failing or likely to fail under the SRM, but the SRM authorities decided not to resolve these banks. Instead, the Italian authorities took over the resolution process (see ECB 2018, 49–51). Italian taxpayer funds were spent before bail-in options were fully utilized. The two banks were eventually liquidated. This episode—together with the earlier "precautionary recapitalization" of Monte dei Paschi and the recent decision to bail out another small, nonsystemic Italian bank, Banca Carige— casts doubt on whether bail-in mechanisms from the EU's single rule book will work in every EU jurisdiction.

A third criticism is that the Dodd-Frank Act strips the Federal Reserve Bank of much of its last-resort lending powers, limiting the Fed from lending money in situations like those faced in 2008 without explicit political authorization. Although this aspect of the act is intended to reduce market expectations of support for SIFIs, it politicizes a crisis response and can lead to worse outcomes if the law's resolution mechanisms are inadequate.

Finally, the process of cross-border resolution remains a thorny issue. There is no clear jurisdiction rule on the power allocation between home and host resolution authorities. The lack of such a rule could prove to be an obstacle to effective global resolution because cross-border cooperation could become difficult during crises due to political sensitivities. As bail-in decisions will have distributional consequences across business units, strong disagreements are likely to arise as decisions are made to determine which subsidiary is bailed in and which is not. When the cross-jurisdictional transfer required for a successful SPOE resolution is too large, regulators may prefer to ring-fence assets in their own jurisdiction and prevent the required transfers. In that case, the planned SPOE resolution could break down, leading to a disorderly liquidation or a tax-funded bailout. Under SPOE, local authorities would need credible guarantees from the consolidating authorities about the resources that would be available to them in case of resolution (Bolton and Oehmke 2018). According to Faia and Weder di Mauro (2015), under multiple point of entry (MPOE) and SPOE with noncooperative authorities, the costs for bail-in-able debt holders are higher than under cooperative SPOE regimes and ring-fencing. The authors also show that banks under those regimes have incentives to reduce their exposure in foreign assets. Work is still needed to identify critical functions to be preserved in resolution via living wills, agreeing on triggers for entry into resolution, coordination on legal issues such as statutory stays on payments, and the total loss-absorbing capacity (TLAC) distribution across home and host jurisdictions.

In November 2015, the Financial Stability Board issued new international standards on the TLAC in the resolution of SIFIs. These new TLAC requirements were issued to increase market discipline and to reduce the possibility of taxpayer funds being used to rescue large financial institutions (FSB 2015). According to the new standards, the TLAC should be made up of securities that can be written down or converted into equity when an SIFI is in distress. These securities can be capital instruments or unsecured debt that can be converted into equity. Because of the tax advantages, in most countries TLAC securities have been in the form of convertible bail-in bonds. The TLAC standard is 16 percent of risk-weighted assets starting in 2019, and it will increase to 18 percent in 2022. SIFIs located in emerging markets have until 2025 and 2028 to meet the same standards. However, this period for emerging market SIFIs will shorten if over the next five years total corporate debt issuance exceeds 55 percent of a given country's GDP. The Single Resolution Board in the EU requires banks to meet a minimum requirement for own funds and eligible liabilities (MREL). This requirement increases the ability of banks to absorb losses and restore their capital position and continue to operate during the aftermath of a financial crisis.

The United States and the EU have statutory requirements that bail-in bondholders must absorb losses before any public money can be put into a troubled bank. If an SIFI were to fail, it would be recapitalized by its private sector long-term creditors using the bail-in bonds, with the idea that the orderly liquidation fund would be used only to provide liquidity support, not to inject capital. In the event of a default, the debt claims would be converted into equity in an automatic process resembling what would typically happen in a Chapter 11 bankruptcy in the United States. Figure 2.6 shows the percentage and number of countries that have implemented requirements for bail-in funding based on the BRSS survey.

The bail-in bonds address two shortcomings of the regulatory regime that was in place before the global financial crisis. First, bail-in bonds provide additional capital to absorb losses, reducing the likelihood that a bank will default and must be liquidated. Second, bail-in bonds reduce the likelihood of a run by uninsured short-term liability holders by increasing the tranche of claims junior to them.

It is possible that, by imposing long-term debt requirements on SIFIs, the new TLAC rules will prompt these banks to increase their leverage, which in turn would increase the probability that they will fail. Critics suggest that SIFIs should instead hold more capital. Although it is more important to avoid default in the first place, it is also important to consider resolution in the event of a default. TLAC requirements, by providing a tranche of equity when a default occurs, give resolution authorities flexibility in creating a new

FIGURE 2.6 Requirements Implemented for Resolving Systemically Important Financial Institutions

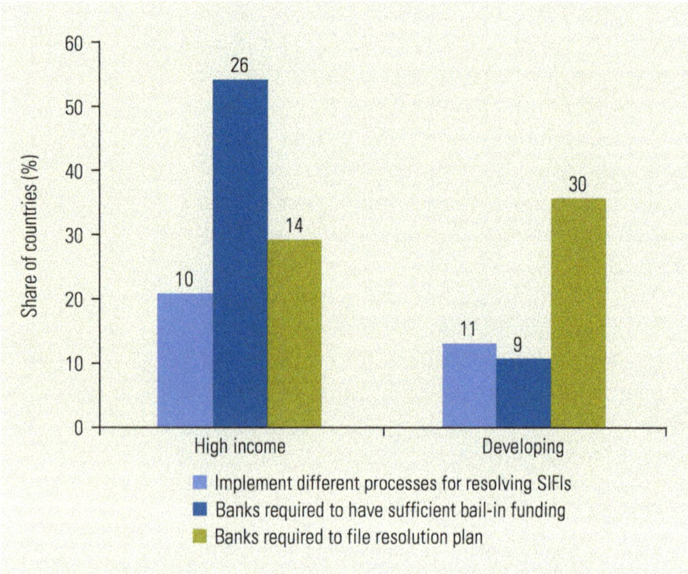

Source: Bank Regulation and Supervision Survey (BRSS), wave 5, https://www.worldbank.org/en/research/brief/BRSS.
Note: This figure shows the number of countries (over the bars) as well as the percentage of countries (height of the bars) that have implemented different resolution schemes for systemically important financial institutions (SIFIs).

entity with capital to continue the operations of a failed bank.

The TLAC system puts bail-in bonds at the forefront for absorbing loses when an SIFI fails. If orderly liquidation works as envisioned by the new regulations, bank losses should be concentrated in bail-in bonds. By implication, other claimants, including some very sophisticated short-term investors, would be more protected by these resolution policies. These reforms therefore have implications for market discipline.

The main effect of bail-in bonds will be to shift monitoring incentives away from short-term liabilities toward longer-term subordinated bonds. Although this shift will reduce runs, as noted earlier, it will also eliminate the disciplinary effects provided by the threat of bank runs. Studies have suggested that short-term debt can reduce potential agency conflicts by exposing managers to more frequent monitoring by the market. Because short-term debt comes up for frequent renewal, a bank and its managers can be scrutinized by lenders and rating agencies before the debt of the bank is rolled over (Rajan and Winton 1995; Hart and Moore 1998).

By contrast, bail-in bondholders would be more exposed to bank losses in the new regulatory regime and would be incentivized to monitor and discipline banks. Although such an outcome would benefit market discipline, the direct corrective action that these bail-in bondholders can take would be limited. Bail-in bonds would account only for a small portion of total liabilities, and their effect on the total cost of funding for banks would be small. At the same time, prices can act as a valuable signal to other debtholders and regulators about the riskiness of banks' assets. The net effect of the TLAC requirement on market discipline thus remains ambiguous.

Finally, implementation of TLAC requirements in emerging markets that lack market depth can be challenging. China's four biggest banks (also the biggest in the world) would have to issue over US$450 billion in bail-in bonds to meet the FSB's loss absorption buffer by 2025 (Bloomberg 2018). This amount is more than double the size of dollar bond issuance from all Chinese corporates last year.

Although some of the reforms just discussed (especially those targeting global systemically important financial institutions) may not apply locally in some developing countries, their implementation in other jurisdictions can have significant spillover effects.[14] In particular, the implementation of reforms may result in a disproportionate tightening or reduction of international and cross-border financial activities in developing countries. A growing reliance on external credit ratings to calculate risk weights may also adversely affect firms in developing countries, which are less likely to be rated or have a verifiable credit history, thereby affecting the availability and cost of external long-term financing.

Macroprudential Rules and Governance Reforms

SIFIs are now subject to enhanced risk management and risk monitoring by supervisors. Figure 2.7 shows the percentage and number of countries in each income group where

FIGURE 2.7 Regulation of Systemic Risk in Systemically Important Financial Institutions

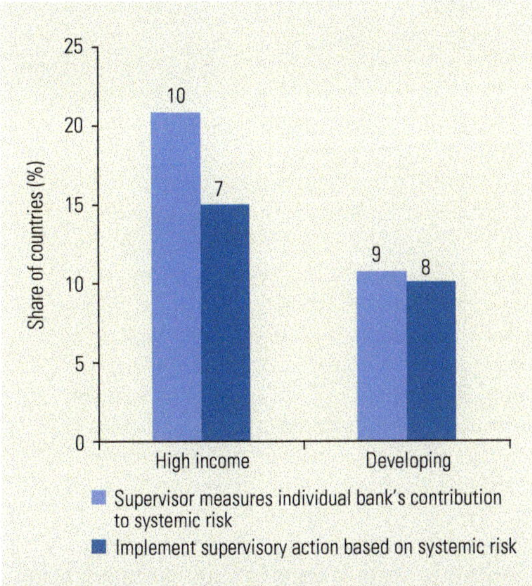

Source: Bank Regulation and Supervision Survey (BRSS), wave 5, https://www.worldbank.org/en/research/brief/BRSS.
Note: This figure shows the number of countries (over the bars) as well as the percentage of countries (height of the bars) in each income group where supervisors explicitly measure and monitor an individual bank's contribution to systemic risk and whether they base supervisory actions on its contribution to systemic risk.

supervisors explicitly measure and monitor an individual bank's contribution to systemic risk. Although a significant percentage of countries take systemic risk into account, that translates into supervisory action for a smaller percentage of countries. As part of the enhanced supervision, most SIFIs are now required to conduct periodic stress tests. These stress tests examine an SIFI's financial response to hypothetical stress scenarios, such as macro shocks, deterioration of asset values, liquidity shortages, and credit defaults. The Federal Reserve under the Dodd-Frank Act in the United States and the European Banking Authority in the EU require SIFIs to engage in periodic stress tests. The stress tests are intended to identify weaknesses in SIFI funding and balance sheets so they can be corrected before problems become larger and spread to other banks. Many SIFIs are also required to establish risk committees to oversee a bank's risk management practices following guidelines set by the Basel Committee on Banking Supervision (BCBS 2015).

Ring-fencing of retail deposits and plain vanilla lending from riskier business lines are another form of SIFI regulation. In the United States, the so-called Volcker Rule limits deposit-taking banks from making risky investments.[15] In the United Kingdom, the Vickers Rule states that financial institutions with deposits in excess of £25 billion are required to segregate those deposit-taking activities from affiliate risks and to restrict retail deposit-taking banks from transferring capital to affiliates.

The global financial crisis also prompted bank governance reforms. Figure 2.8 shows the number and percentage of countries in which the reforms of boards, executive compensation, and risk management processes have been implemented. Corporate governance has improved, but improving the corporate governance of banks—that benefit from a financial safety net when in distress—can backfire. The empirical work in this area suggests that better-governed banks will simply exploit the financial safety net, lowering their levels of capital and taking on more risk (see box 2.4).[16]

FIGURE 2.8 Governance Reforms in Banks

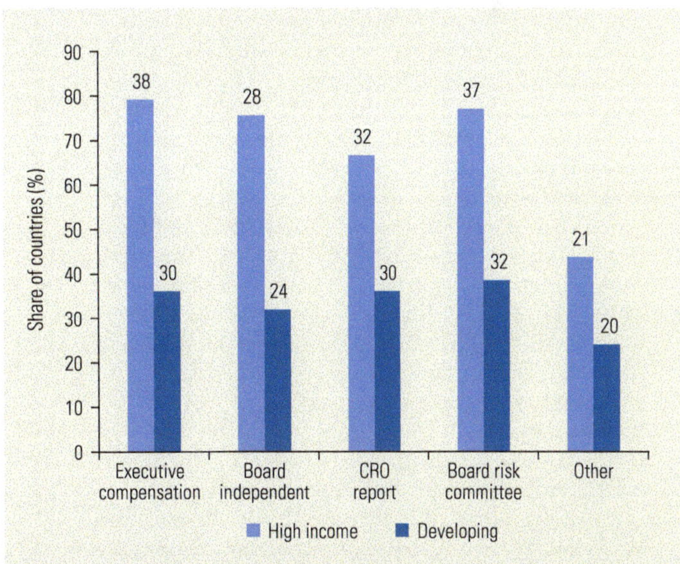

Source: Bank Regulation and Supervision Survey (BRSS), wave 5, https://www.worldbank.org/en/research/brief/BRSS.
Note: This figure shows the number of countries (over the bars) as well as the percentage of countries (height of the bars) in each income group where supervisors implemented governance reforms after the global financial crisis. CRO = Chief Risk Officer.

BOX 2.4 Does Good Governance Lead to Financial Stability?

There was a reexamination of governance and compensation practices of banks after the global financial crisis. Some critics have argued that excessive short-term compensation and the failure of boards to monitor bank executives led directly to the crisis. Although this line of thinking seems intuitive, from a theoretical perspective it is not clear whether better governance would lead to higher risk-taking by executives at banks.

Shareholder-friendly governance better aligns the incentives of bank executives with those of their bank's shareholders. This alignment can lead to higher risk-taking, since the payoffs of shareholders are bounded at zero because of limited liability. Banks' shareholders also benefit from both implicit and explicit guarantees provided by the state. They thus have incentives to take on more risk and more correlated risk in order to exploit the financial safety net. Counterintuitively, it is the banks' executives who are less incentivized to take on excessive risk compared with shareholders. Unlike shareholders, who are likely to hold diversified stock portfolios, executives tend to have their jobs, reputations, and a substantial portion of their personal wealth tied to the performance and health of their firm.

In two papers, Anginer et al. (2016, 2018) examine how CEO compensation and corporate governance are related to the capital and risk-taking policies of financial institutions. They find that shareholder-friendly governance leads to lower capitalization levels and greater stand-alone and systemic risk-taking, especially for larger banks, which tend to benefit more from implicit government guarantees.

In their paper "Corporate Governance and Bank Capitalization Strategies," the authors show that, for an international sample of banks over the period 2003–11, shareholder-friendly corporate governance—in the form of separation of the CEO and chairman of the board roles, intermediate board size, and an absence of anti-takeover provisions—is associated with lower bank capitalization. The authors also examine the share issuance, repurchase, and dividend payout decisions of banks after they experience a negative income shock. Banks with shareholder-friendly corporate governance are more likely to continue to make payouts to bank shareholders in the form dividends and share repurchases after experiencing a major negative income shock. These payouts lead to even lower bank capitalization.

In their second paper, "Corporate Governance of Banks and Financial Stability," the authors examine the relationship between shareholder-friendly corporate governance and the risk-taking behavior of banks. The authors use both stand-alone and correlated risk-taking measures. They find that high levels of shareholder-friendly corporate governance are associated with greater stand-alone and systemic risks for financial institutions compared with that of nonfinancial firms. This finding is consistent with the notion that banks benefit more than nonfinancial firms from financial safety nets.

Anginer et al. (2018) also find that shareholder-friendly corporate governance is associated with greater risk-taking by large banks than small banks. They attribute this finding to market expectations of support for large financial institutions, with larger banks benefiting more from implicit too-big-to-fail guarantees. Figure B2.4.1 illustrates one of the

FIGURE B2.4.1 Corporate Governance of Banks and Leverage

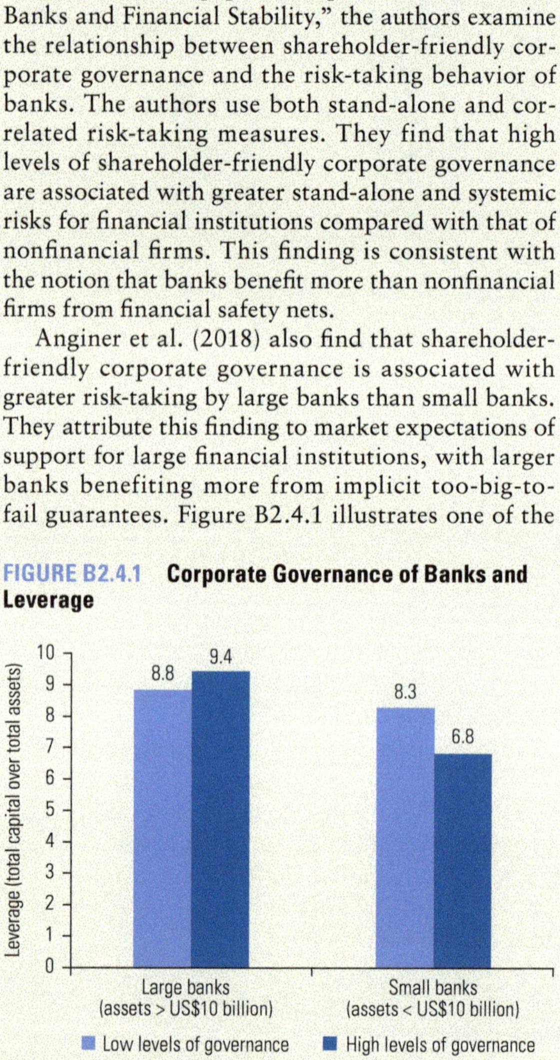

Source: Institutional Shareholder Services and Compustat Global.
Note: Leverage is market leverage computed by dividing the sum of the market value of equity and the book value of liabilities by the market value of equity. Bank size is based on the book value of total assets. The governance measure is based on 44 individual governance attributes related to board size and composition, compensation and ownership, external auditing, and antitakeover measures, available from the Corporate Governance Quotient database assembled by Institutional Shareholder Services (see Anginer et al. 2018 for details). The sample includes international publicly traded banks over 2004–08.

(box continued next page)

BOX 2.4 Does Good Governance Lead to Financial Stability? *(continued)*

findings in the paper. For smaller banks with assets of less than US$10 billion, high levels of corporate governance are associated with lower levels of leverage. For larger banks with assets greater than US$10 billion, however, high levels of governance lead to higher leverage. This finding is consistent with the notion that larger banks benefit more from implicit state guarantees, and shareholder-friendly governance leads to greater risk-taking and shifting in the form of higher leverage.

Both papers have important policy implications. In a world with mispriced financial safety nets and too-big-to-fail policies, shareholder-friendly governance that better aligns managerial incentives with shareholder interests may exacerbate the excessive risk-taking resulting from bank shareholders' incentives to exploit implicit and explicit state guarantees. The authors argue that the first priority should be to address moral hazard issues that result from too-big-to-fail policies.

The macroprudential regulations that have been implemented are not without problems. Critics argue that most of the new regulations focus primarily on regulating banks and other systemically important financial institutions. This entity-focused approach may prove to be too narrow, ignoring other critical elements of the system such as financial markets (Gorton 2009) and the growing importance of fintech and nonfinancial institutions (Buchak et al. 2018; Claessens et al. 2018) in the provision of financial services (see box 2.5). The

BOX 2.5 Shadow Banking in China

The growing importance of the shadow-banking system in China prompted authorities to respond with stricter regulations. Over the past several years, rules and regulations aimed at stabilizing credit growth and safeguarding the financial system have led to the creation of new types of assets around the regulatory perimeter, with commercial banks shifting lending to their investment books (through collaborations with insurance, trust, and securities companies) or off their balance sheets (through bankers' acceptances and entrusted loan arrangements). Although some of these new financial instruments were financed through proceeds from wealth management and trust products, they do not in practice shield financial intermediaries from credit risks. Though these practices can be seen as market-driven responses to credit shortages, they have been increasingly placed under regulatory scrutiny as less visible channels of risk transmission proliferated.

As figure B2.5.1 illustrates, during China's recent decade of rapid credit expansion, different types of financial instruments experienced surges in their utilization, which were followed by periods of relative cooldown and substitution into other shadow financing vehicles as a result of tightening of regulations.

Bankers' acceptances were intended to be a short-term liquidity instrument for trading companies, but were frequently discounted in secondary markets before maturity. They were the most prominent type of nonstandard credit vehicles, although their importance seemed to wane after the China Banking Regulation Commission (CBRC) issued new standards on bank liquidity management in February 2010.

A growing amount of loans were then extended by the less-regulated trust companies, which received financing from commercial banks and insurance companies channeling funding from off–balance-sheet wealth management products (WMPs) as China prepared for the transition to the Basel II capital rules. In March 2013, CBRC announced new bank WMP rules, tightening practices for investment management and information disclosure. A separate

(box continued next page)

BOX 2.5 Shadow Banking in China *(continued)*

FIGURE B2.5.1 Substitution across Allocative Instruments in China

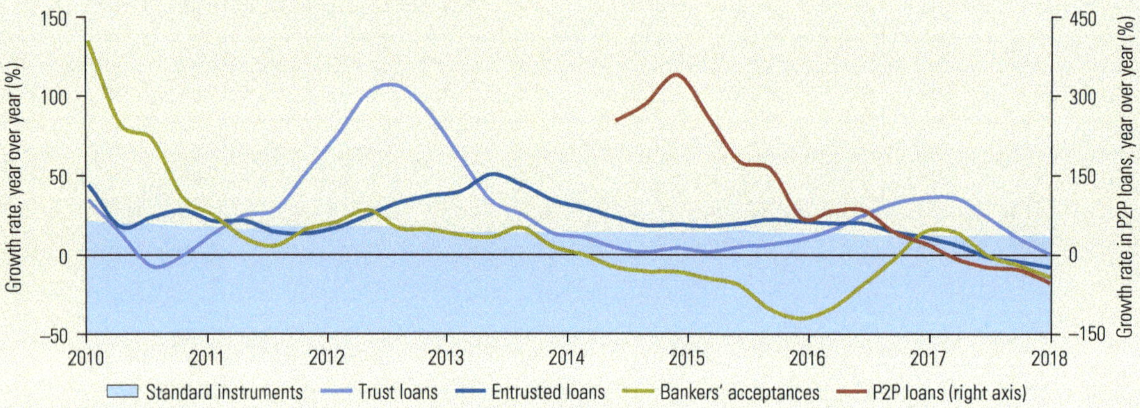

Source: World Bank staff calculations based on statistics from People's Bank of China and Wangdaizhijia, a peer-to-peer (P2P) aggregation portal.
Note: The term "standard instruments" refers to borrowings by nonfinancial companies through bank loans and corporate bonds.

department was also formed within CBRC in July 2014 to specialize in the supervision of WMPs.

In the meantime, banks accelerated their off-balance-sheet custodial business of entrusted lending to serve corporate customers in search of better yields. Such loans benefited (as did WMPs) from a perception of an implicit guarantee, especially when they were intermediated by the larger state-owned banks, despite the fact that the originating trustors were the legal holders of the credit risks. In January 2015, CBRC formalized the rules on entrusted loans, preventing their proceeds from being invested in WMPs, bonds, and equities, and no longer allowing firms to lend on existing bank loans.

Peer-to-peer (P2P) lending and third-party payment platforms began their drastic expansion in 2014. Despite the small base volumes, such practices promised convenience and high returns, and they exposed a growing number of households and corporates to underregulated financial risks. Supervisory oversight in the area has tightened since July 2015, with an emphasis on strengthening financial management, information disclosure, cybersecurity, and the illicit financing safeguards associated with Internet finance.

These episodes seem to suggest two general lessons on the regulatory approach of shadow banking. First, because shadow-banking activities often operate across the supervisory domains for banks, nonbank financial institutions, financial markets, and payment systems, interagency collaboration is often needed to formulate coherent strategies for containing systemic risks. In August 2013, the People's Bank of China was asked to organize coordination conferences on financial regulations by convening banking, insurance, and securities regulators. This arrangement influenced the development of the macroprudential assessment framework implemented in 2016 and was further elevated in July 2017 to become the Financial Stability and Development Committee for determining major plans for financial reforms.

Second, even though gaps and overlaps in regulatory policies can be identified and reduced, it is important to recognize that shadow banking may be driven by broader distortions in the main banking system. The gradual liberalization of lending and deposit interest rates from July 2013 to October 2015 promoted the market's role in determining prices for allocating financial resources. The lifting of a 75 percent cap on bank loan-to-deposit limits in June 2015 also reduced the pressure for credit to flow through nonstandard channels.

extensive and ever-growing regulations also place an undue burden on community banks, putting them at a competitive disadvantage and leading to regulatory arbitrage as nonbank entities enter the market.[17]

The reforms just described have been widely adopted and have succeeded, but many issues remain. SIFIs are better capitalized and financially sounder than they were in 2007. On the bright side, the overall riskiness of the banking sector as measured by the Z-score has improved since the global financial crisis, especially in high-income countries (figure 2.9, panel a). De-leveraging and de-risking have resulted in lower liquidity creation, as evidenced by a decline in the loan-to-deposit ratio (figure 2.9, panel b). However, some balance sheet issues remain.

FIGURE 2.9 Bank Riskiness, Impaired Loans, and Provisions before and after the Global Financial Crisis, by Country Income Group

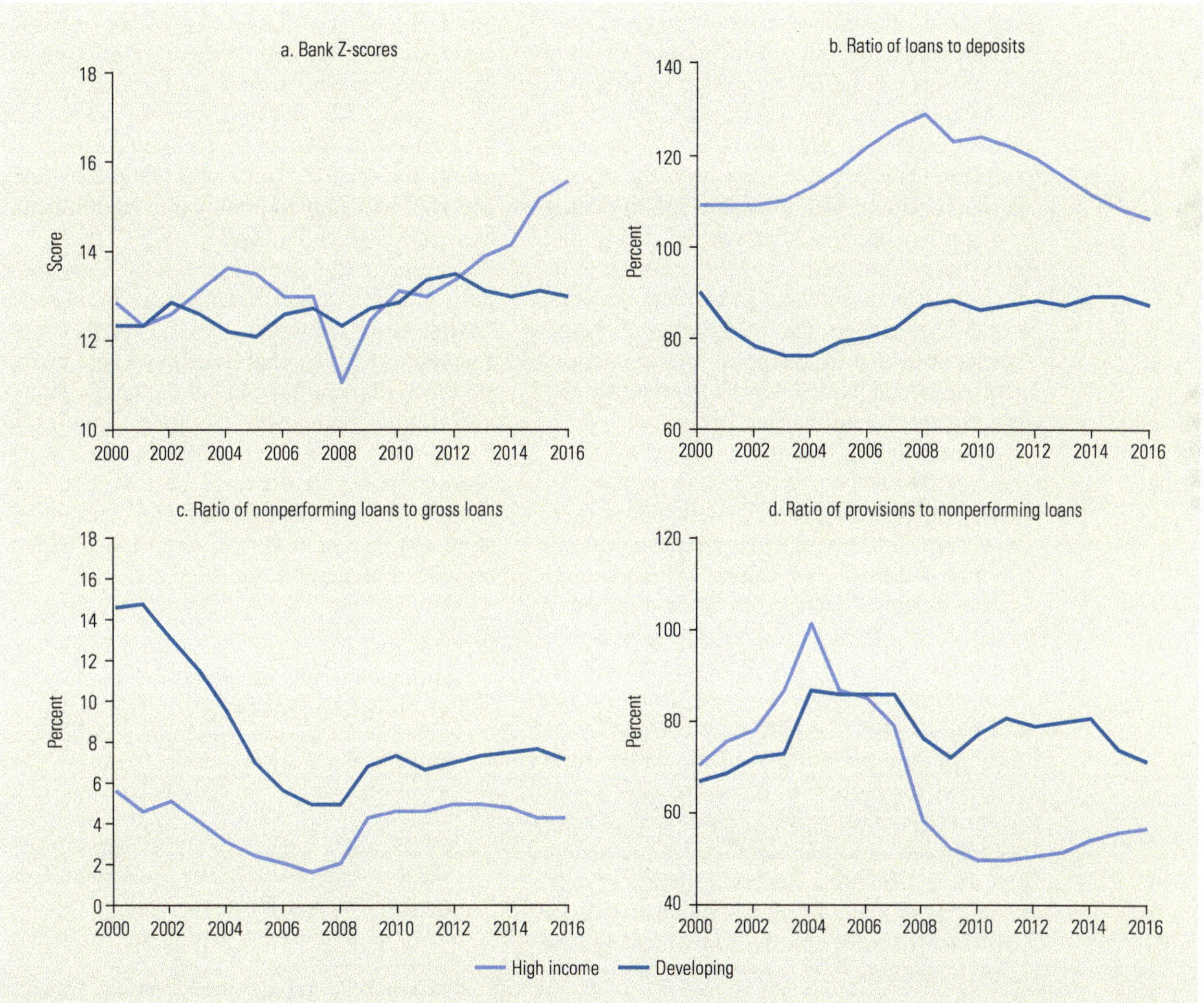

Sources: Global Finance Development Database (World Bank) and World Bank staff calculations.
Note: Bank Z-scores capture the probability of default of a country's banking system. The Z-score compares the buffer of a country's banking system (capitalization and returns) with the volatility of those returns. It is estimated as (ROA+(equity/assets))/sd (ROA), where sd (ROA) is the standard deviation of return on assets (ROA).

Nonperforming loans remain at elevated levels (figure 2.9, panel c). The banks are also underprovisioned for nonperforming loans (figure 2.9, panel d), which puts them at significant risk should a new crisis occur.

POLICY RECOMMENDATIONS

Market discipline has been one of the three pillars of Basel capital regulations and has been recognized by policy makers as an important component of their regulatory frameworks. The global financial crisis exposed important limitations of market discipline and cast doubt on its effectiveness as a prudential tool to rein in excessive risk-taking by banks. Many critics have expressed skepticism at the ability of the private market to identify risks and monitor financial institutions.[18] However, the reason market discipline has not succeeded in reining in risk is not because of private market failure but because of structural impediments such as the presence of implicit guarantees creating moral hazard and the informational asymmetries inherent in financial intermediation, which impeded bank creditors from effectively monitoring and influencing banks.

As emphasized throughout this chapter, incentives are the most important component of market discipline. Market participants must have "skin in the game" to effectively monitor and influence risk-taking. This requires insolvent banks to fail and to be liquidated in an orderly fashion and bank investors and depositors to share in the losses. Recent reforms requiring SIFIs to hold more capital and bail-in debt and new rules for resolution and orderly liquidation are steps in the right direction for putting in place the right set of incentives going forward. These reforms have been widely adopted and have succeeded, but some key policy issues remain. In particular, how cross-border resolution will be implemented and how bail-in funds will be shared between host and home country supervisors remain uncertain. It is also not clear whether bail-in funds will be enough to capitalize bridge banks during resolution to avoid placing taxpayer funds at risk. Finally, it is difficult to quantify the long-term effects of widespread bailouts and blanket guarantees on moral hazard and market discipline.

For developing countries, the principle of proportionality must be kept in mind when implementing policies designed to enhance market discipline. Because developing countries tend to be in the earlier stages of economic and financial sector development, they may lack market depth and scale and may face institutional capacity constraints. For example, the ability of banks to issue bail-in debt depends on the availability of a liquid secondary market to support such issuance. Similarly, some of the recent macroprudential regulations discussed earlier were designed for a more sophisticated banking sector. Social objectives and capacity constraints must be kept in mind in order to avoid placing an undue burden on banks with simple balance sheets that engage in plain vanilla lending and financial intermediation.

Capital regulations are a very important part of getting the incentives right because having more resources at risk curtails excessive risk-taking by shareholders. There is also evidence that capital can substitute for supervision and regulation (Anginer, Demirgüç-Kunt, and Mare 2018), and higher capital requirements can prove to be a simpler and cheaper way of ensuring stability. Thus, chapter 3 covers issues surrounding bank capital regulation in greater depth.

NOTES

1. Although nonbank entities can be classified as SIFIs, this chapter will focus on banks. Later in the chapter, we distinguish between global systemically important banks (G-SIBs) and domestic systemically important banks (D-SIBs).
2. BCBS made a number of revisions to the Pillar 3 framework in the aftermath of the global financial crisis in order to enhance bank disclosure (https://www.bis.org/bcbs/publ/d432.htm).
3. BCBS (1998) reports the following: "Market discipline, however, can only work if market participants have access to timely and reliable information which enables them to assess a bank's activities and the risks inherent in those activities. Proved public disclosure

strengthens market participants' ability to encourage safe and sound banking practices."

4. Icesave is a controversial example. In 2008, Icelandic authorities decided to honor deposit insurance only for domestic depositors, and not for the foreign depositors from whom Landsbanki, a bankrupt Icelandic bank, had collected deposits through its online branch, Icesave. Eventually, the losses of foreign depositors were covered by the British (fully) and Dutch governments (up to €100,000), which hold claims on Landsbanki receivership (Zeissler, Piontek, and Metrick 2014).
5. See, for example, Demirgüç-Kunt and Detragiache (2002); Angkinand and Wihlborg (2008); and Cull, Senbet, and Sorge (2005), among others.
6. Insolvent banks have incentives to take on excessive risks, which result in negative externalities and raise the economic costs of resolution later on (Pyle 1986; Lucas and McDonald 2006).
7. Some of these guarantees were applied to specific financial institutions, such as specific guarantees provided to the later-nationalized Dexia by the Luxembourg and Belgian governments (Laeven and Valencia 2018).
8. The FSB was established after the G-20 London summit in 2009. It is a successor to the Financial Stability Forum, but with an expanded membership and a broader mandate.
9. Methodologies vary. For example, Mauritius adds exposure to large groups as a fifth dimension and uses equal weights (Bank of Mauritius 2016), whereas Pakistan focuses on bank size (exposure) by setting a 3 percent of GDP threshold and having higher weights for the size-related indicator.
10. The Dodd–Frank Wall Street Reform and Consumer Protection Act was signed into law July 21, 2010.
11. The Single Resolution Fund is built up over time with contributions from individual banks in EU member states participating in the banking union. The target size of the fund, however, is expected to be small or about 1 percent of the covered deposits of all banks in EU member states.
12. Indeed, there is some recent empirical evidence showing the market perception of government support is reduced (see, for example, FSB 2018b). However, the estimate of government support tends to be countercyclical (low during good times, high during bad times), and it is very difficult to disentangle default probabilities from the likelihood of government intervention when the default probabilities are low; see Borio, Furfine, and Lowe (2001) and Siegert and Willison (2015).
13. The implicit nature of the too-big-to-fail guarantees implies that the possibility of a bailout may exist in theory but not reliably in practice. The U.S. government had a long-standing policy of "constructive ambiguity" (Freixas 1999; Mishkin 1999) designed to encourage that uncertainty.
14. Briault et al. (2018) report results from a survey of regulators in developing countries on the impacts of the FSB reforms discussed in this section on their banking sectors. Overall, the survey suggests that developing country regulators expect the reforms to be beneficial in the long term but also expect negative spillover costs in the short term.
15. The Volcker Rule has undergone changes over the years and has been challenged in the courts (*Wall Street Journal* 2018).
16. See, for example, Anginer et al. (2016 and 2018).
17. There is also some empirical evidence that fintech firms' activities can also be used to circumvent macroprudential regulation; see, for example, Braggion, Manconi, and Zhu (2018) for the Chinese case.
18. Although there have been some instances of market participants failing ahead of a crisis to sufficiently monitor or react to curb banks' risk-taking behavior because of procyclical and incomplete information, there have been also many cases in which shareholders have actively encouraged banks to take on greater risks in order to match or exceed the performance of their peers.

CHAPTER 3: KEY MESSAGES

- Higher bank capital contributes to financial stability: it provides a cushion for absorbing losses during a crisis or other bank distress; it may improve screening and monitoring by banks; and it tends to curb risk-taking because shareholders have more skin in the game.
- Regulatory capital requirements set out minimum ratios of capital that banks must maintain relative to their risk-weighted and unweighted assets. However, increasing capital requirements can lead some banks to cut lending in the short run.
- Before the global financial crisis, bank regulation in many countries allowed banks to take excessive risk without holding adequate amounts of high-quality capital, such as common equity. The Basel III framework, proposed in 2009 and currently being implemented, aims to increase the quality and quantity of capital. Basel III has been widely adopted in high-income member countries of the Organisation for Economic Co-operation and Development (OECD), with developing countries taking a more cautious approach. Selective adoption of this complex framework is appropriate in settings with limited supervisory capacity.
- Data suggest that banks in high-income OECD countries are holding more regulatory capital relative to their risk-weighted assets now than before the global financial crisis. However, this change appears to be driven by a decrease in risk-weighted assets relative to total assets; regulatory capital relative to total assets did not increase significantly. It is not clear whether banks are taking fewer risks or instead are adjusting their risk models.
- Data also reveal an increase in Tier 1 capital, but regulators have relaxed the rules of what qualifies as Tier 1 capital. Thus not all of the increase may be high-quality common equity and could instead include instruments such as convertible debt, whose performance has not really been tested in times of crisis.
- Implementation of the Basel III framework seems to have reduced lending, at least in the short run, in adopter countries as well as cross-border lending from high-income OECD banks in developing countries.

3

Bank Capital Regulation

The global financial crisis in 2007–09 revealed significant weaknesses in the regulatory and supervisory system, leading to major reform efforts. Experts agree that the crisis stemmed in part from regulatory and supervisory failures (Calomiris 2012, 2017). These failures extended to different areas of banking regulation, but capital regulation was lacking as well, in the sense that it did not provide banks with enough high-quality equity capital to weather the crisis. It also did not sufficiently curb bank risk-taking before the crisis. There is a consensus as well that regulatory weaknesses stemmed in part from the lack of enforcement of existing regulations and the failure to use supervisory powers (Barth, Caprio, and Levine 2012). Therefore, since the financial crisis, regulators have been revamping regulation by, for example, launching the Basel III framework.

Capital regulation is a major element of this reform effort, so it is the subject of this chapter. The chapter begins by defining bank capital and summarizing its main functions. It then discusses the reasons for regulating bank capital and reviews efforts to standardize capital regulation across countries (Basel I and II). The chapter subsequently turns to the effects of capital regulation on financial access and stability. It reviews the role of capital in the global financial crisis and the regulatory responses that followed (Basel III). It then describes postcrisis trends in the adoption of capital regulation and its effects on capital holdings, stability, and access. The chapter concludes with policy recommendations.

DEFINITIONS AND FUNCTIONS OF BANK CAPITAL

In an economic sense, bank capital consists of the value of equity owned by shareholders. Bank economic capital can be defined as the value of the equity of a bank that can withstand losses. It has the lowest priority if the bank liquidates. Although there are several types of equity instruments (for example, common stock, contributed capital, and retained earnings), equity consists mainly of the profits retained by a bank or obtained from selling shares to investors. However, measuring equity is not simple because its value depends on how all financial instruments and on– and off–balance sheet assets of banks are valued (Berger, Herring, and Szegö 1995). Equity measured by its book value reflects the assets and liabilities that a bank reports on its balance sheet, thereby ignoring most off–balance sheet items and providing a historical accounting value rather than a current one. Equity measured by its market value reflects the value of the bank according to the stock market. For this measure, however, the market may not have the information needed to accurately price all bank assets.

It is important to distinguish bank economic capital from regulatory capital. Regulatory capital is the amount of capital required of banks by their financial regulator to fund their investments, such as extending loans to borrowers or purchasing bonds. It is commonly measured in the form of a ratio, where the numerator corresponds to the amount of regulatory capital and is segmented into layers or tiers. The definition of regulatory capital also allows counting some nonequity financial instruments as capital—such as reserves, hybrid capital instruments, or subordinated term debt—up to some limits (see box 3.1 for details). The denominator of the ratio, or the regulatory measure of risk exposure, corresponds to the assets of the bank, which can be unweighted or weighted by risk. In theory, weighting assets by risk requires banks to hold more capital against portfolio items with higher risk. In practice, however, measuring risk exposure is difficult. Several approaches that have been used only weakly reflect the actual risk of bank operations and

BOX 3.1 Types of Regulatory Capital

As illustrated in table B3.1.1, different types of regulatory capital have different characteristics in terms of liquidity and incentives. To account for these differences, regulatory bank capital is often divided into tiers, which rank instruments according to their subordination (or priority of payment in case of liquidation) and maturity (and thus their capacity to absorb losses). Tier 1 capital broadly consists of the safest types of capital that can absorb losses without disrupting operations, whereas Tier 2 capital consists of instruments considered less safe.

TABLE B3.1.1 Examples of Regulatory Capital Instruments and Key Characteristics

Instrument	Characteristics
Equity capital (common stock, retained earnings)	The instruments constituting the shareholders' equity and considered the core capital of a bank. Equity capital is the most secure and liquid form of capital to absorb losses in the event of a financial emergency.
Disclosed reserves	Published reserves originated by appropriations of retained earnings or other surplus set aside to cover future losses.
Cumulative preferred stock	Securities considered hybrid capital instruments because they share characteristics of debt instruments (that is, they pay fixed dividends). They can be converted into equity when a trigger event occurs. In terms of subordination, these instruments have priority over equity capital.
Revaluation reserves	An accounting term used by banks in revaluating an asset. These instruments are more difficult to liquidate and price because calculating their value is difficult.
Undisclosed reserves	Not a very common instrument, but accepted as capital by some regulators. This type of reserve is created from a profit that has not appeared in the normal retained profits of a bank.
Loan provisions, loan and lease-loss reserves	Money that a bank has set aside on a loan to provide for expected future losses on loans and leases.
Subordinated term debt	Debt that ranks lower than ordinary deposits in the bank. To be considered capital, it must comply with regulatory guidelines on its characteristics, and its initial maturity should be of more than five years. In terms of subordination, these instruments have priority over preferred stock.

may be manipulated by banks (Berger, Herring, and Szegö 1995).

A key function of capital is that it allows banks to sustain unexpected losses, while still honoring deposit withdrawals and other obligations. On a bank's balance sheet, capital is equal to the difference between assets, such as loans and investments, and liabilities, mostly deposits. If the assets of a bank are worth less than its liabilities, capital can thus act as a buffer in absorbing unexpected shocks, allowing the bank to remain solvent and continue operations (Berger, Herring, and Szegö 1995; Diamond and Rajan 2000; Valencia 2016). Higher capitalization should therefore help banks reduce default risk and increase their likelihood of survival during periods of financial turmoil.

A second important function of capital is to provide top management and shareholders of banks with incentives for effective risk management. Moral hazard incentives naturally encourage excessive risk-taking by any entities with debt. These incentives are exacerbated for banking organizations because of their very high leverage and the existence of imperfectly priced deposit insurance that absorbs some of the losses from risk-taking without fully charging for the expected losses. Moral hazard incentives may be even greater for large institutions that believe they are too big to fail and will be bailed out by government. Capital helps offset these incentives because shareholders take the hit when bank losses are absorbed by the core capital of the bank. In principle, the more core capital shareholders contribute, the greater is their skin in the game. By forcing bank owners to put more skin in the game, capital requirements can help curtail excessive risk-taking. Laeven, Ratnovski, and Tong (2016), using data on large banks across 56 countries, empirically analyze the factors associated with systemic risk during the global financial crisis. They find a negative correlation between Tier 1 capital and systemic risk that increases in magnitude with bank size. Berger and Bouwman (2013), studying five financial crises in the United States, including the global crisis, find that higher equity capital ratios improve the likelihood of survival of banks of all size classes during these crises.

CAPITAL REGULATION: WHY AND HOW?

In the absence of regulatory minimum capital requirements, banks may have incentives to maintain insufficient equity capital ratios from a social standpoint. A key reason banks may choose not to raise enough equity is the presence of negative externalities when a bank fails (Aiyar, Calomiris, and Wieladek 2015). Bank failure has large private and social costs in the form of credit supply contraction and loss of economic output, which are not internalized by bank managers or shareholders.

A second reason banks may not hold enough equity stems from the presence of safety nets such as deposit insurance and bailouts. Safety nets protect depositors, but they also indirectly subsidize risk-taking by banks because depositors no longer need to monitor or discipline banks. To the extent that other uninsured creditors are protected, monitoring is further weakened. Thus safety nets weaken the role of the market in encouraging banks to maintain adequate capital (Calomiris 2012).

Banks' corporate governance and compensation schemes can further incentivize banks to hold less equity. Compensation schemes that reward executives for short-term gains in profits encourage them to take more risks. Thus bank managers may have incentives to maintain high default risk at the expense of shareholders. In addition, as Anginer et al. (2016) document using data from a sample of international banks, banks with corporate governance policies that are more shareholder-friendly tend to adopt riskier capitalization strategies. This behavior is consistent with the incentives of shareholders to shift risk toward safety nets.

Capital requirements are therefore an important tool for monitoring banks. When properly implemented, capital requirements incentivize banks to improve their risk management (Calomiris 2012; World Bank 2012). Moreover, capital can substitute for supervision and oversight in reducing bank risk. Empirical evidence corroborates that in countries where supervision and regulation are costlier, the role of capital in systemic stability is stronger (see box 3.2).

However, regulating bank capital is not simple, because regulation can distort the risk-taking incentives of banks. Incentives for risk-taking are potentially among the most important sources of financial instability (World Bank 2012). Badly designed regulations or indirect subsidies from safety nets can exacerbate bank risk-taking by, for example, tempting banks to make riskier loans. Banks may also be encouraged to become "too big to fail" by growing larger, "too interconnected to fail" by becoming more connected with large banks, or "too many to fail" by engaging in herding behavior to improve their chances of bailouts (Acharya and Yorulmazer 2007; Berger, Roman, and Sedunov, forthcoming). A challenge for regulators is to identify how banks respond in practice to regulatory changes and to adapt regulation in such a way that banks' risk-taking incentives are best aligned with those of regulators. One suggestion by Čihák, Demirgüç-Kunt, and Johnston (2013) is the use of incentive audits to help regulators identify incentive misalignments in the financial sector. A push for better disclosure of information can also reduce excessive bank risk-taking by making bank operations more transparent. One concrete way would be disclosing information regarding how banks manage risk, which supervisors across various countries already collect via CAMELS ratings.

Basel I was the first international initiative to define and regulate capital. In the early 1980s, U.K. and U.S. regulators pioneered the requirement of minimum capital-to-assets ratios for banks, triggering their adoption in various other countries (Jackson et al. 1999; Rose 2014). In 1988, as a response to an international debt crisis that originated in Latin America, the Basel Committee on Banking and Supervision (BCBS) published the first set of minimum capital requirements for banks, now known as Basel I, with the goal of promoting a sound and stable international banking system. Basel I implemented for the first time higher capital requirements for assets that were perceived to have more credit risk, capital requirements for off–balance sheet activities, and capital requirements that were similar across nations. Although

BOX 3.2 Capital as a Complement to Weak Supervisory Capacity

Analysis of cross-country data reveals a negative and statistically significant relationship between the total regulatory capital ratio of banks and their systemic risk measures. Anginer, Demirgüç-Kunt, and Mare (2018) use data on publicly traded banks across countries to study whether this relationship varies according to the institutional environment, information availability, and monitoring efficiency of bank regulators.

Their study relies on several measures of supervisory capacity and information availability to examine the influence of the institutional environment on the relationship between the systemic risk of individual banks and capital ratios. Overall, this relationship becomes much stronger in countries with weaker institutional environments, where monitoring banks, either via private or public channels, is more challenging and where information about firms and banks is scarcer.

These results suggest that capital exerts a greater impact in banking sectors where the supervisory power of regulators is limited and the institutional environment is weaker. A message emerging from this research is that enhancing the quality and quantity of bank capital can mitigate the adverse effects of a lack of supervisory capacity and information availability. Such a message is particularly relevant for developing countries, where regulating and supervising banks can be prohibitively costly.

the minimum capital requirements agreed to in Basel I originally focused on international banks and were intended for member countries of the Bank for International Settlements (BIS), most banking regulators worldwide ended up adopting them and imposing them on virtually all the banks in their jurisdictions (Goodhart 2011).

Basel I induced banks to maintain higher capital ratios, but its simplicity in measuring risks led to regulatory arbitrage. With the aim of setting a simple risk-weighted asset (RWA) approach, Basel I categorized bank assets and off–balance sheet activities into four credit risk levels that were assigned risk weights of 0 percent, 20 percent, 50 percent, or 100 percent. This broad risk-weighting approach implies that within each risk level there is great variation in the quality of assets. For example, the 100 percent risk category includes all commercial loans irrespective of their credit quality. This ranking of risk also encouraged banks to engage in arbitrage because in a given risk bucket they had no incentives to hold the highest-quality assets with low expected returns, and instead had incentives to hold assets of the lowest quality with high expected returns. Regulatory capital ratios ended up being uninformative about the actual risks that banks were taking (Ferguson 2003). Furthermore, because the Basel standards were calculated using book value accounting measures of capital rather than market values and because accounting practices differ across countries, Basel I was not fully effective in standardizing practices with respect to capital. In addition, its focus on credit risk left key exposures related to liquidity and operational risks unattended, making it almost redundant for the few, yet complex, large international banks.[1]

In 2004 a revised capital framework, Basel II, replaced Basel I. Basel II was set forth with the objectives of better aligning the risk-taking of banks with their required regulatory capital and better reflecting the sophistication and complexity of bank operations. Basel II is built on three pillars: (1) minimum capital requirements; (2) supervisory oversight on behalf of national regulators; and (3) stronger market discipline in the form of information disclosure on capital, risk exposures, and risk assessment processes. Table 3.1 compares Basel I and Basel II. Key features of Basel II were (1) a new definition of regulatory capital, expanding from two to three tiers; (2) two new methodologies to measure credit risk (the denominator of the regulatory capital ratio); and (3) the inclusion of operational risks, defined as risks related to loss from inadequate or failed processes.

Basel II offered a more complex framework for measuring capital requirements and credit risk. It allowed banks to choose one of two approaches to measuring credit risk. The standardized approach (SA) measures credit risk in a manner that resembles the risk buckets used under Basel I. But there are two differences: the number of risk categories increases substantially, and risk weights are determined by assessments from authorized external credit assessment institutions. Subject to the approval of their supervisor, banks can also select the internal ratings–based (IRB) approach, which allows banks to use their internal rating models for credit risk—that is, subject to the approval of regulators, banks develop in-house models for computing the risk parameters of their portfolios.

Even though these new approaches were designed to improve risk sensitivity, the complexity of the calculation of capital requirements increased substantially. Whereas the regulatory capital ratio under Basel I was transparent and easily verifiable by regulators and market participants, the more complex credit risk measures, in particular the IRB approach, made it more challenging for supervisors and investors to monitor financial institutions properly.[2] The imbalance in resources between banks and regulators plays against regulators because they have to understand and evaluate the increasingly sophisticated risk assessment and management tools of banks (Danielsson et al. 2001). Moreover, the use of credit-rating agencies has been shown to be problematic because their ratings do not properly reflect actual risks, and riskier firms are tempted to forgo ratings in order to obtain cheaper loans (Danielsson et al. 2001).

TABLE 3.1 Key Characteristics of Basel I and II

	Basel I	Basel II
Regulatory capital	Regulatory capital consists of Tier 1 + Tier 2 capital.[a] Tier 1 capital consists of disclosed reserves, and noncumulative perpetual preferred stock.[b] Tier 2 capital consists of supplementary capital instruments: undisclosed reserves, revaluation reserves, general provisions or loan loss reserves, hybrid debt capital instruments, and subordinated term debt.	Regulatory capital consists of Tier 1 + Tier 2 + Tier 3 capital. Tier 1 and Tier 2 capital remain unchanged. Tier 3 capital is added to help banks meet the required minimum capital for market risks and is subject to the approval of national regulators. Tier 3 capital consists of short-term subordinated debt (with a maturity of at least two years).
Credit risk measurement	Assets of banks are classified into four groups according to their risk and are weighted according to fixed weights of 0 percent, 20 percent, 50 percent, and 100 percent. Assets with no credit risk such as cash are weighted 0 percent, whereas assets such as commercial loans are weighted 100 percent.	Regulators and banks can select from two methodologies to measure credit risk: 1. Standard approach. Bank assets are bundled in categories and weighted according to fixed risk weights. 2. Internal ratings–based approach. The risk weight of a loan is determined by the internal models of banks.[c]
Regulatory capital ratio	Calculated as the ratio of value of regulatory capital to the sum of credit and market risk-weighted assets (RWA):[d] $\frac{\textit{regulatory capital}}{\textit{credit RWA + market RWA}}$ The minimum required regulatory capital is set at 8 percent, with at least 4 percent in the form of Tier 1 capital and 2 percent in the form of common equity.	Consists of the value of the ratio of regulatory capital to the sum of credit, market, and operational risk-weighted assets (RWA):[e] $\frac{\textit{regulatory capital}}{\textit{credit RWA + market RWA + operational}}$ The minimum required regulatory capital remains unchanged, at 8 percent, with at least 4 percent in the form of Tier 1 capital and 2 percent in the form of common equity.

a. The following limits were imposed on regulatory capital: Tier 2 capital cannot exceed 100 percent of Tier 1 capital; subordinated term debt cannot exceed 50 percent of Tier 1 capital; loan provisions must include only valuations of latent but unidentified losses; and revaluation reserves will face a discount of 55 percent.
b. Under certain restrictions, additional instruments can be counted as Tier 1 but cannot exceed 15 percent of total Tier 1 capital—for example, instruments that have a step-up or minority interest in equity accounts of consolidated subsidiaries.
c. The standard approach resembles the approach under Basel I. The difference is that the number of risk categories grows and weights are assigned by an approved external credit-rating institution. Under the IRB approach, banks determine the risk weight of a loan based on the loan's probability of default, loss given default, exposure at default, and effective maturity.
d. Market risks stemming from movements in interest rates, foreign exchanges, and equity exposures are also subject to a capital charge, with the corresponding methodologies described in BCBS (2004).
e. See BCBS (2004) for the capital requirement methodology for operational risk.

The greater complexity of credit risk measures increased the opacity of the operations and risk management of banks. That situation in turn raised the costs of regulators and market participants to validate the accuracy of reported capital ratios (Haldane 2011), weakening the effectiveness of supervisors (Pillar 2) and market discipline (Pillar III). The global financial crisis revealed that the growth of highly complex, interconnected, nontransparent institutions and instruments was not matched with disclosure of the information needed to monitor them effectively (World Bank 2012).

Although capital requirements are intended to increase the stability of the banking sector, social costs may be associated with them. It is argued that increasing capital requirements can induce changes in the supply of credit of banks, potentially hurting households and firms in need of financing. Social costs may also take the form of reduced bank profitability. The next sections examine the evidence for these social costs and whether capital requirements have succeeded in improving financial stability.

BANK CAPITAL AND CREDIT SUPPLY

Theoretical studies of the role of bank capital in lending reach different conclusions. Some theories predict that greater capital can help banks expand lending. Increasing capital can improve the capacity of banks to raise funding, compete more effectively for deposits and loans, and better protect them from deposit risk when economic conditions deteriorate (Kishan and Opiela 2000; Calomiris and Mason 2003; Calomiris and Wilson 1998). Other theories point to the fact that lending increases bank risk, whereas capital absorbs risk and therefore expands banks' lending capacity (Bhattacharya and Thakor 1993; Allen and Santomero 1998; Allen and Gale 2004; Repullo 2004; Von Thadden 2004; Coval and Thakor 2005). These theories also generalize beyond banks' lending to their ability to create liquidity for the public (Berger and Bouwman 2009).

Other theories argue that greater capital may reduce bank lending. Diamond and Rajan (2000, 2001) suggest that bank capital may impede bank lending and liquidity creation by making the capital structure of banks less fragile. Fragile capital structures encourage banks to commit to monitoring their borrowers because depositors can run on the bank. Capital may also reduce liquidity creation because it "crowds out" or replaces deposits, which are an important source of liquidity creation (see, for example, Gorton and Winton 2017).

Empirical studies are mixed on the effects of capital on lending, with the results often differing by bank size. Cross-country evidence on major international banks suggests that better-capitalized banks face lower funding costs, allowing them to increase lending (Gambacorta and Shin, forthcoming). Consistent with this evidence, Berger and Bouwman (2009) find that capital has a positive effect on the more general measure of bank output, liquidity creation, for large U.S. banks, primarily driven by off–balance sheet loan commitments. However, the results are reversed for small U.S. banks and for banks in other nations (Lei and Song 2013; Horvath, Seidler, and Weill 2014; Fungacova, Weill, and Zhou 2017). However, measuring the causal effect of capital on lending is difficult because movements in capital are often the response of changing economic conditions, which also affect the demand for loans.[3] Therefore, variation in bank lending may jointly result from changes in the demand for as well as the supply of loans. The empirical studies discussed in the rest of this section have found ways to isolate movements in the supply of credit from responses in the demand for credit and thus have advanced our understanding of the impact that capital has on bank lending and firms' economic outcomes.

Capital can help banks smooth the supply of credit during crisis years. In times of economic turmoil, banks with larger capital buffers are somewhat protected from cuts in lending. Carlson, Shan, and Warusawitharana (2013) find evidence of this by comparing the loan growth of neighboring banks in the United States (that is, banks operating in a same location). By exploiting variation across local banks within a metropolitan area, they control for changes in the demand for credit because neighboring banks are likely to face the same economic conditions, and thus any difference in loan growth can be attributed to the difference in credit supply related to capital ratios. They find that during the global financial crisis years (2008–10) banks with higher capital ratios tended to have stronger loan growth, but not in the years before or after. One question discussed in box 3.3 is whether recapitalization for banks in distress is a plausible policy tool to contain a systemic crisis.

Capital also smooths bank lending in times of monetary policy contractions. Jiménez et al. (2012) exploit the universe of bank loan applications to study how the supply of credit by Spanish banks responds in times of monetary policy contractions. Important in this setting is the fact that the monetary policy in Spain is fairly exogenous because it is set for the euro area as a whole. They find that under tighter monetary and economic conditions, lending to the same firm differs across banks, and those with lower capital are the ones that resort to cutting lending.

The supply of bank lending can be affected by negative shocks to capital. To the extent that firms are dependent on bank finance, a bank credit crunch induced by a shortage of capital can further hinder economic activity (Bernanke and Lown 1991). Capital crunches can result from different factors. One factor is

BOX 3.3 Is Bank Recapitalization an Effective Policy Tool for Banks in Distress?

The design of recapitalization programs is not a trivial matter, because these interventions should protect the interests of taxpayers, reduce the moral hazard incentives of banks, and ensure that only banks in desperate straits—and yet with a real chance of survival—are rescued (Demirgüç-Kunt and Servén 2010). Theory also suggests that saving the financial system is best achieved by rescuing the strong over the weak banks (Choi 2014). To achieve these goals, recapitalization programs must impose tough criteria that guarantee real costs for all the responsible parties and ensure the right incentives for restructured banks going forward. Recapitalization interventions should also rely on the private sector to decide which banks to help—for example, by basing eligibility for the program on securing at least some fraction of capital via private sector funding.

Most studies of the impact of bank recapitalizations have found that these interventions can increase the supply of loans and spur firm growth (Laeven and Valencia 2013; Li 2013; Berger and Roman 2017; Berger, Makaew, and Roman, forthcoming; Chu, Zhang, and Zhao, forthcoming), although some studies find mixed or no effects on credit supply (Black and Hazelwood 2013; Duchin and Sosyura 2014). On an aggregate basis, findings suggest that recapitalizations can improve the real economy (Berger and Roman 2017) and reduce systemic risk in the short term (Berger, Roman, and Sedunov, forthcoming). However, injecting capital into banks appears to help only if banks are sufficiently recapitalized (Giannetti and Simonov 2013). Cross-country empirical evidence further shows that providing distressed banks with timely support during a recession also helps reduce the duration of the recession. According to Homar and van Wijnbergen (2017), recapitalization shortens severe recessions by two years and lighter ones by six months.

One downside of bank recapitalization is that it potentially shifts banks' appetite for risk, as evidence from Indonesia supports. Using data on the universe of commercial banks in Indonesia from 1993 to 2008, Poczter (2016) finds that even though bank recapitalization after the Asian financial crisis of 1997 increased bank lending, it also boosted bank risk in the years that followed. The effect on bank risk was concentrated among banks that were recapitalized, whereas nonrecapitalized banks actually reduced their risk. Recapitalizations in the United States have also been found to increase moral hazard incentives to lend to riskier borrowers (Duchin and Sosyura 2014; Berger, Makaew, and Roman, forthcoming) and may increase systemic risk in the long run (Berger, Roman, and Sedunov, forthcoming).

Some recent research suggests that recapitalizations by the private sector, usually referred to as bail-ins, may have advantages over government recapitalizations. In the United States, bail-ins are the current practice under the Orderly Liquidation Authority (OLA), and in Europe under the Bank Recovery and Resolution Directive (BRRD) and the Single Resolution Mechanism (SRM). Berger et al. (2018) find that bail-ins provide much better incentives than government recapitalizations for banks to hold higher capital ratios during normal times and raise them when they become distressed, although bail-ins may entail other problems.

stricter capital requirements, whereby banks can shrink lending to achieve a higher capital ratio (Thakor 1996; Watanabe 2007; Van Hoose 2008; Calomiris 2012; Aiyar, Calomiris, and Wieladek 2014a). This might happen if it were costly for banks to raise equity. If adverse selection costs due to asymmetric information penalize the stock prices of issuing banks, banks would be discouraged from raising equity in the first place (Aiyar, Calomiris, and Wieladek 2014b). Other factors include increased borrower defaults, the collapse of asset prices (Bernanke 1983; Peek and Rosengren 1995b), or the tightening of monetary policy, whereby an increase in the policy rate can reduce banks' profits and potentially their capital (Van den Heuvel 2002).

Bank and loan-level data confirm that capital shortfalls from capital contractions or increased capital requirements reduce lending. Several studies of the U.S. credit crunch in the early 1990s find that reduced capital from loan losses and increased capital requirements contributed to a contraction in the supply of credit for banks (Bernanke and Lown 1991; Berger and Udell 1994; Hancock, Laing, and Wilcox 1995; Peek and Rosengren 1995a, 1995b). Similarly, other studies exploiting a series of natural experiments as sources of exogenous capital shocks reach similar findings. Peek and Rosengren (1997) find that a negative capital shock in Japan was transmitted to Japanese bank branches in the United States. In response, those branches significantly reduced their lending to U.S. firms that were not affected by the shock.

Recent empirical evidence further corroborates that banks reduce their lending as capital requirements increase. Aiyar, Calomiris, and Wieladek (2015) argue that because raising equity is costly, banks often opt to reduce their lending when they need to raise their equity-to-asset ratios. Brun, Fraisse, and Thesmar (2013) find that in France, when banks transitioned from Basel I to Basel II, their capital requirements fell by 2 percent, which led to a 10 percent increase in loan size and substantial increases in employment and investment. In the United Kingdom, a 1 percentage point increase in required equity ratios was found to contract lending in the short term by approximately 6 percent (Aiyar, Calomiris, and Wieladek 2015). Gropp et al. (2019) exploit a capital exercise conducted in 2011 by the European Banking Authority (EBA) on a subset of European banks to identify the impact of higher capital requirements on capital ratios and lending. The authors document that the banks subject to this exercise engaged in asset shrinking by reducing their exposures to corporate and retail borrowers.

Some scholars, however, argue that there are ways to increase capital requirements while limiting the effects on loan supply. Admati and Hellwig (2013) claim that the higher cost of equity is not a valid reason for not requiring banks to increase their equity. They argue that better-capitalized banks may not be affected by the costs of raising equity because they have more retained earnings to fund their growth and face proportionally lower costs of issuing equity. Furthermore, they suggest that regulators can help undercapitalized banks reduce the negative stigma of issuing bank equity by, for example, imposing a timetable for equity issuance. To help banks build capital, higher capital requirements should be accompanied by requirements for banks to quickly meet them by restricting dividend and other equity payouts. Although, in the short term, undercapitalized banks may contract lending as a response to increased capital requirements, once banks are better capitalized, they could be able to restore their credit supply.

Increasing capital in the short run is expensive, but having higher capital in the long run does not necessarily hurt bank profitability. Theory suggests that the relations between bank capital ratios may be either negative (Modigliani and Miller 1963) or positive (Allen, Carletti, and Marquez 2011). In reality, higher bank capital can either reduce or increase bank profitability, depending on economic and financial conditions and where a bank is relative to its target capital ratio. Most banks have capital ratios that exceed regulatory capital requirements. Bank capital ratio targets are largely determined by market trade-offs between the tax benefits of lower capital and the lower costs of debt and equity afforded by higher capital (Berger 1995). Because changing capital quickly is costly, actual capital ratios may deviate significantly from targets, altered by earnings shocks and other events, and banks do adjust to these targets over time (Berger et al. 2008). Empirical research on U.S. banks suggests that higher capital enhances the profitability of small banks during both normal times and financial crises and improves the profitability of large banks during financial crises (Berger and Bouwman 2013).

Capital requirements that increase in bad times are more likely to affect lending and economic output. When economic conditions are good, firms are better able to overcome tightening of bank credit induced by increased capital requirements. In turmoil years, replacing bank credit with other sources is more challenging. Thus countercyclical capital requirements may help reduce the negative effects on lending. Conversely, approaches such as risk-sensitive capital regulation that link capital requirements with the risk of different assets more directly can exacerbate lending procyclicality because measures of asset risk change with economic conditions. Under these approaches, capital requirements may further prompt lending to drop during a downturn and rise during periods of economic growth (Danielsson et al. 2001; Kashyap and Stein 2004; Repullo and Suarez 2012).

Indeed, empirical evidence shows that risk-sensitive capital regulation deters bank lending in bad times. When implementing Basel II, German banks were allowed to choose between two methodologies to calculate their regulatory capital: the standard approach and the internal ratings-based approach.[4] Whereas capital requirements under the standard approach are determined the moment loans are issued and are fixed thereafter, the required capital under IRB changes over time as banks update the default probabilities of their loans. Because banks that opted for the IRB approach phased it in over time, Behn, Haselmann, and Wachtel (2016) exploit the failure of Lehman Brothers to examine how the credit conditions of a given firm in the IRB pool of one bank and the SA pool of another IRB bank changed. After the shock, banks reduced loans to the same firm by 2.1–3.9 percentage points more when capital requirements for the loan were based on internal ratings (IRB) than when they were based on fixed risk weights (SA).

Overall, a large body of evidence has advanced understanding of how capital requirements can affect access to finance; yet several other questions remain unanswered. What is the longer-term impact of adjustments to capital requirements on loan supply, and how long does it take banks to weather the increased requirements? What effect would a large change in capital requirements have on lending supply? Because most empirical studies rely on local and relatively small changes in capital requirements, extrapolating their findings may not be very informative (Aiyar, Calomiris, and Wieladek 2015). Admati and Hellwig (2013) find that substantially higher equity capital requirements in the long term can help banks improve their lending decisions and reduce excessively risky investments.

CAPITAL AND FINANCIAL STABILITY

Theory predicts that higher bank capital can lower bank risk-taking in at least two ways. First, banks will improve their screening and monitoring of borrowers (Holmstrom and Tirole 1997; Coval and Thakor 2005; Allen, Carletti, and Marquez 2011; Mehran and Thakor 2011). Second, greater capitalization can give banks incentives to choose less risky asset portfolios (Furlong and Keeley 1989; Calomiris and Kahn 1991; Rochet 1992; Freixas and Rochet 2008).

Some argue, however, that higher bank capital may also lead to more risk-taking through two potential channels. First, if higher capital implies a greater number of shareholders, owners may exert less effort as their ownership becomes diluted (Besanko and Kanatas 1996). Second, because increasing equity lowers the return on equity (ROE), banks may invest in riskier projects as capital increases to seek higher returns and to bring ROE back up (Koehn and Santomero 1980; Dell Ariccia, Laeven, and Marquez 2014). These incentives may increase because of greater expectations of a bailout. For large banks, additional capital may thus increase risk-taking because they want to benefit from the upside and perceive little downside (Calem and Rob 1999).

Empirical evidence supports the view that higher bank capital leads to less bank risk. In a sample of almost all U.S. banks for 1984–2010, higher capital, measured as the ratio of equity to total assets, was associated with a greater probability of survival during noncrisis times (Berger and Bouwman 2013). This result reflects a correlation and is not necessarily causal. However, a study comparing Belgian banks with other European banks between 2003 and 2007 provides causal evidence of the effects of a bank capital increase that was caused by a 2006 tax reform (Schepens 2016). Banks increased their retained earnings in response to the tax reform, and the resulting increase in capital, again measured as the ratio of equity to total assets, led to reduced risk-taking both in terms of a lower ratio of nonperforming loans to total loans and in terms of lower volatility of returns on assets.

However, higher capital during normal times appears to lower risk-taking mostly for small banks, not large ones. Both Berger and Bouwman (2013) and Schepens (2016) find that the risk-mitigating effects of higher capital are mostly concentrated among smaller banks. These findings are in line with the argument that larger banks may be willing to take more risks because they are likely to be saved by a bailout when in distress.

In times of crisis, greater capital is associated with better performance by banks of all sizes. In crisis years, both small and large U.S. banks are more likely to survive if they have more capital (Berger and Bouwman 2013). Beltratti and Stulz (2012), after assessing a sample of 164 large banks in 32 countries with more than US$50 billion in assets, learned that those with more Tier 1 capital to risk-weighted assets had significantly higher stock market returns during the global financial crisis. These findings may reflect the following two channels. First, capital can act as a "cushion" for absorbing losses in a crisis. Second, banks with more capital (as opposed to debt) suffer less from the debt overhang problem, in which existing debt is so great that a bank cannot easily borrow more money (Myers 1977).

CAPITAL AND THE GLOBAL FINANCIAL CRISIS: CAUSES AND REGULATORY RESPONSES

Although higher capital helped banks weather the 2007–09 financial crisis, capital requirements in many countries were not sufficient to avert the crisis. For 164 large banks in 32 countries, stricter capital regulation did not come with higher stock market returns during the crisis (Beltratti and Stulz 2012). Similarly, a study of over 3,000 banks in 86 countries finds no relationship between Basel Core Principle compliance and bank risk over the period 1999–2006 (Demirgüç-Kunt and Detragiache 2011). Data on all publicly traded European and U.S. banks over the period 1991–2014 also reveal that banks in countries with more stringent capital requirements contributed less to systemic risk only after, but not before, the financial crisis (Bostandzic and Weiß, forthcoming). On the other hand, in a sample of almost 400 banks in 70 developing countries, stricter capital regulation was associated with lower bank risk over the period 2002–08 (Klomp and De Haan 2014, 2015). In the same way, stricter capital requirements were associated with lower bank risk in 13 Central and Eastern European countries over the period 1998–2005 (Agoraki et al. 2011). A possible explanation for these different findings is that regulation may have been more effective in developing countries than in high-income countries because it was simpler.

Capital regulation before the global financial crisis was often too complex and discretionary to be effective. According to data from the fourth round of the Bank Regulation and Supervision Survey (BRSS) covering 143 countries, countries directly affected by the crisis had less stringent and more complex definitions of capital, giving banks greater discretion in how they satisfied capital requirements. Banks in crisis countries also exhibited lower Tier 1 capital ratios than those in noncrisis countries (Čihák et al. 2013). Further evidence from 381 banks in 12 countries suggests that risk-weighted capital ratios lacked credibility during the crisis (see box 3.4). For these 381 banks, capital was associated with higher stock market returns during the financial crisis, but this relationship is stronger when capital is measured by a simple leverage ratio (regulatory capital divided by total assets) rather than a risk-adjusted regulatory capital ratio, particularly for larger banks, which tend to have the most discretion in Basel II risk calibrations (Demirgüç-Kunt, Detragiache, and Merrouche 2013).

Regulations in place before the financial crisis diluted the quality of capital. All countries directly hit by the crisis allowed Tier 2 capital

BOX 3.4 Bank Capital: Lessons from the Global Financial Crisis

Demirgüç-Kunt, Detragiache, and Merrouche (2013), using Bankscope data, have examined the relationship between bank capital and stock market returns around the time of the global financial crisis. Their sample consists of 381 banks in 12 countries covering the period 2005:Q1–2009:Q1. The authors also present estimation results for a subsample that consists of only 91 banks with assets above US$50 billion in eight countries.

The empirical analysis relates stock market returns in quarter t to bank capital in quarter $t - 1$, controlling for other bank characteristics. The authors estimate this relationship separately for the precrisis period (up to 2007:Q2) and the crisis period (2007:Q3–2009:Q1).

The paper examines different measures of capital to determine which measure showed the strongest correlation with stock returns—that is, the authors look at a Basel II measure of regulatory capital, defined as Tier 1 + Tier 2 capital to risk-weighted assets, as well as a nonrisk-based leverage ratio, defined as Tier 1 + Tier 2 capital to total assets. They also disaggregate capital into various levels of quality, looking separately at Tier 1, common equity, and Tier 2 capital.

The results show that higher capital was linked with higher stock returns during the financial crisis. This relationship is stronger for large banks. It is also much stronger when capital is measured as a simple leverage ratio than a risk-weighted ratio. This finding may reflect the fact that market participants viewed the risk adjustment under the Basel rules as subject to manipulation or at least not reflective of true risk for large banks.

Another finding is that higher-quality capital—Tier 1 capital and common equity—displayed a stronger correlation with subsequent stock market returns than Tier 2 capital, especially for larger banks.

The results have several policy implications. First, they support the view that a stronger capital position is an important asset during a crisis, suggesting that an emphasis on strengthening capital requirements is appropriate. Second, introduction of a minimum leverage ratio to supplement minimum risk-weighted capital requirements is important because properly measuring risk exposure is very difficult, especially for large and complex financial organizations. Finally, a greater emphasis on "higher quality capital," in the form of Tier 1 capital or common equity, is justified.

in regulatory capital, and 81 percent allowed Tier 3 capital, compared with 86 percent and 27 percent of noncrisis countries, respectively (Čihák et al. 2013). However, these types of capital appeared to be less relevant for mitigating the crisis. As described in box 3.4, Tier 1 capital, particularly common equity, showed the strongest link with banks' stock market returns during the crisis.

The global financial crisis also highlighted that banks' assets were riskier than risk measurement suggested, pointing to issues with the existing risk models. Several studies have provided evidence that banks use accounting discretion to underreport their risk positions, and approaches such as the IRB may give banks more opportunity to manipulate their credit risk measures. Huizinga and Laeven (2012) find that during the U.S. mortgage crisis, banks overstated the value of their distressed assets and their regulatory capital. They further point out that banks select valuation techniques that yield relatively high asset values. Mariathasan and Merrouche (2014) use cross-sectional data on 115 banks from OECD member countries to document that banks, particularly undercapitalized ones, lower their reported riskiness after their IRB approval. This decline in risk is more modest when supervisory capacity is high.

The global financial crisis thus exposed the weaknesses of existing capital regulation, so the Basel III norms were proposed in 2009 to improve the quantity and quality of capital and address these weaknesses. As further described in box 3.5, major features of the capital requirements under Basel III relative to Basel II are that Basel III (1) requires a higher share of common equity and Tier 1 capital; (2) introduces two new capital buffers—the

BOX 3.5 Basel III

The Basel III norms were proposed in 2009. Most of the regulatory changes have been phased in gradually, for completion by 2019. What follows are summaries of some of the key features of Basel III aimed at improving both the quality and quantity of capital.

More common equity
Basel III increases the common equity ratio from 2 percent to 4.5 percent of risk-weighted assets, with an additional "capital conservation" buffer of 2.5 percent of common equity, bringing the total to 7 percent. The capital conservation buffer implies that regulators will impose constraints on a bank's discretionary distributions when common equity falls into the buffer range. This step prevents the kind of market failure that occurred during the global financial crisis. Some banks continued to make large distributions even though their financial condition and the outlook for the sector were deteriorating. Much of this activity was driven by a collective action problem, in which reductions in distributions were perceived as a signal of weakness; and in fact the distributions ended up weakening banks and the sector (BCBS 2010). Basel III also introduces a "countercyclical buffer" of 0–2.5 percent of common equity, to be applied at the discretion of country supervisors when credit growth is judged to result in an unacceptable buildup of systematic risk. This buffer of capital ensures that the banking system is protected against future potential losses.

Same overall capital requirement, but more Tier 1
Basel III increases the Tier 1 capital requirement from 4 percent to 6 percent. The total risk-adjusted capital requirement remains unchanged, at 8 percent.

Stricter definition of capital—no more Tier 3
Banks can meet the difference between the total capital requirement and the Tier 1 requirement with Tier 2 capital—that is, Basel III eliminates Tier 3 capital.

Leverage ratio
Basel III imposes a supplemental minimum 3 percent leverage ratio to serve as a backstop to the risk-based capital requirement. This leverage ratio is calculated as Tier 1 capital to total assets and thus is not based on risk-weighted assets.

Liquidity requirements
Basel III introduces a liquidity coverage ratio that requires banks to have enough high-quality liquid assets to withstand a 30-day stressed funding scenario specified by supervisors. It also defines a longer-term structural net stable funding ratio that is designed to address liquidity mismatches. This ratio covers the entire balance sheet and provides incentives for banks to use stable sources of funding.

FIGURE B3.5.1 A Comparison of the Capital Requirements for Basel II and III

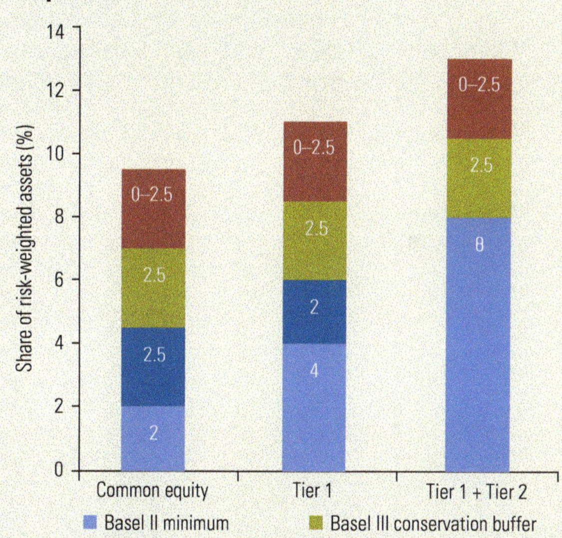

Source: World Bank staff calculations.

capital conversion buffer and the countercyclical capital buffer—that increase overall capital requirements; and (3) contains a stricter definition of capital—that is, it limits what can be considered as regulatory capital. Basel III also adds a nonrisk-based leverage ratio, and it includes liquidity requirements, for example, to ensure that enough high-quality liquid resources are available for survival for one month in the face of a stress scenario.

Chapter 1 discusses these liquidity requirements, as well as stress tests, in more detail.

ADOPTION OF POST–GLOBAL FINANCIAL CRISIS CAPITAL REGULATION

In BRSS 2019, all countries reported using one of the Basel regimes, but many were still using Basel I or Basel II. High-income countries have adopted Basel III more quickly than middle- and low-income countries. In 2016, 85 percent of high-income countries were using Basel III, followed by about half of upper-middle-income countries and a third of lower-middle-income countries. Only one low-income country, Nepal, reported using Basel III.

Basel III's adoption varies greatly across regions. In 2016 more than two-thirds of countries in the South Asia and the Middle East and North Africa (MENA) regions reported using Basel III. By contrast, adoption of Basel standards has been slow in the Latin America and the Caribbean (LAC) and Sub-Saharan Africa (SSA) regions, where close to half of countries continued to use Basel I in 2016 (figure 3.1).[5] Overall, countries in the same region tend to follow the same Basel regime. This pattern is in line with evidence from 102 countries indicating that a country is more likely to implement reforms in financial sector supervision if nearby countries also undertake such reforms (Masciandaro and Romelli 2018).

Both Basel II and III were designed to fit the needs of the more sophisticated banking sectors of Basel Committee members. Thus the rules proposed under these agreements may be overly complex for banking sectors in many developing countries. The reliance of Basel II and III on market discipline and strong supervisory capacity can even have an adverse effect on banking sectors of countries with weaker institutional environments and where market discipline and supervisory capacity are thin (Barth, Caprio, and Levine 2008). With poor oversight of banks, regulators may become lax, and banks may be tempted to take on more risk. Box 3.6 discusses in greater detail the approach that developing countries are taking when moving beyond Basel I.

FIGURE 3.1 Percentage of Countries Following Each Basel Regime, by Region

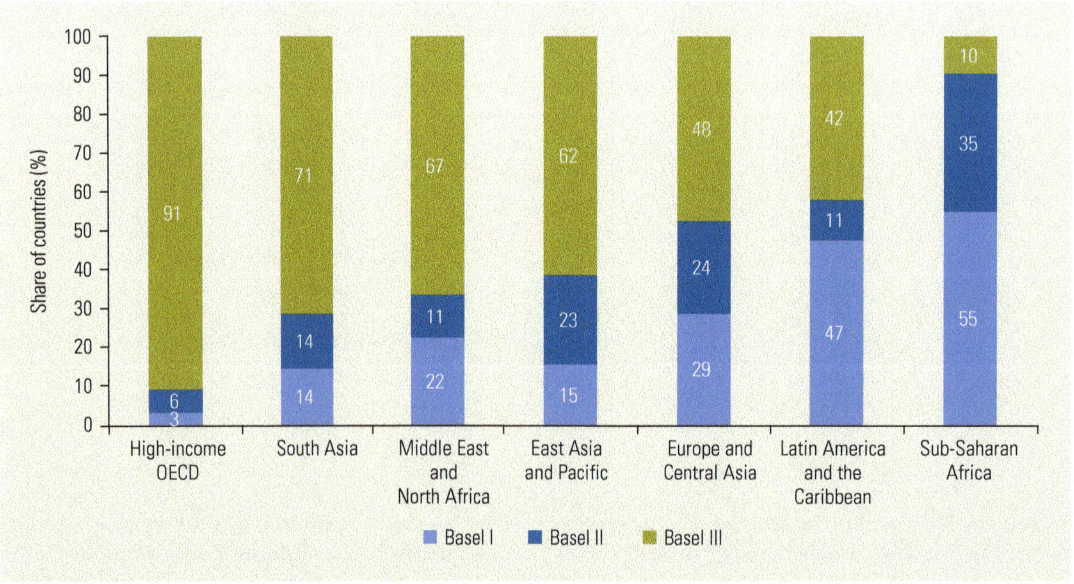

Source: Bank Regulation and Supervision Survey (BRSS), wave 5, https://www.worldbank.org/en/research/brief/BRSS.
Note: This figure is based on 2016 data from 133 countries. Not all high-income OECD countries use Basel III. Chile follows Basel I, and Austria and Latvia follow Basel II. OECD = Organisation for Economic Co-operation and Development.

BOX 3.6 Adoption of Basel II and III in Developing Countries: Why and How?

Relying on case studies and cross-country data, Beck, Jones, and Knaack (2018) explore why developing countries outside Basel Committee membership decide to adopt Basel II or III. In many cases, countries wish to move beyond Basel I to signal sophistication and strong domestic regulatory standards. Upgrading from Basel I may also ease coordination between home and host country supervisors. Peer countries also may play a role in the form of either peer pressure or peer learning. And international organizations such as the World Bank and the International Monetary Fund tend to recommend to countries that they adopt Basel II or Basel III.

That said, regulators in developing countries seem to have followed the principle of proportionality in their adoption of elements of Basel II and III. Beck, Jones, and Knaack (2018), Hohl et al. (2018), and Jones and Zeitz (2017) document that although many nonmember countries of the Bank for International Settlements are taking steps to implement Basel II, regulators cautiously decide which components to adopt. Because of the complexity of the Basel standards, nonmember countries may not have the infrastructure or supervisory capacity needed to effectively monitor compliance. Moreover, the benefits of Basel II may not offset the implementation costs in countries with only a few large international banks.

Data from BRSS 2019 shows consistent patterns, in that the more complex additions of Basel II and III were adopted only by countries with more sophisticated banking sectors (Anginer et al. 2019). Although all countries that moved beyond Basel I reported relying on the standard approach to measure credit risk (which is quite similar to the simple risk-weighted assets approach used in Basel I), adoption of the more complex internal ratings–based (IRB) approach is highly correlated with income, with very low to zero adoption rates among countries in the Latin America and the Caribbean, Sub-Saharan Africa, and South Asia regions (see figure B3.6.1).

FIGURE B3.6.1 Percentage of Countries Adopting the Internal Ratings–Based (IRB) Approach, by Region

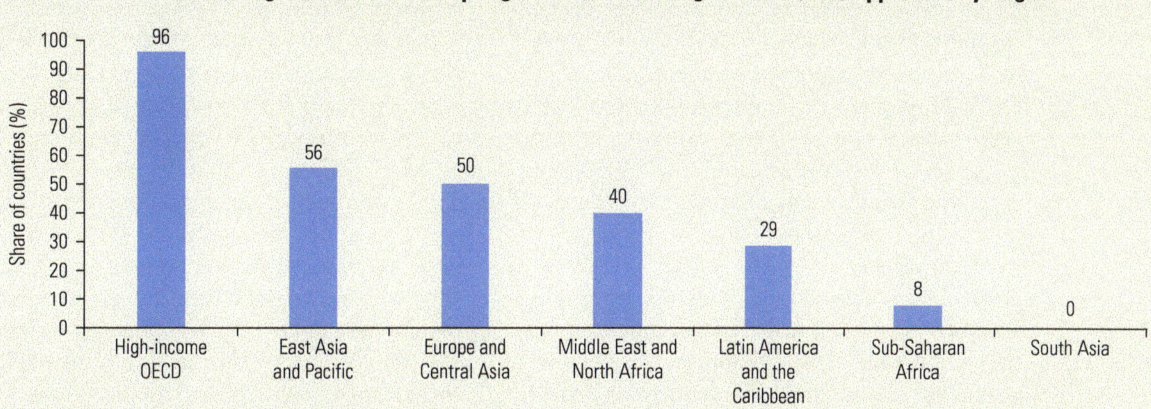

Source: Bank Regulation and Supervision Survey (BRSS), wave 5, https://www.worldbank.org/en/research/brief/BRSS.
Note: Information for 2016 from supervisors of 77 countries that adopted Basel II or III. OECD = Organisation for Economic Co-operation and Development.

Most Basel III countries have a capital conservation buffer, but only about 70 percent introduced a countercyclical capital buffer. In most regions, virtually all Basel III countries reported having a capital conservation buffer in 2016. The two exceptions are the LAC and SSA regions, where only three-fourths and two-thirds, respectively, of Basel III countries put in place a capital conversion buffer. Adoption rates of the countercyclical capital buffer are lower in all regions, except MENA. MENA is the only region in which all Basel III countries reported using both buffers in 2016 (figure 3.2). Although 70 percent of Basel

FIGURE 3.2 Percentage of Countries with Capital Buffers, by Region

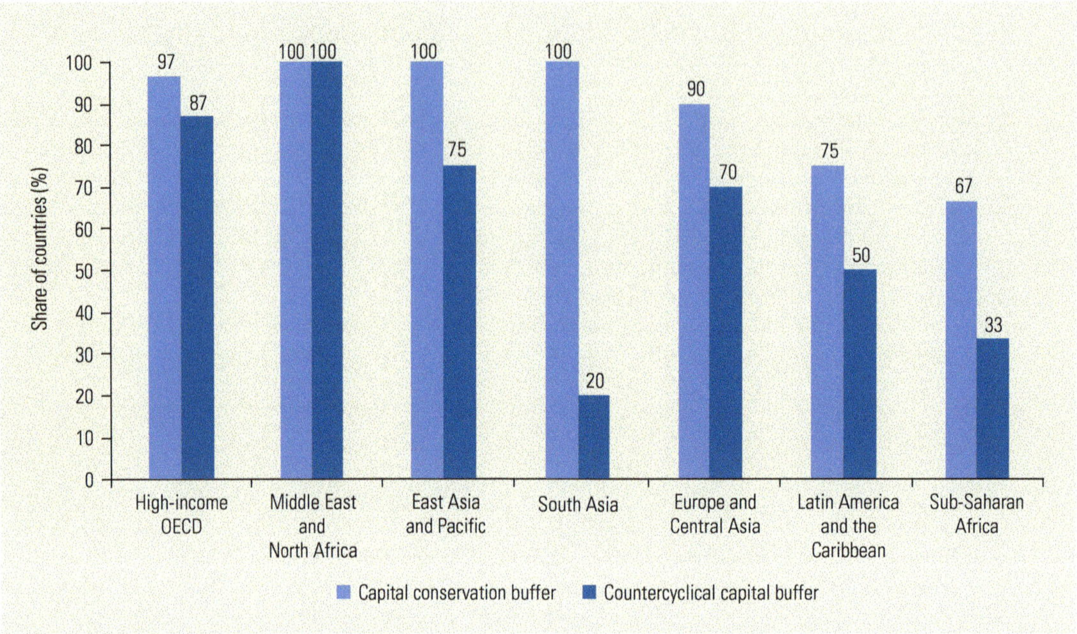

Source: Bank Regulation and Supervision Survey (BRSS), wave 5, https://www.worldbank.org/en/research/brief/BRSS.
Note: This figure is based on 2016 data from 70 countries that reported using Basel III. Data on the countercyclical capital buffer refer to having this buffer in place, even if it is currently not "turned on." OECD = Organisation for Economic Co-operation and Development.

III countries report having a countercyclical capital buffer in place, this buffer was "turned off" for most countries at the end of 2016. Only 15 percent of countries with the buffer report that it had a nonzero value at that time.

Apart from countries in the MENA region and South Asia, relatively few Basel III countries had implemented a leverage ratio requirement in 2016. In the MENA and South Asia regions, 67 and 60 percent of Basel III countries, respectively, reported having a leverage ratio requirement. However, across other regions the percentage of Basel III countries with such a requirement was lower, varying between 20 and 38 percent. Interestingly, some countries following Basel I or II also have in place leverage ratio requirements, most notably in South Asia. In the East Asia and Pacific (EAP) and Europe and Central Asia (ECA) regions, as well as high-income OECD countries, the percentage of countries with a leverage ratio requirement is greater among Basel I and II countries than among Basel III countries (figure 3.3). The size of the required minimum leverage ratio is typically 3 percent for Basel III countries, with some using higher ratios, up to 5 percent, and it is 5 or 6 percent for non-Basel III countries, up to a maximum of 10 percent (Tajikistan).

Basel III has arguably increased countries' compliance and reporting costs, leading some to adopt proportional frameworks for bank regulation. Some elements of Basel III, such as the introduction of liquidity requirements, may contribute significantly to increasing the regulatory burden for banks because supervisors need more data to monitor and verify the elements. Some countries are thus using or contemplating proportional regimes that exempt certain banks from some of the standard (Basel) regulatory requirements and specify alternative rules for qualifying banks. For example, Brazil, the European Union, Japan, Switzerland, the United States, and Hong Kong SAR, China, apply the standard Basel framework only to banks bigger than a certain size; and of those, Brazil and the United States apply the framework only to

FIGURE 3.3 Percentage of Countries with a Leverage Ratio Requirement, by Region and Basel Regime

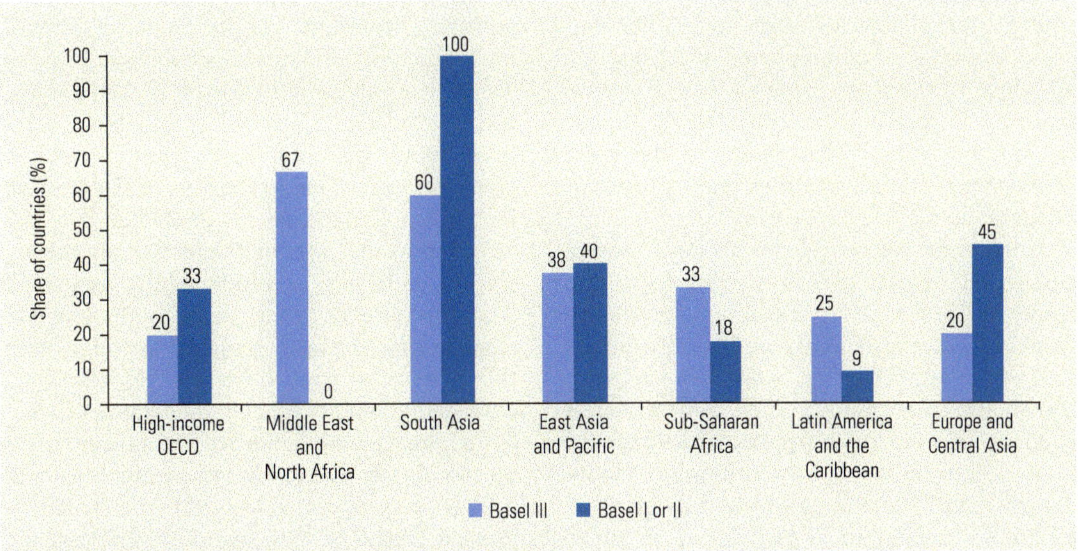

Source: Bank Regulation and Supervision Survey (BRSS), wave 5, https://www.worldbank.org/en/research/brief/BRSS.
Note: This figure is based on 2016 data from 70 countries that reported using Basel III, and 63 countries that reported using Basel I or II. OECD = Organisation for Economic Co-operation and Development.

banks with sufficiently large foreign operations (Castro Carvalho et al. 2017).

Over time, the definition of Tier 1 capital seems to have become laxer in some countries, highlighting that the Basel frameworks leave room for discretion. Basel III sought to increase the quality of capital by eliminating Tier 3 capital and by raising the percentage of Tier 1 versus Tier 2 capital (see box 3.5). However, like Basel II the Basel III guidelines allow some financial instruments that are not common equity to count as Tier 1 capital. Interestingly, over time supervisors seem to have changed the way in which these guidelines are applied. In 2016 a higher percentage of countries allowed hybrid debt capital instruments, asset revaluation gains, and subordinated debt to count as Tier 1 capital than in 2010 (figure 3.4). The change here is greatest for asset revaluation gains. The percentage of countries allowing this item to count as Tier 1 increased from 14 in 2010 to 43 in 2016.

FIGURE 3.4 Percentage of Countries Allowing Items as Part of Tier 1 Capital, 2010 and 2016

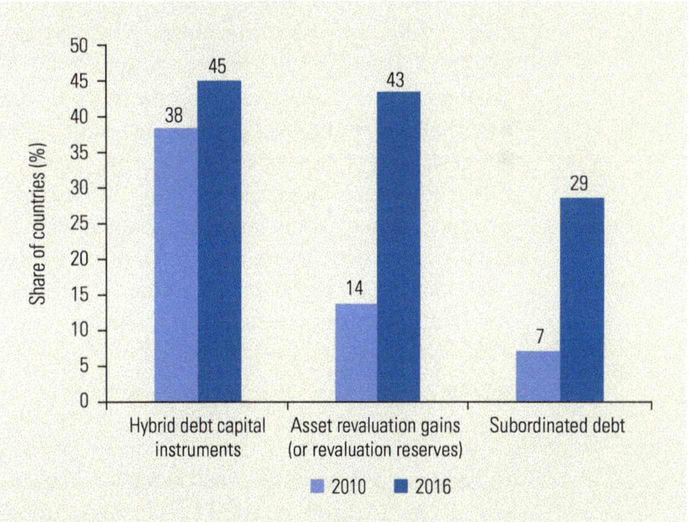

Source: Bank Regulation and Supervision Survey (BRSS), wave 5, https://www.worldbank.org/en/research/brief/BRSS.
Note: This figure is based on 2010 data from 115 countries and 2016 data from 133 countries.

In practice, however, most of the Tier 1 capital that banks hold appears to be common equity. Systematic and comprehensive information on which types of instruments go into banks' Tier 1 capital holdings is lacking. Bankscope, which compiles data from banks' balance sheets, includes information on hybrid capital and subordinated debt, but the data on the over 90 percent of banks reporting Tier 1 capital in Bankscope are missing. By contrast, data on common equity are available for most banks. The values of common equity reported in Bankscope are close to the total value of Tier 1 capital reported, suggesting that most Tier 1 capital is common equity. This finding is the same in countries that allow other types of instruments to count as Tier 1 capital.

Contingent convertible bonds (CoCos) are being used as part of Tier 1 capital in some countries, but it is not clear how well they work in practice. CoCos or bailable bonds are debt instruments that can be converted to equity after a triggering event, such as a fall in stock prices below a prespecified threshold or a decline in regulatory capital to below a threshold. These bonds can thus provide additional capital to absorb losses in times of crisis (see also chapter 2). CoCos may be easier and less costly to issue than equity, and, compared with equity, they can provide similar or even stronger incentives for sound risk management (Calomiris and Herring 2011).[6] However, it is unclear how well CoCos work in practice. For example, Fiordelisi, Pennacchi, and Ricci (forthcoming) describe a Spanish bank that failed before reaching any of the triggers for its CoCos. This scenario could be avoided by designing CoCos differently, as suggested by Calomiris and Herring (2011), but it illustrates how theory may differ from practice when such adverse events occur. CoCos are also not a viable option for countries lacking an appropriate financial market for issuing contingent debt instruments.

EFFECTS OF POSTCRISIS CAPITAL REGULATION

In high- and middle-income countries, the ratio of Tier 1 capital to total regulatory capital has increased since the global financial crisis. From 2005 to 2017, the ratio of Tier 1 capital to total regulatory capital increased from 75 to about 90 percent in high-income countries and from 75 to about 85 percent in middle-income countries (figure 3.5). In low-income countries, the ratio of Tier 1 capital to total regulatory capital has not changed much since 2005, but it started out at an elevated level (over 90 percent). These data from the International Monetary Fund's Financial Soundness Indicators do not include a breakdown of Tier 1 capital, so it is not clear whether the increase in Tier 1 capital comes from common equity or from other types of capital. However, according to the bank balance sheet data from Bankscope for 2009–12, for 101 large banks in 23 jurisdictions that are mostly OECD countries, common equity increased. About two-thirds of the rise in common equity stemmed from higher retained earnings, with the other third from other sources, including new share issues (Cohen and Scatigna 2016).

In high-income countries, the ratio of capital to risk-weighted assets has caught up with middle-income countries since the global financial crisis. In high-income countries, the ratio of regulatory capital to risk-weighted assets was lower than that in middle- and low-income countries before the crisis—about 12 percent, compared with 16–18 percent (figure 3.6). Since the crisis, high-income countries have caught up with middle-income countries: both high- and middle-income countries now have a ratio of regulatory capital to risk-weighted assets of about 18 percent. Low-income countries have increased their ratio of regulatory capital to risk-weighted assets up to 22 percent.

However, the ratio of capital to total assets has increased by much less. High-income countries also started out with a lower leverage ratio (defined as the ratio of regulatory capital to total assets), at about 7 percent, compared with 11–14 percent in middle- and low-income countries (figure 3.7). The leverage ratio has increased slightly in high-income countries, standing at 9 percent in 2017, but it is still lower than those of middle- and low-income countries. Upper-middle-income and low-income countries also both saw a slight increase in their leverage ratio, while lower-middle-income countries experienced a slight decline.

In high-income countries, the ratio of risk-weighted assets to total assets has steadily decreased, from 61 percent in 2005 to 50 percent in 2017. In middle- and low-income countries, this ratio has remained higher: in 2017 it was about 65 percent (figure 3.8). In line with these numbers, Cohen and Scatigna (2016) find that large banks increased their total assets from 2009 to 2012, but risk-weighted assets increased less than total assets. The decline in risk-weighted assets relative to total assets could be driven by a shift toward safer assets. However, only patchy data on banks' asset holdings are available from Bankscope and the Financial Soundness Indicators; thus we are not able to verify whether such a shift toward safer assets took place. An alternative explanation for the decrease in risk-weighted assets relative to total assets is that banks have adjusted their internal risk models to lower risk weights.

Although Basel III was mainly adopted in high-income countries, it has implications for lending in developing countries as banks adjust their assets and cross-border operations. For example, Berrospide et al. (2017) find that tighter U.S. capital regulation reduced lending by large U.S. global banks in other countries. At the same time, high capital requirements seem to change to whom banks lend in other countries. Ongena, Popov, and Udell (2013) analyze business lending by 155 banks to firms in 16 countries in the ECA region, where bank subsidiaries have tended to rely more on parent funding than in other regions, such as LAC. They find that higher minimum capital requirements in domestic markets are associated with lower bank lending standards abroad (more lending to opaque firms but not other firms). This finding may imply that banks take advantage of laxer host country regulation to try to make up abroad for the inability to engage in high-risk, high-return lending at home.

Evidence suggests that Basel III also slowed down bank lending in adopting countries, at least in the short run. Several studies have used economic models and empirical results from pre-Basel III times to extrapolate the effect of Basel III on lending (see Cosimano and Hakura 2011; Gambacorta 2011; BCBS 2016). These studies find that Basel III would have a negative effect on bank lending, although this effect would vary across

FIGURE 3.5 Tier 1 Capital to Total Regulatory Capital, by Country Income Group

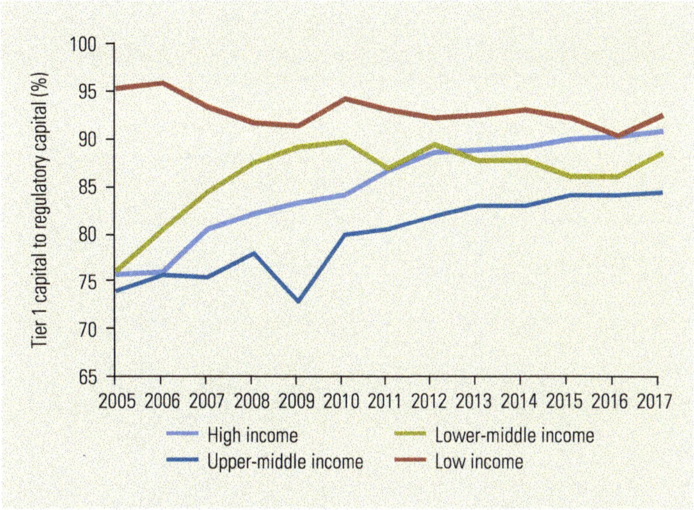

Source: World Bank staff calculations based on data from Financial Soundness Indicators (database, International Monetary Fund).
Note: The Financial Soundness Indicators (FSI) provide country-level data on total capital and assets holdings of the banking sector, as reported by participating countries to the IMF. Tier 1 capital to regulatory capital is calculated as total Tier 1 capital divided by regulatory capital of the banking sector. Country-level ratios are then averaged by country income group using a simple average. Country coverage increases over time, moving from 28 countries in 2005, to 70 in 2008, and to 114 in 2016.

FIGURE 3.6 Total Regulatory Capital to Risk-Weighted Assets, by Country Income Group

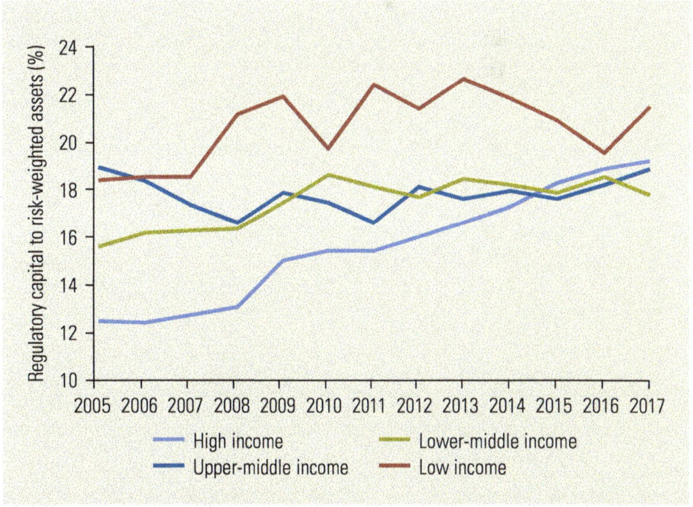

Source: World Bank staff calculations based on data from Financial Soundness Indicators (database, International Monetary Fund).
Note: The Financial Soundness Indicators (FSI) provide country-level data on total capital and assets holdings of the banking sector, as reported by participating countries to the IMF. Regulatory capital to risk-weighted assets is calculated as total regulatory capital divided by risk-weighted assets of the banking sector. Country-level ratios are then averaged by country income group using a simple average. Country coverage increases over time, moving from 28 countries in 2005, to 74 in 2008, and to 116 in 2016.

FIGURE 3.7 Total Regulatory Capital to Total Assets (Leverage Ratio), by Country Income Group

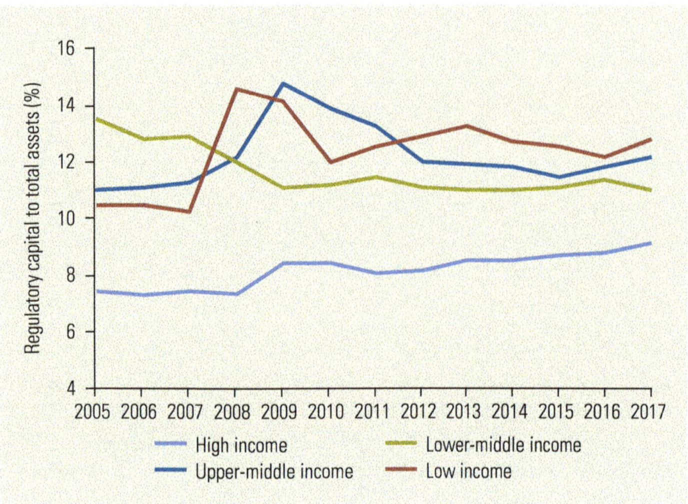

Source: World Bank staff calculations based on data from the Financial Soundness Indicators (database, International Monetary Fund).
Note: The Financial Soundness Indicators (FSI) provide country-level data on total capital and assets holdings of the banking sector, as reported by participating countries to the IMF. Regulatory capital to total assets is calculated as total regulatory capital divided by total assets of the banking sector. Country-level ratios are then averaged by country income group using a simple average. Country coverage increases over time, moving from 25 countries in 2005, to 65 in 2008, and to 107 in 2016.

FIGURE 3.8 Risk-Weighted Assets to Total Assets, by Country Income Group

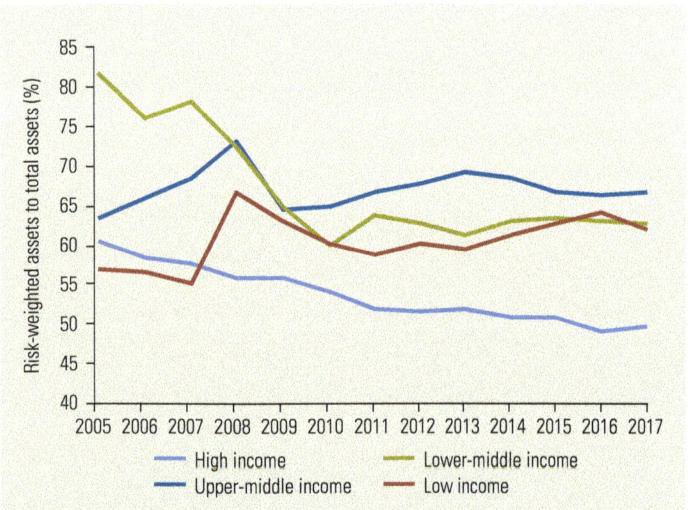

Source: World Bank staff calculations based on data from Financial Soundness Indicators (database, International Monetary Fund).
Note: The Financial Soundness Indicators (FSI) provide country-level data on total capital and assets holdings of the banking sector, as reported by participating countries to the IMF. Risk-weighted assets to total assets is calculated as risk-weighted assets divided by total assets of the banking sector. Country-level ratios are then averaged by country income group using a simple average. Country coverage increases over time, going from 25 countries in 2005, to 65 in 2008, and to 107 in 2016.

countries. For example, countries with higher costs of raising equity would be more affected. Direct evidence on the effects of Basel III is still scarce. An exception is a paper on Peru, which introduced bank-specific capital buffers when it adopted Basel III. Fang et al. (2018) use this bank-level variation in capital requirements to measure the effect on lending. In line with other studies, their results show that higher capital requirements had a negative impact on bank lending, but this effect was short-lived, lasting about six months. In the Peruvian case, banks seem to have been able to raise additional capital, in part thanks to the early announcement of reforms, the relatively slow speed of implementation, and the high profitability of banks.

Countercyclical capital buffers appear to smooth credit for firms across the business cycle, increasing firm growth and survival. Jiménez et al. (2017) use data from Spain to analyze the impact that capital buffers have on credit supply and firm outcomes. They exploit the introduction of and changes in dynamic provisioning over time. They find that banks use the stored buffers in bad times to continue lending, and that tightening capital in good times has little impact on firms because they switch to other credit sources. Such a switch may be entirely appropriate because these other sources would not carry government guarantees, and thus they may be well positioned to absorb risk. The effects measured in this study are substantial: increasing capital buffers by 1 percentage point expands firms' credit by 9 percentage points, employment by 6 percentage points, and survival by 1 percentage point. A caveat is that countercyclical capital buffers can undermine monetary policy (Calomiris 2012).

Liquidity requirements can enhance the role of bank capital in sustaining lending by large banks during a crisis. In their study of U.S. commercial banks over the period 1993–2010, Kim and Sohn (2017) find no evidence that bank liquidity mattered for the relationship between bank capital and lending in small and medium-sized banks. For large banks, however, greater liquidity was associated with a stronger positive correlation between bank capital and lending, particularly during the global financial crisis. These findings suggest that Basel III liquidity requirements complement capital requirements and can help smooth lending by large banks during times of crisis.

POLICY RECOMMENDATIONS

Proportionality. One set of regulations may not fit all countries. Regulations tailored to the needs of developed countries—with their more sophisticated banks, more complex operations, and stronger supervisory power—may not be appropriate for the banking sectors of developing countries. The observed selective and gradual adoption of Basel II and III is thus appropriate. Rather than adopting overly complex capital requirement approaches, regulators in developing countries should focus on simpler capital ratios and give priority to building up supervisory capacity that improves enforcement and better monitoring of their local financial systems.

Simple is better. A simple capital ratio appears to be more reliable than a risk-weighted ratio. In the global financial crisis, the market relied primarily on a simple measure of leverage for valuing bank stocks—capital to total assets—instead of relying on capital to risk-weighted assets (see, for example, box 3.4). Risk-weighted models tend to be less informative because measuring risk exposure is very difficult, especially for large and complex financial organizations. Although a simple leverage ratio may make it possible for banks to hold overly risky assets, it also avoids manipulation of risk weights and is relatively transparent and verifiable (Haldane 2011; Calomiris 2012). Overall, then, the leverage ratio introduced under Basel III seems appropriate as a complement to the risk-weighted ratio. Setting the minimum value at 3 percent is a topic for more research because some analysts advocate much higher levels (Admati 2016).

Quality matters. The low quality of regulatory capital contributed to the global financial crisis, implying that the focus of Basel III on common equity is warranted. Under Basel II, part of regulatory capital (Tiers 2 and 3) had a low loss absorptive capacity, contributing to risk-taking before the crisis and leaving banks in trouble during the crisis. Basel III sought to improve the quality of equity by eliminating Tier 3 capital and increasing the minimum common equity requirement. These changes appear to have indeed led to an increase in Tier 1 capital, but there is also evidence that some regulators have relaxed the definition of Tier 1 capital. It is thus important to carefully monitor exactly what banks are holding as part of Tier 1.

Increases in the quantity and quality of capital since the global financial crisis can foster financial stability, but the increases appear to have reduced access to credit, at least in the short run. There is, however, little direct evidence on the effect of Basel III regulation on credit access in high-income OECD countries, which are the main adopters of Basel III. According to a study of Peru by Fang et al. (2018), Basel III reduced bank lending, but only in the short run. Moreover, several studies suggest that tightening of regulation in high-income OECD countries has led banks from these countries to lend less in developing countries. The effects on lending may be mitigated by allowing banks to increase capital with contingent convertible bonds, but experience with these instruments remains limited. It is not clear how well they will perform in practice, and they are not an option for countries without developed capital markets.

Greater transparency, information disclosure, and monitoring are needed to ensure that banks are not tempted to circumvent regulation. Based on the data available through BankScope and public sources, it is not possible to determine what exactly banks are holding as Tier 1 capital. It would thus be useful for market participants to have more information about the types of instruments that banks hold and how they are meeting their Tier 1 requirements. Information is also lacking on the types of assets that banks have, making it difficult to know why their risk-weighted assets relative to total assets have fallen over time. Thus, although on the surface it looks as though banks may now be holding more equity and safer assets than before the global financial crisis, the numbers may be providing a false sense of security.

NOTES

1. See Jackson et al. (1999) for a thorough discussion of the impact of Basel I regulation.
2. As Haldane (2011) notes, the number of risk categories under Basel II exploded for the larger, more complex banks, moving from fewer than 10 to over 200,000. This change implies that the number of calculations needed to determine the regulatory capital ratio of this size bank rose to over 200 million.
3. Further evidence also finds that the composition of borrowers among banks of varying degrees of capital is not random. "Bank-dependent" firms are more likely to seek financing from banks with greater capital (Schwert 2018).
4. Under the standard approach, the capital required for a loan is similar to that of Basel I because it is determined by fixed risk weights. By contrast, under the IRB approach banks use their own estimates of four risk parameters to determine the risk weight of a loan. The four parameters are probability of default, loss given default, exposure at default, and effective maturity of the loan.
5. These percentages are driven in part by small countries because most larger countries within each region have adopted Basel III.
6. However, Berg and Kaserer (2015) show that in some cases CoCo bonds can magnify equity holders' incentives to increase the riskiness of assets and decrease incentives to raise new equity in a crisis.

Statistical Appendixes

This section consists of two appendixes.

Appendix A presents basic country-by-country data on financial system characteristics around the world. It also reports averages of the same indicators for peer groups of countries, together with summary maps. It is an update on information from the 2017/2018 *Global Financial Development Report.*

Appendix B provides additional country-by-country information on key aspects of market discipline, bank capital regulation, and supervision around the world. It is specific to the 2019/2020 *Global Financial Development Report.*

These appendixes present only a small part of the Global Financial Development Database (GFDD), available at http://www.worldbank.org/financialdevelopment, and of the Bank regulation and Supervision Survey, available at https://www.worldbank.org/en/research/brief/BRSS.

APPENDIX A
BASIC DATA ON FINANCIAL SYSTEM CHARACTERISTICS, 2015–17

TABLE A.1 Economies and Their Financial System Characteristics, 2015–17

Economy	Financial institutions				Financial markets			
	Private credit by deposit money banks to GDP (%)	Account at a formal financial institution (%, age 15+)	Bank lending-deposit spread (%)	Bank Z-score	Stock market capitalization to GDP (%)	Market capitalization, excluding top 10 companies, to total market capitalization (%)	Stock market turnover ratio (%)	Stock price volatility
Afghanistan	3.5	14.5		11.7				
Albania	34.6	39.3	7.3	17.0				
Algeria	21.8	42.8	6.3	20.6	0.2			
Andorra				19.1				
Angola	19.7	29.3	11.1	10.2				
Antigua and Barbuda	49.1		7.5	34.4				
Argentina	12.3	47.9	6.8	6.9	10.4	32.9	7.2	35.4
Armenia	44.7	45.3	4.9	9.2				
Aruba	63.1		4.9	25.1				
Australia	133.4	99.5	3.3	14.8	96.4	58.6	63.2	13.8
Austria	83.0	98.2		25.5	27.7	42.9	30.0	19.5
Azerbaijan	31.5	28.6	8.4	6.9				
Bahamas, The	52.7		3.5	15.9				
Bahrain	71.4	82.6	4.2	16.1	62.1	24.5	1.9	7.3
Bangladesh	39.4	41.0	3.9	7.1	31.1			11.0
Barbados	80.8		7.4	15.3	67.9			
Belarus	21.9	81.2	2.7	3.0				
Belgium	61.4	98.6		17.6	82.8		28.5	18.1
Belize	54.9	48.2	7.5	9.6				
Benin	22.3	31.9	2.3	9.9				
Bermuda				17.5				21.8
Bhutan	46.3	33.7	10.8	27.7				
Bolivia	52.2	51.2	6.3	9.8				
Bosnia and Herzegovina	52.6	58.8	3.5	18.0				11.6
Botswana	31.2	44.8	5.3	8.4				3.6
Brazil	63.1	70.0	36.5	15.4	36.1	49.3	79.7	25.2
Brunei Darussalam	41.6		5.2	10.0				
Bulgaria	52.6	72.2	6.1	8.4				12.0
Burkina Faso	29.1	23.3	3.7	7.5				
Burundi	15.6	6.9		18.3				
Cabo Verde	60.5		7.2	23.5				
Cambodia	73.4	17.8		12.8				
Cameroon	14.5	26.9		9.8				
Canada	164.5	99.7	2.6	13.4	120.5	70.2	62.2	12.4
Cayman Islands				11.1				

(table A.1 continues next page)

TABLE A.1 Economies and Their Financial System Characteristics, 2015–17 *(continued)*

	Financial institutions				Financial markets			
Economy	Private credit by deposit money banks to GDP (%)	Account at a formal financial institution (%, age 15+)	Bank lending-deposit spread (%)	Bank Z-score	Stock market capitalization to GDP (%)	Market capitalization, excluding top 10 companies, to total market capitalization (%)	Stock market turnover ratio (%)	Stock price volatility
Central African Republic	12.3	13.7		6.7				
Chad	9.1	8.8		7.0				
Chile	77.5	73.8	1.8	6.8	84.6	54.9	12.2	11.2
China	146.6	80.2	2.8	22.4	65.7	85.6	338.4	26.9
Colombia	45.7	44.9	7.5	7.1	34.2	27.5	12.6	15.9
Comoros	25.7		8.8					
Congo, Dem. Rep.	5.7	15.0	15.9	3.6				
Congo, Rep.	22.4	23.3		6.3				
Costa Rica	56.0	67.8	10.3	17.3	5.0			23.7
Croatia	61.4	86.1	7.2	5.0	37.5		2.0	8.7
Cuba				5.9				
Curaçao				8.8				
Cyprus		88.7		10.9	13.5		3.2	20.7
Czech Republic	49.5	81.0	3.5	13.8				15.1
Côte d'Ivoire	21.9	14.8	1.3	14.5	35.1		4.7	
Denmark	166.4	99.9		20.3				19.3
Djibouti	27.9		10.0	16.0				
Dominica	49.0		6.3	8.0				
Dominican Republic	25.1	54.8	8.0	29.0				
Ecuador	28.6	50.9		5.2				
Egypt, Arab Rep.	27.1	32.1	5.5	20.2	15.0	52.5	30.8	23.7
El Salvador	47.3	29.3		23.6				
Equatorial Guinea	15.4							
Eritrea	11.8							
Estonia	66.7	98.0	4.0	7.7				9.4
Eswatini	19.4		7.2	11.7				
Ethiopia		34.8		9.2				
Fiji	66.7		2.9	14.2				
Finland	93.0	99.8		12.9				17.8
France	95.1	94.0		22.5	86.6		53.2	19.8
Gabon	13.6	34.0		12.4				
Gambia, The	5.3		13.2	10.1				
Georgia	50.8	61.2	2.7	5.3				
Germany	76.1	99.1		24.8	50.1	57.2	78.0	19.5
Ghana	17.2	42.3		8.2				7.6
Gibraltar				22.3				
Greece	108.3	85.5		6.8	21.4	32.1	35.5	38.1
Grenada	54.5		7.0	13.6				

TABLE A.1 Economies and Their Financial System Characteristics, 2015–17 *(continued)*

Economy	Financial institutions: Private credit by deposit money banks to GDP (%)	Financial institutions: Account at a formal financial institution (%, age 15+)	Financial institutions: Bank lending-deposit spread (%)	Financial institutions: Bank Z-score	Financial markets: Stock market capitalization to GDP (%)	Financial markets: Market capitalization, excluding top 10 companies, to total market capitalization (%)	Financial markets: Stock market turnover ratio (%)	Financial markets: Stock price volatility
Guatemala	32.3	43.5	7.7	18.6				
Guinea	9.5	14.6		7.1				
Guinea-Bissau	9.1		5.3	6.3				
Guyana	36.5		11.8	17.9				
Haiti	16.7	28.2	7.9	14.4				
Honduras	53.3	42.9	10.9	32.4				
Hong Kong SAR, China	209.3	95.3	5.0	16.3	1039.6	65.5	53.2	17.9
Hungary	35.0	74.9	1.6	7.2	15.9	3.5	42.2	17.3
Iceland	84.7			3.4				13.2
India	48.7	79.8		16.7	70.8	74.7	54.7	14.6
Indonesia	31.6	48.4	4.5	6.0	43.5	51.9	21.2	14.7
Iran, Islamic Rep.	59.3	93.4	5.2	5.0	24.0		12.9	
Iraq	9.2	20.3		30.1				
Ireland	50.4	95.3		12.0	41.5	9.0	18.8	19.2
Israel	64.3	92.8	3.0	28.6	69.4	47.6	26.3	11.6
Italy	84.8	93.8		12.1	28.0		341.2	26.2
Jamaica	29.1	78.3	12.4	9.3				14.9
Japan	102.8	98.2	0.7	15.9	106.1	84.7	111.1	21.4
Jordan	71.8	42.1	5.0	52.7	63.2	34.6	11.3	6.6
Kazakhstan	29.8	58.7		3.2	21.2	12.6	4.8	21.7
Kenya	30.9	55.7	6.9	19.7				11.3
Korea, Rep.	130.6	94.9	1.8	10.4	91.0	68.4	139.0	11.7
Kosovo	2 34.9	52.3						
Kuwait	98.0	79.8	2.8	16.0				9.7
Kyrgyz Republic	20.5	38.3	20.1	16.4				
Lao PDR		29.1		5.6				21.3
Latvia	46.7	93.2		7.3				16.2
Lebanon	94.8	44.8	1.7	34.1	22.4		5.8	7.2
Lesotho	16.3	33.3	9.7	10.2				
Liberia		21.6	9.6	5.3				
Libya	48.0	65.7	3.5	34.2				
Lithuania	40.7	82.9		7.0				7.5
Luxembourg	97.3	98.8		44.1	94.8		0.2	20.1
Macao SAR, China	107.1		5.2	17.5				
Madagascar	12.7	9.6	44.0	6.8				
Malawi	10.2	23.0	32.7	13.4				
Malaysia	118.6	85.1	1.6	18.3	125.9	65.0	30.2	9.3
Maldives	27.1		6.8	13.8				

(table A.1 continues next page)

TABLE A.1 Economies and Their Financial System Characteristics, 2015–17 *(continued)*

Economy	Financial institutions				Financial markets			
	Private credit by deposit money banks to GDP (%)	Account at a formal financial institution (%, age 15+)	Bank lending-deposit spread (%)	Bank Z-score	Stock market capitalization to GDP (%)	Market capitalization, excluding top 10 companies, to total market capitalization (%)	Stock market turnover ratio (%)	Stock price volatility
Mali	23.3	18.2	3.2	7.8				
Malta	82.0	97.4		21.8	36.8	13.0	2.1	7.1
Mauritania	2.6	19.0	11.8	23.4				
Mauritius	98.7	89.5	3.7	15.8	64.2		5.1	4.5
Mexico	23.9	35.4	3.6	19.9	33.1	47.5	28.9	13.3
Micronesia, Fed. Sts.	22.6		15.4	22.7				
Moldova	26.6	43.8	3.4	6.7				
Mongolia	52.2	93.0	6.7	19.6				16.5
Montenegro	47.7	68.4		6.6				12.4
Morocco	63.0	28.4		43.6	50.7	26.1	6.4	9.4
Mozambique	30.4	33.0	9.2	5.0				
Myanmar	18.9	25.6	5.0	3.2				
Namibia	50.1	77.3	4.3	8.7	17.9		3.9	22.6
Nepal	68.0	45.4		27.8				
Netherlands	111.9	99.6		11.1	101.6		59.0	18.0
New Zealand	148.5	99.2	1.8	23.5	41.1	54.9	13.6	8.4
Nicaragua	33.9	28.4	10.3	19.0				
Niger	15.0	9.5	2.9	14.8				
Nigeria	14.3	39.4	8.4	15.7	9.1	24.8	6.5	18.9
North Macedonia	48.1	76.6	4.5	5.0				
Norway	118.7	99.7		10.6	56.5	30.2	49.2	18.8
Oman	69.0		2.3	20.2	46.0	53.6	9.1	11.7
Pakistan	15.4	18.0	3.9	10.5	27.1		36.8	12.7
Panama	76.7	45.8	5.4	43.8	23.7		1.9	5.7
Papua New Guinea	18.2		8.0	7.4				
Paraguay	40.2	31.1	14.9	15.1				
Peru	35.8	42.2	13.8	16.9	37.4	40.7	4.1	14.0
Philippines	41.7	31.8	3.9	18.0	81.0	57.6	14.7	15.5
Poland	52.1	86.7		8.8	30.2		37.0	17.3
Portugal	113.6	92.3		12.9	28.7		68.7	19.7
Puerto Rico		69.7						
Qatar	72.5		2.1	21.8	95.2	28.4	13.4	18.2
Romania	27.7	57.6	4.7	6.6				
Russian Federation	53.6	75.8	5.6	6.2	34.8	38.9	28.8	18.9
Rwanda	19.9	36.7	9.9	8.5				
Samoa	43.9		6.6	9.7				
San Marino	108.0			9.4				
Saudi Arabia	55.3	71.7		19.5	67.6	43.0	71.6	21.4

TABLE A.1 Economies and Their Financial System Characteristics, 2015–17 *(continued)*

Economy	Financial institutions				Financial markets			
	Private credit by deposit money banks to GDP (%)	Account at a formal financial institution (%, age 15+)	Bank lending-deposit spread (%)	Bank Z-score	Stock market capitalization to GDP (%)	Market capitalization, excluding top 10 companies, to total market capitalization (%)	Stock market turnover ratio (%)	Stock price volatility
Senegal	26.0	20.4	0.9	13.3				
Serbia	42.9	71.4	8.0	14.8				10.6
Seychelles	26.0		8.9	10.2				
Sierra Leone	5.1	12.4	14.0	4.6				
Singapore	124.0	97.8	5.2	22.2	209.1	66.1	30.0	12.0
Slovak Republic	54.1	84.2		17.7				18.8
Slovenia	47.8	97.5		4.0	13.0	89.4	5.9	12.2
Solomon Islands	21.3		10.2					
Somalia		7.9						
South Africa	65.5	67.4	3.2	15.1	280.6	68.5	38.8	15.7
South Sudan	1.6	8.6	10.4	7.8				
Spain	112.6	93.8		21.1	62.5	22.0	98.0	22.0
Sri Lanka	36.2	73.6	2.3	12.8	23.5	61.3	6.3	8.2
St. Kitts and Nevis	53.9		6.7	13.3				
St. Lucia	75.8		6.6	2.8				
St. Vincent and the Grenadines	50.5		7.1	11.7				
Sudan	7.8	15.3		16.0				
Suriname	31.0		5.3	7.6				
Sweden	126.5	99.7		14.5				18.4
Switzerland	170.6	98.4	2.9	15.6	220.1		61.3	16.6
Syrian Arab Republic				9.6				
São Tomé and Príncipe	24.3		15.8	3.0				
Taiwan, China		94.2		16.5		69.8		
Tajikistan	19.1	47.0	22.7	16.9				
Tanzania	13.5	21.0	6.0	12.6				24.0
Thailand	113.1	81.0	3.2	7.5	99.2	65.5	74.6	13.3
Timor-Leste	7.6		12.9					
Togo	36.9	34.1	2.1	3.4				
Tonga	34.1		5.0					
Trinidad and Tobago	36.9	80.8	7.2	31.0				
Tunisia	74.5	36.8		34.6	19.7		10.5	6.7
Turkey	60.0	67.7		8.1	21.0	60.4	186.4	21.2
Turkmenistan		40.6		3.1				
Uganda	13.6	32.8	10.7	13.9				
Ukraine	41.2	62.9	7.9	4.0	4.4			25.8
United Arab Emirates	78.9	87.4		27.1	59.4	24.2	22.8	17.6
United Kingdom	131.4	96.4		11.8	111.7			14.5
United States	50.9	93.1		29.8	145.2	74.9	151.1	13.1

(table A.1 continues next page)

TABLE A.1 Economies and Their Financial System Characteristics, 2015–17 *(continued)*

Economy	Financial institutions				Financial markets			
	Private credit by deposit money banks to GDP (%)	Account at a formal financial institution (%, age 15+)	Bank lending-deposit spread (%)	Bank Z-score	Stock market capitalization to GDP (%)	Market capitalization, excluding top 10 companies, to total market capitalization (%)	Stock market turnover ratio (%)	Stock price volatility
Uruguay	27.6	63.9	9.9	6.0				
Uzbekistan		37.1		7.4				
Vanuatu	66.8		2.2	2.8				
Venezuela, RB	30.4	73.2	5.5	3.9				41.7
Vietnam	112.5	30.0	2.4	13.5	34.7		43.2	15.3
West Bank and Gaza	37.9	25.0		16.7	25.3		12.0	
Yemen, Rep.		6.4		13.1				
Zambia	12.4	35.8	4.2	9.3				
Zimbabwe	17.3	28.2		3.5				

Source: Data from and calculations based on the Global Financial Development Database. For more information, see Čihák et al. 2013.
Note: Empty cells indicate the lack of data.

NOTES

Economy: A territorial entity for which statistical data are maintained and provided internationally on a separate and independent basis (not necessarily a state as understood by international law and practice). The term, used interchangeably with *country*, does not imply political independence or official recognition by the World Bank.

Table layout: The layout of the table follows the 4x2 matrix of financial system characteristics introduced in the 2013 *Global Financial Development Report*, with four variables approximating the depth, access, efficiency, and stability of financial institutions and financial markets, respectively.

Additional data: The table above presents a selection of the information available in the Global Financial Development Database, accompanying this report. For additional variables, historical data, and detailed metadata, see the full data set at http://www.worldbank.org/financialdevelopment.

Period covered: The table shows averages of values during 2015–17, where available.

Averaging: Each observation is an arithmetic average of the corresponding variable over 2015–17.

Visualization: To illustrate where an economy observation is in relation to the global distribution of the variable, the table includes four bars to the left of each observation. The four-bar scale is based on the location of the economy in the statistical distribution of the variable in the Global Financial Development Database. Values below the 25th percentile show only one bar colored dark blue; values equal to or greater than the 25th and less than the 50th percentile show two bars colored dark blue; values equal to or greater than the 50th and less than the 75th percentile show three bars colored dark blue; and values greater than the 75th percentile show four bars colored dark blue. At the economy level, bars are calculated using winsorized and rescaled values, as described in the 2013 and 2017/2018 *Global Financial Development Report.* Specifically, the 5th and 95th percentiles for each variable for the entire pooled economy-year data set are calculated, and the top and bottom 5 percent of observations are truncated; that is, all observations from the 5th percentile to the minimum are replaced by the value corresponding to the 5th percentile, and all observations from the 95th percentile to the maximum are replaced by the value corresponding to the 95th percentile. To standardize all the variables to a 0–100 scale, each score is rescaled by the maximum and the minimum for each indicator. The rescaled indicator can be interpreted as the percent distance between the worst (0) and the best (100) financial development outcome, defined by the 5th and 95th percentiles of the original distribution (for further information, see the 2013 *Global Financial Development Report*). The four bars to the left of the economy name show the unweighted arithmetic average of the rescaled variables (dimensions) for each economy. This average is reported only for those countries where data for 2015–17 are available for at least four variables (dimensions).

Private credit by deposit money banks to GDP (%) measures the domestic private credit to the real sector by deposit money banks as a percentage of local currency GDP. Data on domestic private credit to the real sector by deposit money banks are from the International Financial Statistics (IFS), line FOSAOP/22D, published by the International Monetary Fund (IMF). Local currency GDP is also from IFS.

Account at a formal financial institution (%, age 15+) measures the percentage of adults with an account (self or together with someone else) at a bank, credit union, another financial institution (e.g., cooperative, microfinance institution), or the post office (if applicable), including adults who report having a debit card. The data are from the Global Financial Inclusion (Global Findex) Database (Demirgüç-Kunt and Klapper 2012; Demirgüç-Kunt et al. 2018).

Bank lending-deposit spread (%) is lending rate minus deposit rate. Lending rate is the rate charged by commercial or similar banks on loans to the private sector. Deposit interest rate is the rate paid by those banks for demand, time, or savings deposits. The lending and deposit rates are from the International Financial Statistics (IFS), lines FILR/60P and FIDR/60L, respectively.

Bank Z-score is calculated as [ROA + (equity / assets)] / (standard deviation of ROA). To approximate the probability that an economy's banking system defaults, the indicator compares the system's buffers (returns and capitalization) with the system's riskiness (volatility of returns). Return on Assets (ROA), equity, and assets are economy-level aggregate figures (calculated from underlying bank-by-bank unconsolidated data from Bankscope and Orbis Bank Focus).

Stock market capitalization to GDP (%) measures the capitalization of all equity markets as percentage of GDP. Market capitalization (also known as market value) is the share price times the number of shares outstanding. Listed domestic companies are the domestically incorporated companies listed on the economy's stock exchanges at the end of the year. Listed companies do not include investment companies, mutual funds, or other collective investment vehicles. Data are from the World Federation of Exchanges (WFE) and are compiled and reported by the *World Development Indicators* (WDI).

Market capitalization, excluding top 10 companies, to total market capitalization (%) measures the ratio of market capitalization, excluding the top 10 largest companies, to total market capitalization. The World Federation of Exchanges (WFE) provides data at the exchange level. This information is then aggregated at the economy level by taking a simple average of the data on the individual exchanges.

Stock market turnover ratio (%) is the total value of shares traded during the period divided by the average market capitalization for the period. Average market capitalization is calculated as the average of the end-of-period values for the current period and the previous period. Data are from the World Federation of Exchanges (WFE) and are compiled and reported by the *World Development Indicators* (WDI).

Stock price volatility is the 360-day standard deviation of the return on the primary national stock market index. The data are from Bloomberg.

MAP A.1 DEPTH—FINANCIAL INSTITUTIONS

To approximate financial institutions' depth, this map uses domestic private credit to the real sector by deposit money banks as a percentage of local currency GDP. Data on domestic private credit to the real sector by deposit money banks are from the International Financial Statistics (IFS), line FOSAOP/22D, published by the International Monetary Fund (IMF). Local currency GDP is also from IFS. The four shades of blue in the map are based on the average value of the variable in 2015–17: the darker the blue, the higher the quartile of the statistical distribution of the variable.

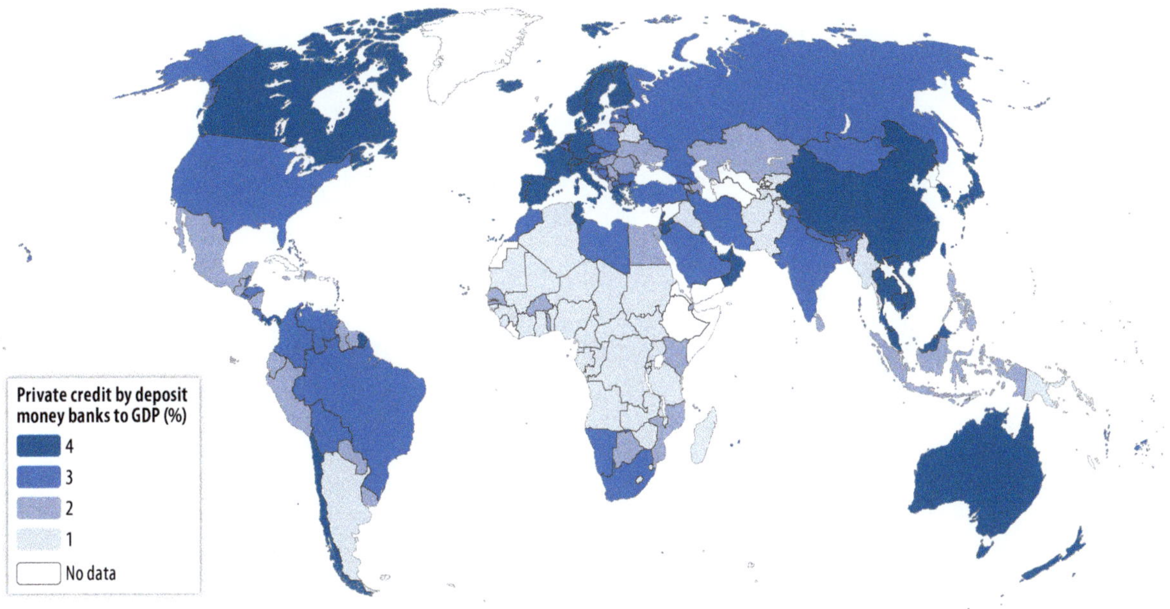

TABLE A.1.1 Depth—Financial Institutions

Private credit by deposit money banks to GDP (%)	Number of economies	Average	Median	Standard deviation	Minimum	Maximum	Weighted average
World	176	52.2	45.2	38.4	1.6	209.3	85.8
By developed/developing economies							
Developed economies	57	84.4	77.5	40.6	12.3	209.3	83.5
Developing economies	119	36.8	30.9	25.8	1.6	146.6	90.1
By income level							
High income	57	84.4	77.5	40.6	12.3	209.3	83.5
Upper-middle income	49	48.8	44.7	27.7	9.2	146.6	106.5
Lower-middle income	43	35.1	30.9	21.9	2.6	112.5	39.9
Low income	27	17.6	15.0	13.4	1.6	68.0	18.5
By region							
High income: OECD	33	94.3	93.0	38.3	35.0	170.6	83.9
High income: non-OECD	24	70.8	66.0	40.4	12.3	209.3	77.4
East Asia and Pacific	17	58.2	43.9	41.8	7.6	146.6	133.2
Europe and Central Asia	18	38.5	38.1	12.8	19.1	60.0	50.6
Latin America and the Caribbean	23	42.0	40.2	14.4	16.7	75.8	46.2
Middle East and North Africa	11	48.7	48.0	26.3	9.2	94.8	42.8
South Asia	8	35.6	37.8	20.2	3.5	68.0	44.3
Sub-Saharan Africa	42	21.6	15.9	18.4	1.6	98.7	27.3

Source: Global Financial Development Database, 2015–17 data.
Note: Weighted average by current GDP. OECD = Organisation for Economic Co-operation and Development.

MAP A.2 ACCESS—FINANCIAL INSTITUTIONS

To approximate access to financial institutions, this map uses the percentage of adults (age 15+) who reported having an account at a formal financial institution. The data are taken from the Global Financial Inclusion (Global Findex) Database. The four shades of blue in the map are based on the value of the variable in 2017: the darker the blue, the higher the quartile of the statistical distribution of the variable.

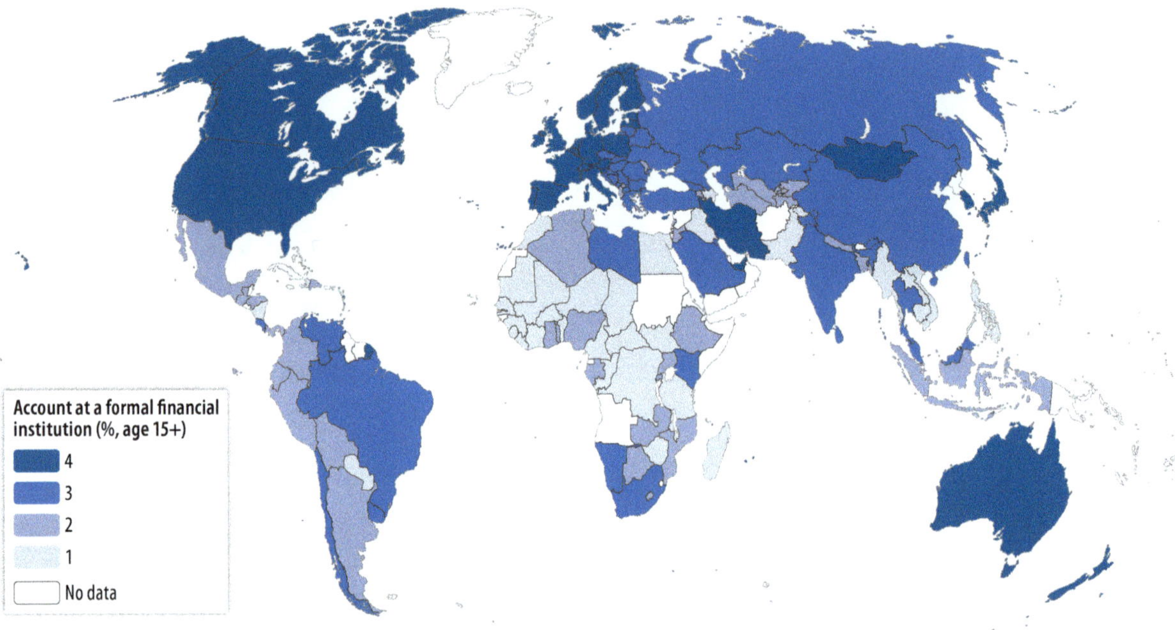

TABLE A.1.2 Access—Financial Institutions

Account at a formal financial institution (%, age 15+)	Number of economies	Average	Median	Standard deviation	Minimum	Maximum	Weighted average
World	143	58.0	54.8	29.4	8.6	99.9	65.4
By developed/developing economies							
Developed economies	47	89.6	94.0	12.6	45.8	99.9	91.7
Developing economies	96	42.5	38.8	21.8	8.6	93.4	60.1
By income level							
High income	47	89.6	94.0	12.6	45.8	99.9	91.7
Upper-middle income	37	58.0	58.7	18.9	20.3	93.4	72.3
Lower-middle income	34	39.7	36.3	18.1	14.8	93.0	56.8
Low income	25	23.4	21.6	11.3	8.6	47.0	24.4
By region							
High income: OECD	32	94.1	96.9	7.2	73.8	99.9	94.4
High income: non-OECD	15	80.2	82.9	16.4	45.8	97.8	67.4
East Asia and Pacific	10	52.2	40.1	29.3	17.8	93.0	69.3
Europe and Central Asia	20	55.4	58.2	14.9	28.6	81.2	64.3
Latin America and the Caribbean	15	46.3	43.5	15.1	28.2	73.2	53.5
Middle East and North Africa	10	43.1	39.4	21.8	20.3	93.4	48.0
South Asia	6	45.4	43.2	27.2	14.5	79.8	67.4
Sub-Saharan Africa	35	30.1	26.9	18.9	8.6	89.5	32.1

Source: Global Financial Development Database, 2017 data.
Note: Weighted average by current GDP. OECD = Organisation for Economic Co-operation and Development.

MAP A.3 EFFICIENCY—FINANCIAL INSTITUTIONS

To approximate the efficiency of financial institutions, this map uses the spread (difference) between lending rate and deposit interest rate. Lending rate is the rate charged by banks on loans to the private sector, and deposit interest rate is the rate paid by commercial or similar banks for demand, time, or savings deposits. The lending and deposit rates are from IFS, lines FILR/60P and FIDR/60L, respectively. The four shades of blue in the map are based on the average value of the variable in 2015–17: the darker the blue, the higher the quartile of the statistical distribution of the variable.

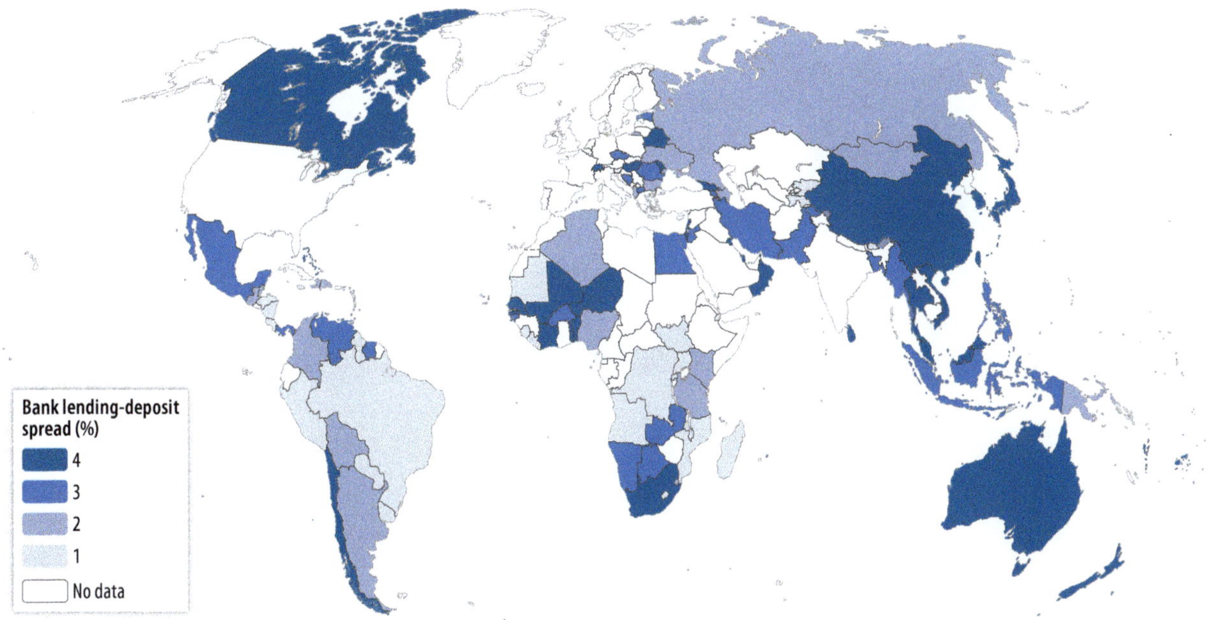

TABLE A.1.3 Efficiency—Financial Institutions

Bank lending-deposit spread (%)	Number of economies	Average	Median	Standard deviation	Minimum	Maximum	Weighted average
World	122	7.3	5.6	6.3	0.7	44.0	5.1
By developed/developing economies							
Developed economies	29	4.4	4.0	2.4	0.7	9.9	2.3
Developing economies	93	8.2	6.6	6.9	0.9	44.0	6.7
By income level							
High income	29	4.4	4.0	2.4	0.7	9.9	2.3
Upper-middle income	40	7.0	5.9	5.7	1.6	36.5	6.9
Lower-middle income	32	7.7	7.0	4.5	1.3	20.1	5.3
Low income	21	11.2	9.2	10.6	0.9	44.0	10.5
By region							
High income: OECD	11	2.4	2.6	1.0	0.7	4.0	1.8
High income: non-OECD	18	5.6	5.2	2.2	2.1	9.9	5.3
East Asia and Pacific	16	5.8	4.7	4.0	1.6	15.4	3.0
Europe and Central Asia	13	7.7	5.6	6.4	2.7	22.7	5.7
Latin America and the Caribbean	21	9.9	7.7	6.8	3.6	36.5	21.0
Middle East and North Africa	6	5.6	5.4	2.7	1.7	10.0	5.3
South Asia	5	5.6	3.9	3.4	2.3	10.8	3.7
Sub-Saharan Africa	32	9.3	7.8	8.8	0.9	44.0	7.2

Source: Global Financial Development Database, 2015–17 data.
Note: Weighted average by current GDP. OECD = Organisation for Economic Co-operation and Development.

MAP A.4 STABILITY—FINANCIAL INSTITUTIONS

To approximate the stability of financial institutions, this map uses the Z-score for commercial banks. The indicator is estimated as follows: [ROA + (equity / assets)] / (standard deviation of ROA). Return on assets (ROA), equity, and assets are economy-level aggregate figures (calculated from underlying bank-by-bank unconsolidated data from Bankscope). The indicator compares the banking system's buffers (returns and capital) with its riskiness (volatility of returns). The four shades of blue in the map are based on the average value of the variable in 2015–17: the darker the blue, the higher the quartile of the statistical distribution of the variable.

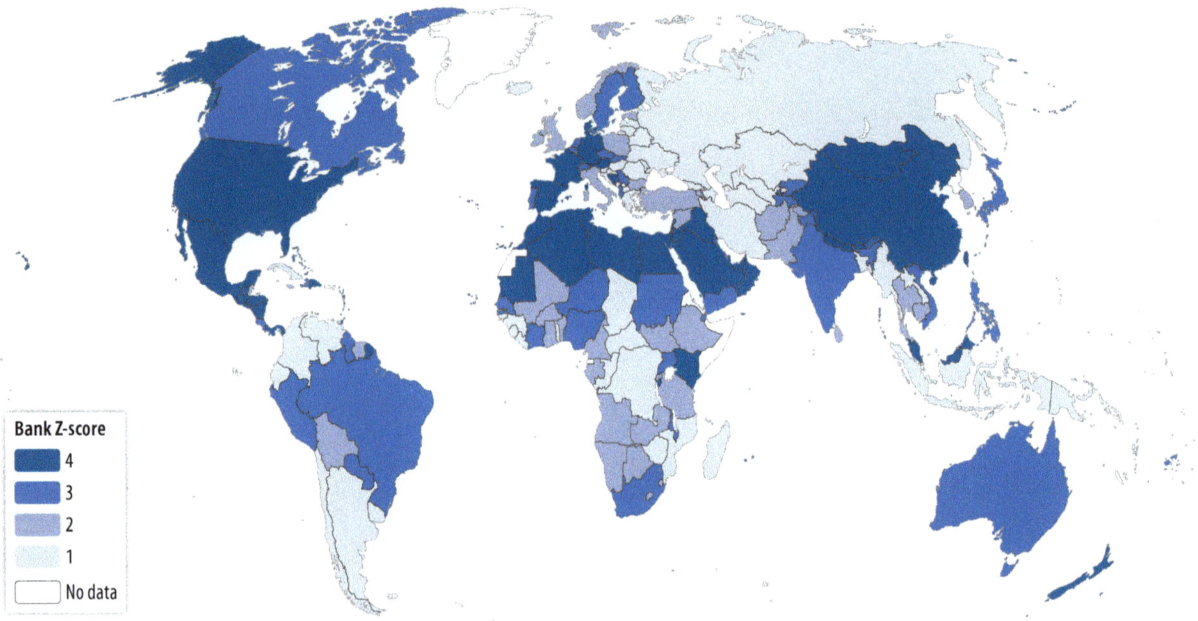

TABLE A.1.4 Stability—Financial Institutions

Bank Z-score	Number of economies	Average	Median	Standard deviation	Minimum	Maximum	Weighted average
World	185	14.2	12.9	8.8	2.8	52.7	20.1
By developed/developing economies							
Developed economies	64	16.4	15.5	8.6	3.4	44.1	21.6
Developing economies	121	13.1	10.2	8.7	2.8	52.7	17.1
By income level							
High income	64	16.4	15.5	8.6	3.4	44.1	21.6
Upper-middle income	49	13.6	11.7	9.6	2.8	52.7	18.2
Lower-middle income	42	14.6	13.2	9.1	2.8	43.6	14.2
Low income	30	10.0	8.9	5.3	3.4	27.8	10.5
By region							
High income: OECD	33	15.4	13.4	8.6	3.4	44.1	21.9
High income: non-OECD	31	17.4	16.3	8.7	5.0	43.8	17.5
East Asia and Pacific	15	12.2	12.8	6.8	2.8	22.7	20.3
Europe and Central Asia	19	8.8	6.9	5.1	3.0	18.0	6.8
Latin America and the Caribbean	24	13.9	14.0	7.6	2.8	32.4	16.0
Middle East and North Africa	13	25.4	20.6	14.1	5.0	52.7	20.7
South Asia	8	16.0	13.3	7.8	7.1	27.8	15.3
Sub-Saharan Africa	42	10.4	9.2	5.1	3.0	23.5	13.2

Source: Global Financial Development Database, 2015–-17 data.
Note: Weighted average by current GDP. OECD = Organisation for Economic Co-operation and Development.

MAP A.5 DEPTH—FINANCIAL MARKETS

To approximate the depth of financial markets, this map uses stock market capitalization as a percentage of GDP. Market capitalization (also known as market value) is the share price times the number of shares outstanding. Listed domestic companies are the domestically incorporated companies listed on the economy's stock exchanges at the end of the year. Listed companies do not include investment companies, mutual funds, or other collective investment vehicles. Data are from World Federation of Exchanges (WFE), and are compiled and reported by the *World Development Indicators*. The four shades of blue in the map are based on the average value of the variable in 2015–17: the darker the blue, the higher the quartile of the statistical distribution of the variable.

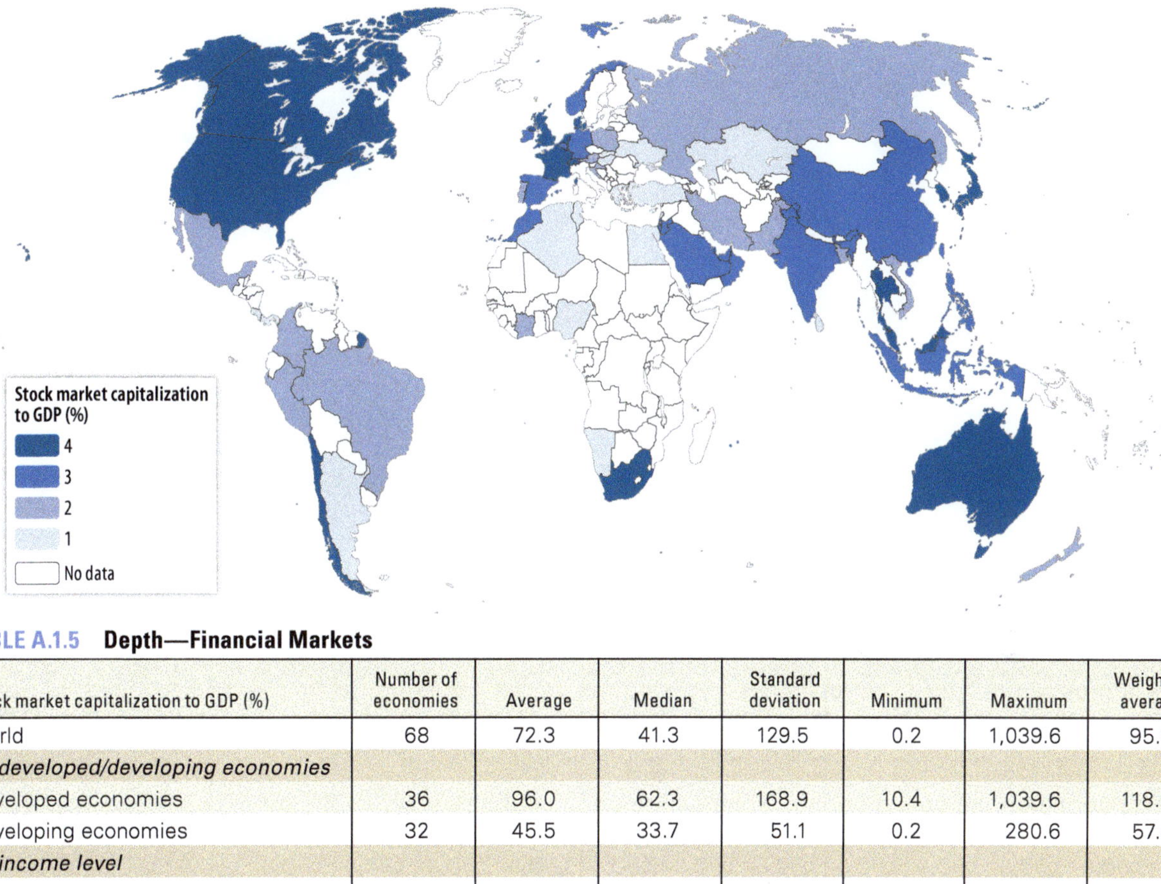

TABLE A.1.5 Depth—Financial Markets

Stock market capitalization to GDP (%)	Number of economies	Average	Median	Standard deviation	Minimum	Maximum	Weighted average
World	68	72.3	41.3	129.5	0.2	1,039.6	95.9
By developed/developing economies							
Developed economies	36	96.0	62.3	168.9	10.4	1,039.6	118.2
Developing economies	32	45.5	33.7	51.1	0.2	280.6	57.0
By income level							
High income	36	96.0	62.3	168.9	10.4	1,039.6	118.2
Upper-middle income	18	54.8	34.5	64.8	0.2	280.6	58.9
Lower-middle income	14	33.6	29.1	21.9	4.4	81.0	50.3
Low income	0						
By region							
High income: OECD	23	73.4	69.4	48.2	13.0	220.1	113.6
High income: non-OECD	13	136.1	59.4	276.2	10.4	1,039.6	187.1
East Asia and Pacific	6	75.0	73.4	34.4	34.7	125.9	66.4
Europe and Central Asia	4	20.3	21.1	12.4	4.4	34.8	28.0
Latin America and the Caribbean	5	29.2	34.2	13.6	5.0	37.4	34.6
Middle East and North Africa	8	27.6	23.2	20.1	0.2	63.2	21.8
South Asia	4	38.1	29.1	22.0	23.5	70.8	62.2
Sub-Saharan Africa	5	81.4	35.1	113.3	9.1	280.6	119.3

Source: Global Financial Development Database, 2015–17 data.
Note: Weighted average by current GDP. OECD = Organisation for Economic Co-operation and Development.

MAP A.6 ACCESS—FINANCIAL MARKETS

To approximate access to financial markets, this map uses the ratio of market capitalization, excluding the top 10 largest companies, to total market capitalization. The World Federation of Exchanges (WFE) provides data on the exchange level. This variable is aggregated up to the economy level by taking a simple average over exchanges. The four shades of blue in the map are based on the average value of the variable in 2015–17: the darker the blue, the higher the quartile of the statistical distribution of the variable.

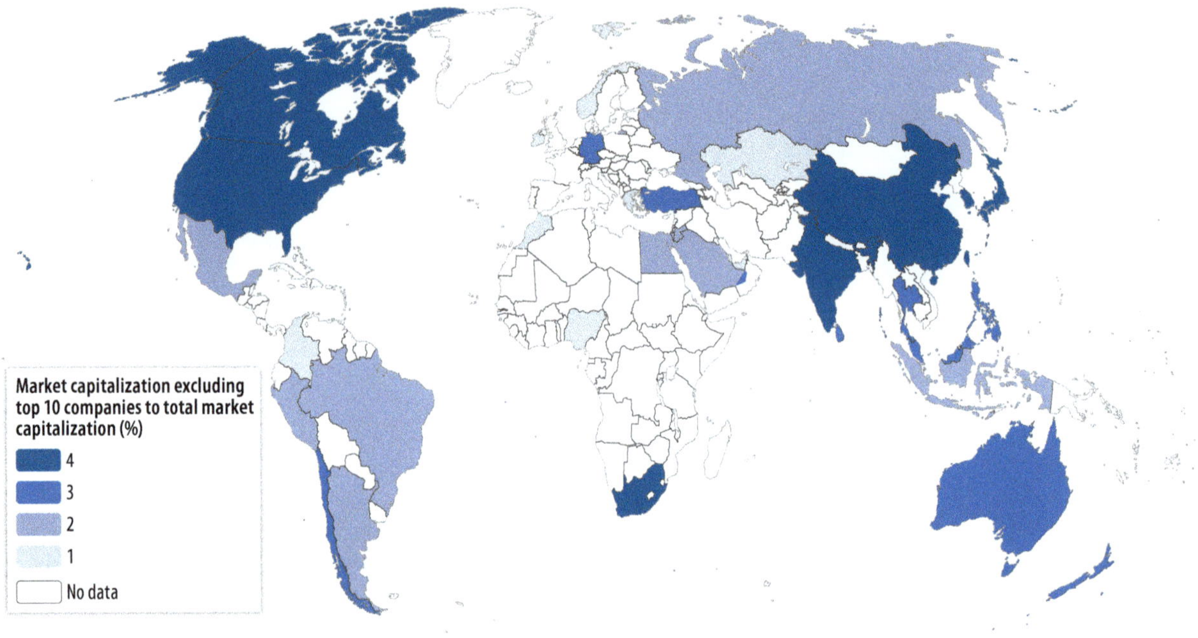

TABLE A.1.6 Access—Financial Markets

Market capitalization, excluding top 10 companies, to total market capitalization (%)	Number of economies	Average	Median	Standard deviation	Minimum	Maximum	Weighted average
World	41	49.0	52.5	20.0	9.0	85.6	69.4
By developed/developing economies							
Developed economies	22	48.4	54.2	21.2	9.0	84.7	69.3
Developing economies	19	49.7	51.9	19.1	12.6	85.6	69.5
By income level							
High income	22	48.4	54.2	21.2	9.0	84.7	69.3
Upper-middle income	12	49.7	48.4	20.3	12.6	85.6	71.5
Lower-middle income	7	49.9	52.5	18.3	24.8	74.7	61.2
Low income	0						
By region							
High income: OECD	12	53.6	56.1	21.3	9.0	84.7	71.3
High income: non-OECD	10	42.1	37.9	20.5	13.0	69.8	42.7
East Asia and Pacific	5	65.1	65.0	12.7	51.9	85.6	81.5
Europe and Central Asia	3	37.3	38.9	23.9	12.6	60.4	44.8
Latin America and the Caribbean	4	41.2	44.1	9.9	27.5	49.3	46.4
Middle East and North Africa	3	37.7	34.6	13.4	26.1	52.5	44.7
South Asia	2	68.0	68.0	9.5	61.3	74.7	74.2
Sub-Saharan Africa	2	46.7	46.7	30.9	24.8	68.5	43.6

Source: Global Financial Development Database, 2015–17 data.
Note: Weighted average by current GDP. OECD = Organisation for Economic Co-operation and Development.

MAP A.7 EFFICIENCY—FINANCIAL MARKETS

To approximate the efficiency of financial markets, this map uses the total value of shares traded during the period divided by the average market capitalization for the period. Average market capitalization is calculated as the average of the end-of-period values for the current period and the previous period. Data are from World Federation of Exchanges (WFE), and are compiled and reported by the *World Development Indicators*. The four shades of blue in the map are based on the average value of the variable in 2015–17: the darker the blue, the higher the quartile of the statistical distribution of the variable.

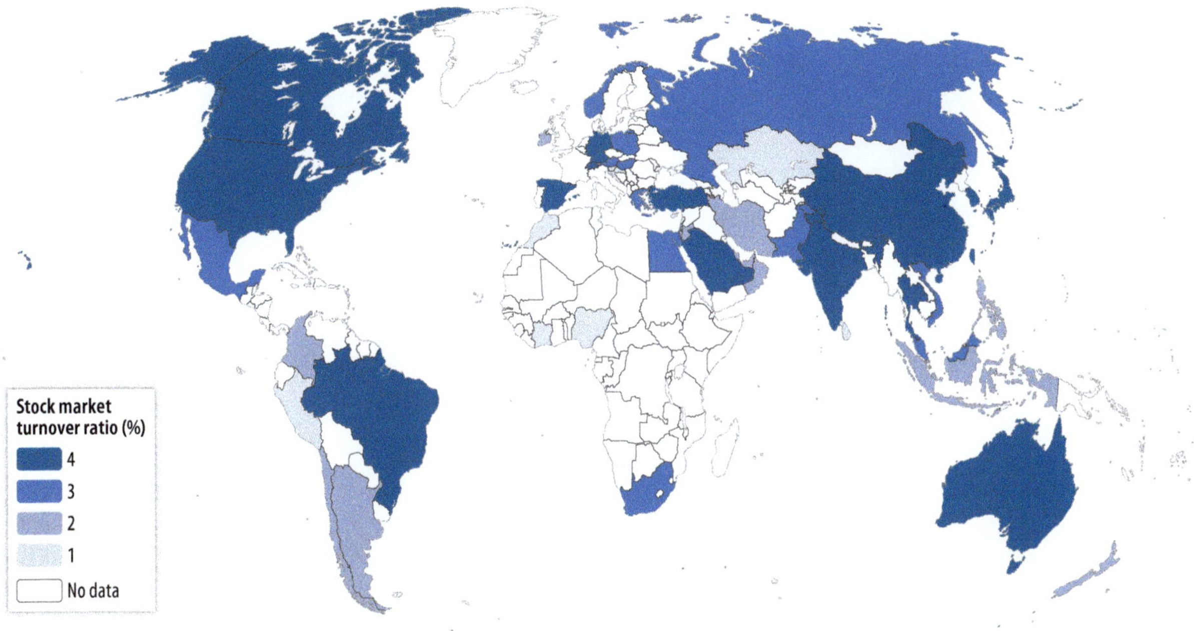

TABLE A.1.7 Efficiency—Financial Markets

Stock market turnover ratio (%)	Number of economies	Average	Median	Standard deviation	Minimum	Maximum	Weighted average
World	56	42.0	27.6	56.5	0.2	338.4	141.3
By developed/developing economies							
Developed economies	30	41.7	30.0	40.9	0.2	151.1	112.6
Developing economies	26	42.3	17.9	71.4	4.1	338.4	187.7
By income level							
High income	30	41.7	30.0	40.9	0.2	151.1	112.6
Upper-middle income	15	57.5	28.8	91.1	4.1	338.4	227.9
Lower-middle income	11	21.6	14.7	17.3	4.7	54.7	36.8
Low income	0						
By region							
High income: OECD	19	54.5	42.2	43.8	0.2	151.1	118.3
High income: non-OECD	11	19.7	9.1	23.3	1.9	71.6	34.4
East Asia and Pacific	6	87.1	36.7	124.9	14.7	338.4	289.8
Europe and Central Asia	3	73.4	28.8	98.6	4.8	186.4	82.9
Latin America and the Caribbean	4	31.3	20.8	33.9	4.1	79.7	53.4
Middle East and North Africa	6	13.2	11.7	9.1	5.8	30.8	17.5
South Asia	3	32.6	36.8	24.5	6.3	54.7	51.3
Sub-Saharan Africa	4	13.8	5.8	16.7	4.7	38.8	19.4

Source: Global Financial Development Database, 2015–17 data.
Note: Weighted average by current GDP. OECD = Organisation for Economic Co-operation and Development.

MAP A.8 STABILITY—FINANCIAL MARKETS

To approximate the stability of financial markets, this map uses the 360-day standard deviation of the return on the primary national stock market index. Data are from Bloomberg. The four shades of blue in the map are based on the average value of the variable in 2015–17: the darker the blue, the higher the quartile of the statistical distribution of the variable.

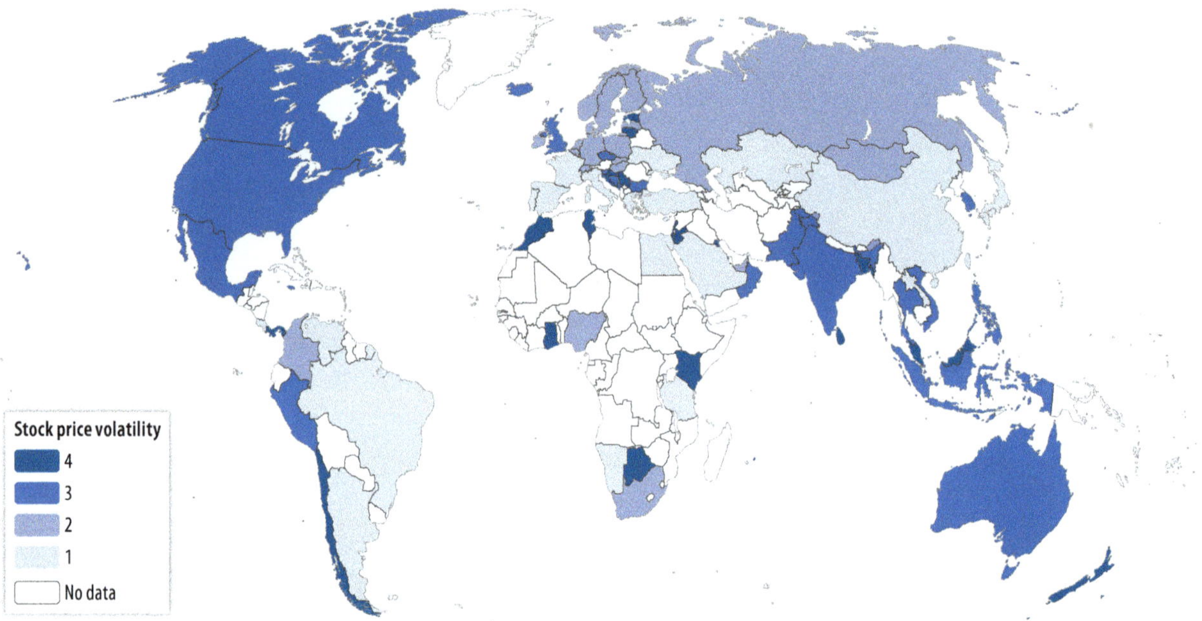

TABLE A.1.8 Stability—Financial Markets

Stock price volatility	Number of economies	Average	Median	Standard deviation	Minimum	Maximum	Weighted average
World	88	16.1	15.6	6.9	3.6	41.7	18.2
By developed/developing economies							
Developed economies	48	16.5	17.5	6.4	5.7	38.1	16.5
Developing economies	40	15.6	14.7	7.5	3.6	41.7	21.7
By income level							
High income	48	16.5	17.5	6.4	5.7	38.1	16.5
Upper-middle income	23	15.9	14.0	8.6	3.6	41.7	23.7
Lower-middle income	16	14.6	14.7	5.7	6.7	25.8	15.1
Low income	1	24.0	24.0		24.0	24.0	24.0
By region							
High income: OECD	33	17.2	17.8	5.4	8.4	38.1	16.3
High income: non-OECD	15	14.9	12.0	8.1	5.7	35.4	20.5
East Asia and Pacific	8	16.6	15.4	5.3	9.3	26.9	24.8
Europe and Central Asia	8	16.8	15.6	5.8	10.6	25.8	19.7
Latin America and the Caribbean	7	21.2	15.9	10.2	13.3	41.7	20.0
Middle East and North Africa	5	10.7	7.2	7.3	6.6	23.7	16.8
South Asia	4	11.6	11.9	2.7	8.2	14.6	13.9
Sub-Saharan Africa	8	13.5	13.5	8.0	3.6	24.0	16.5

Source: Global Financial Development Database, 2015–17 data.
Note: Weighted average by current GDP. OECD = Organisation for Economic Co-operation and Development.

APPENDIX B

SELECTED INDICATORS OF MARKET DISCIPLINE, CAPITAL REGULATION, AND SUPERVISION

TABLE B.1 Economies and Their Market Discipline, Capital Regulation, and Supervision

	Market discipline				Capital regulation			Supervision
Economy	Deposit insurance limit of retail depositors	Top 10 banks rated by international credit-rating agencies (%)	Bank governance and risk management framework publicly available	Enforcement actions publicly available	Minimum capital ratio	Minimum Tier 1 ratio	Minimum leverage ratio	Supervisors with post-graduate degrees (%)
Albania	4.9	30	1	0	12	6		53
Angola		20	1		10	10		33
Antigua and Barbuda		0	1	1	8	6		25
Argentina		60	1	0	8	6		25
Armenia	5.8	50	1	0	12	8		7.4
Aruba		0	0	0	14			22
Australia	3.7	100	1	0	8	6		50
Austria	2.5	90	1	0	8	6		34
Azerbaijan	4.8	80	1	0	10	5	5	14
Bahrain		0	1	1	12.5	9		
Bangladesh		0	0	0	10	6	3	80
Belarus		50	1	1	10	6	3	13.1
Belgium	2.7	90	1	0	8	6	2	45
Belize		0	0	0	9	4.5		17
Benin	2.9		0	0	8			100
Bermuda		50	1	1	11.63	6	5	
Bhutan		0	1		10	5	5	50
Bolivia		100	0	0	10	7		2.5
Bosnia and Herzegovina	5.7	0	0	0	12	9	6	18.5
Botswana		0	1	1	15	7.5		57
Brazil	8.2	100	1	0	9.875	6		63
British Virgin Islands		90	0	1	12	12		0
Bulgaria	14.8	50	1	0	8	6		100
Burkina Faso	3.9		0	0	8			100
Burundi		0	0	0	4 14.5	12.5	7	3
Cabo Verde		0	1		10			83
Canada	1.8	100	1	0	8	6	3	
Cayman Islands		90	1	0	10	6		50
Chile	0.3	100	1	0	8	0	3	24
China		100	1	1	8	6	4	
Colombia		100	1	0	9			72
Comoros								

(table B.1 continues next page)

TABLE B.1 Economies and Their Market Discipline, Capital Regulation, and Supervision *(continued)*

Economy	Market discipline				Capital regulation			Supervision
	Deposit insurance limit of retail depositors	Top 10 banks rated by international credit-rating agencies (%)	Bank governance and risk management framework publicly available	Enforcement actions publicly available	Minimum capital ratio	Minimum Tier 1 ratio	Minimum leverage ratio	Supervisors with post-graduate degrees (%)
Congo, Dem. Republic					10	7		
Cook Islands		50	0	0	10	5		0
Costa Rica		60	1	0	10			100
Côte d'Ivoire	1.5		0	0	8			100
Croatia	8.9	70	1	1	8	6		20
Curaçao		40	0	1	10.5	5		49
Cyprus	4.6	40	1		8	6		88
Czech Republic	6.0	70	1	1	8	6		15
Denmark			0	1	8	4.5		
Djibouti		20	0	1	12	12		8
Dominican Republic	1.6	10	0	0	10			76
Ecuador	5.3	0	0	0	9	9		30
El Salvador	2.7	100	1	0	12	12	7	17
Estonia	6.1	0	1	0	8	4.5		100
Eswatini								
Fiji		70	0	0	12			15
Finland	2.5	90	1	0	8	6		
France	3.0	100	1	0	8	6		10
Gambia		0	0		10	10		54.5
Georgia		30	0	0	10.5	8.5		
Germany	2.6	100	1	1	8	6		43.34
Ghana		0	1	0	10			82
Gibraltar		0	0	1	8	8	3	0
Greece	6.1	10	1	0	8	6		95
Guatemala	0.6	100	0	0	10	5		63
Guernsey		0	0	0	10.5	8.5		40
Guinea-Bissau	3.4		0	0	8			100
Guyana		0	1	0	8	4		27
Haiti		0	0	0	12			33
Honduras	4.1	80	1	0	10			92
Hong Kong SAR, China	1.5	100	1	0	8	6		72
Hungary	8.6	80	1	1	8	6		
Iceland		90	1	1	8	6	3	88
India		100	1	1	9	7	4.5	30
Indonesia	42.2	90	1	1	8	6		26.3
Ireland	1.7	100	1	1	8	6		

TABLE B.1 Economies and Their Market Discipline, Capital Regulation, and Supervision *(continued)*

Economy	Market discipline				Capital regulation			Supervision
	Deposit insurance limit of retail depositors	Top 10 banks rated by international credit-rating agencies (%)	Bank governance and risk management framework publicly available	Enforcement actions publicly available	Minimum capital ratio	Minimum Tier 1 ratio	Minimum leverage ratio	Supervisors with post-graduate degrees (%)
Israel		60	1	0	12.5			50
Italy	3.6	100	1	1	8	6		14
Japan		100	1	1	8	6		
Jersey		100	1	0	10	5		0
Jordan	17.2	60	1	0	12	8.5	4	50
Kenya	0.7	30	1	0	14.5	10.5		80
Korea, Republic		100	1		8	6		
Kosovo	1.2	10	0	0	12	8	7	41
Kuwait		100	1	0	13	11	3	12
Kyrgyz Republic	2.6	0	1	1	12	6	8	
Latvia	7.8	10	1	0	8	6		
Lebanon	0.4	40	1	1	14	11		51
Lesotho		0		0				90
Liberia		0	1	0	10	5	5	65
Liechtenstein		20	1	0	8	6		33
Lithuania	7.4	80	1	0	8	6		97.5
Luxembourg	1.1	100	1	0	8	6		0
Macao SAR, China	0.8	30	1	0	8	4		78
Madagascar		0	0	0	8			0
Malawi		0	1	1	15	10	3	54
Malaysia	6.2	90	1	0	8	6		
Maldives	0.2	50	0	0	12	6	5	27
Mali	2.9		0	0	8			100
Malta	4.4	0	1	0	8	4.5	3	25
Marshall Islands		0	0	1	15	15		50
Mauritania		0	0	1	10	6		50
Mauritius		20	1	0	10	8		15
Mexico	13.6	100	1	0	8	6		11.15
Moldova	0.1	0	1	0	16			1.56
Montenegro	7.9	0	0	0	10			20
Montserrat				1				75
Morocco	2.8	80	1	1	12	9		94
Mozambique	0.8	0	0	0	8	4		20
Namibia		0	1	0	10	7	6	26
Nepal		0	0	0	11	6	4	100
Netherlands	2.4	90	1	1	8	6		

(table B.1 continues next page)

TABLE B.1 Economies and Their Market Discipline, Capital Regulation, and Supervision *(continued)*

	Market discipline				Capital regulation			Supervision
Economy	Deposit insurance limit of retail depositors	Top 10 banks rated by international credit-rating agencies (%)	Bank governance and risk management framework publicly available	Enforcement actions publicly available	Minimum capital ratio	Minimum Tier 1 ratio	Minimum leverage ratio	Supervisors with post-graduate degrees (%)
New Zealand		100	1	0	8	6		69
Nicaragua	4.9	50	0	0	10	8	3.75	56.67
Niger	6.2		0	0	8			100
Nigeria		100	1	0	10			90
North Macedonia	6.5	0	1	0	8	6		52
Norway	3.4	100	1	1	8	6		70
Oman	3.5	90	1	0	12.625			55
Pakistan		0	1	0	10.65	8.15		80
Palau		0	0	0	12	6	5	100
Panama		60	1	0	8	6	3	39
Papua New Guinea		70	0		12	8	6	8
Paraguay		0	1	0		8		33
Peru	4.7	80	1	0	10	5		47
Philippines	3.6	90	1	0	10	7.5	5	94
Poland	8.8	100	0		8	6		
Portugal	5.5	80	1	0	8	6		22
Qatar		100	1	1	13.5	10.5	3	8
Romania	11.6	70	1	0	8	6		4
Russian Federation	2.4	100	1	0	8	6		
Rwanda	0.9	50	1	1	15	10		95
Samoa		10	0		24.5	19.9		28.6
San Marino	2.4	0	0	0	11			7
São Tomé and Príncipe		0	0	0	12	6		90
Saudi Arabia	2.7	100	1	1	9.625	7.625	3	4
Senegal	1.8		0	0	8			100
Serbia	9.6	0	1	0	12	6		43.5
Seychelles		0	1	0	12	6		5
Singapore	0.6	100	1	0	10	8		26
Slovak Republic	6.7	100	1	1	8	6		2
Slovenia	5.1	50	1		8	6	3	35
South Africa		90	1	0	9.75	7.5	4	34
Spain		100	1	1	8	6		18
Sri Lanka	0.5	100	1	0	10	5		29
Suriname		0	1	0	10	6		42
Sweden		100	1	0	8	6		
Switzerland	1.3	100	1	0	8	6		70

TABLE B.1 Economies and Their Market Discipline, Capital Regulation, and Supervision *(continued)*

	Market discipline				Capital regulation			Supervision
Economy	Deposit insurance limit of retail depositors	Top 10 banks rated by international credit-rating agencies (%)	Bank governance and risk management framework publicly available	Enforcement actions publicly available	Minimum capital ratio	Minimum Tier 1 ratio	Minimum leverage ratio	Supervisors with post-graduate degrees (%)
Taiwan, China		100	1	0	8.625	6.625	3	65.46
Tajikistan	2.5	10	0	0	12		10	0
Tanzania	7.1		1	0	14.5	12.5		
Thailand	71.1	80	1	0	8.5	6		70
Togo	3.8		0	0	8			100
Tonga		0	0	1	15			0
Trinidad and Tobago	1.2	20	1	0	8	4		100
Tunisia	7.6	80	1	1	10	7		100
Turkey		100	1	0	8	6	3	12
Turks and Caicos Islands		50	0	1		11		80
Uganda	1.4	0	1	0	12	8		78
Ukraine	3.6	100	1	1	10			
United Kingdom	2.8	100	1	0	8	6	3	44
United States	4.3	100	1	1	8	6	4	
Uruguay	0.5	100	1	0	8	5.33	4	35
Vanuatu		60	0	0	12	6		57
Vietnam	1.0		0	0				50
West Bank and Gaza	3.3	0	1	0	12	8		32.5
Zimbabwe	0.7				12	6	6	100

Source: Data from and calculations based on the Bank Regulation and Supervision Survey. For more information, see Anginer et al. 2019.
Note: Empty cells indicate the lack of data.

NOTES

Additional data: Table B.1 presents information from the 2019 World Bank's global Bank Regulation and Supervision Survey on key aspects of bank capital regulation, market discipline, and supervision.

Period covered: The table shows the most recently available data for 2016.

Economy: A territorial entity for which statistical data are maintained and provided internationally on a separate and independent basis (not necessarily a state as understood by international law and practice). The term, used interchangeably with *country,* does not imply political independence or official recognition by the World Bank.

Deposit insurance limit of retail depositors: Basic deposit insurance limit for retail depositors (for example, households and unincorporated businesses) as of end of 2016. Data are converted to U.S. dollars using, wherever it is needed, the exchange rate with U.S. dollars as per the last trading day of 2016. Figures are then standardized using the 2016 gross domestic product per capita in U.S. dollars at nominal values.

Top 10 banks rated by international credit-rating agencies (%): Percentage of the top ten banks (in terms of total domestic assets) rated by international credit rating agencies (for example, Moody's, Standard & Poor's). If there are fewer than 10 banks operating in the banking system, the percentage is provided with respect to the total number of banks in the banking system.

Bank governance and risk management framework publicly available: Whether banks disclose to the supervisors the governance and risk management framework. It takes a value of 1 if banks disclose the information to the bank supervisory agency, 0 otherwise.

Enforcement actions publicly available: Whether bank regulators/supervisors are required to make public formal enforcement actions, which include cease-and-desist orders and written agreements between a bank regulatory/supervisory body and a banking organization. It takes a value of 1 if bank regulators/supervisors disclose publicly the information, 0 otherwise.

Minimum capital ratio: The minimum required risk-based regulatory capital ratio (as a percentage of risk-weighted assets) as of the end of 2016.

Minimum Tier 1 ratio: The minimum regulatory Tier 1 capital ratio (as a percentage of risk-weighted assets) as of the end of 2016.

Minimum leverage ratio: The minimum required leverage ("gearing") ratio as of the end of 2016.

Supervisors with postgraduate degrees (%): Percentage of bank supervisors with postgraduate degrees, such as an MBA (master of business administration), CPA (certified public accountant), or CFA (certified financial analyst).

Bibliography

Acharya, V. V., D. Anginer, and A. J. Warburton. 2017. "The End of Market Discipline? Investor Expectations of Implicit Government Guarantees." http://dx.doi.org/10.2139/ssrn.1961656.

Acharya, V. V., R. Engle, and D. Pierret. 2014. "Testing Macroprudential Stress Tests: The Risk of Regulatory Risk Weights." *Journal of Monetary Economics* 65: 36–53.

Acharya, V. V., R. Engle, and M. Richardson. 2012. "Capital Shortfall: A New Approach to Ranking and Regulating Systemic Risks." *American Economic Review* 102 (3): 59–64.

Acharya, V. V., I. Gujral, N. Kulkarni, and H. S. Shin. 2011. "Dividends and Bank Capital in the Financial Crisis of 2007–2009." NBER Working Paper 16896, National Bureau of Economic Research, Cambridge, MA.

Acharya, V. V., and T. Yorulmazer. 2007. "Too Many to Fail—An Analysis of Time-Inconsistency in Bank Closure Policies." *Journal of Financial Intermediation* 16: 1–31.

Admati, A. R. 2016. "The Missed Opportunity and Challenge of Capital Regulation." *National Institute Economic Review* 235 (1): R4–R14.

Admati, A. R., and M. Hellwig. 2013. *The Bankers' New Clothes: What's Wrong with Banking and What to Do about It: Updated Edition.* Princeton, NJ: Princeton University Press.

Agoraki, M. E., K. Manthos, D. Delis, and F. Pasiouras. 2011. "Regulations, Competition and Bank Risk-Taking in Transition Countries." *Journal of Financial Stability* 7 (1): 38–48.

Ait-Sahalia, Y., J. Andritzky, A. Jobst, S. Nowak, and N. Tamirisa. 2012. "Market Response to Policy Initiatives during the Global Financial Crisis. "*Journal of International Economics* 87 (1): 162–77.

Aiyar, S., C. W. Calomiris, and T. Wieladek. 2014a. "Does Macro-Prudential Regulation Leak? Evidence from a UK Policy Experiment." *Journal of Money, Credit and Banking* 46: 181–214.

———. 2014b. "Identifying Channels of Credit Substitution When Bank Capital Requirements Are Varied." *Economic Policy* 29 (77): 45–77.

———. 2015. "Bank Capital Regulation: Theory, Empirics, and Policy." *IMF Economic Review* 63 (4): 955–83.

Allen, F., A. Babus, and E. Carletti. 2009. "Financial Crises: Theory and Evidence." *Annual Review of Financial Economics* 1 (1): 97–116.

Allen, F., E. Carletti, and R. Marquez. 2011. "Credit Market Competition and Capital Regulation." *Review of Financial Studies* 24: 983–1018.

Allen, F., and D. Gale. 2004. "Financial Intermediaries and Markets." *Econometrica* 72: 1023–61.

Allen, F., and A. M. Santomero. 1998. "The Theory of Financial Intermediation." *Journal of Banking and Finance* 21: 1461–85.

Almansi, A. A. 2018a. *Cyber-Security Survey: Self-Assessments.* Washington, DC: World Bank. http://pubdocs.worldbank.org/en/654221432913965267/Aquiles-Almansi-World-Bank-Cyber-Seminar-18-19-May.pdf.

———. 2018b. *Financial Sector's Cybersecurity: Regulations and Supervision.* FCI Insight. Washington, DC: World Bank. http://documents.worldbank.org/curated/en/686891519282121021/Financial-sector-s-cybersecurity-regulations-and-supervision.

Anginer, D., A. C. Bertay, R. Cull, A. Demirgüç-Kunt, and D. S. Mare. 2019. "Bank Regulation and Supervision Ten Years after the Global Financial Crisis." Policy Research Working Paper WPS9044, World Bank, Washington, DC.

Anginer, D., and A. Demirgüç-Kunt. Forthcoming. "Bank Runs and Moral Hazard: A Review of Deposit Insurance. In *Handbook of Banking.*

Anginer, D., A. Demirgüç-Kunt, H. Huizinga, and K. Ma. 2016. "Corporate Governance and Bank Capitalization Strategies." *Journal of Financial Intermediation* 26: 1–27.

———. 2018. "Corporate Governance of Banks and Financial Stability." *Journal of Financial Economics* 130 (2): 327–46.

Anginer, D., A. Demirgüç-Kunt, and D. S. Mare. 2018. "Bank Capital, Institutional Environment and Systemic Stability." *Journal of Financial Stability* 37: 97–106.

Anginer, D., A. Demirgüç-Kunt, and M. Zhu. 2014. "How Does Competition Affect Bank Systemic Risk?" *Journal of Financial Intermediation* 23 (1): 1–26.

Angkinand, A., and C. Wihlborg. 2008. "Deposit Insurance, Risk-Taking and Banking Crises: Is There a Risk-Minimizing Level of Deposit Insurance Coverage?" Center for Law, Economics and Financial Institutions at CBS Working Paper.

Ashcraft, A. B., and T. Schuermann. 2008. "Understanding the Securitization of Subprime Mortgage Credit." Federal Reserve Bank of New York Staff Report No. 318.

Bank of Mauritius. 2016. *Domestic-Systemically Important Banks (D-SIBs) in Mauritius.* St. Louis, Mauritius.

Barlevy, G., and P. Veronesi. 2003. "Rational Panics and Stock Market Crashes." *Journal of Economic Theory* 110: 234–63.

Barth, J. R., C. Brummer, T. Li, and D. E. Nolle. 2013. "Systemically Important Banks (SIBs) in the Post-Crisis Era: The Global Response, and Responses around the Globe for 135 Countries." Milken Institute, Santa Monica, CA.

Barth, J. R., G. J. Caprio, and R. Levine. 2001. "The Regulation and Supervision of Banks around the World: A New Database." Policy Research Working Paper WPS2588, World Bank, Washington, DC.

———. 2008. *Rethinking Bank Regulation: Till Angels Govern.* Cambridge: Cambridge University Press.

———. 2012. *Guardians of Finance: Making Regulators Work for Us.* Cambridge, MA: MIT Press.

Basel Consultative Group. 2014. *Impact and Implementation Challenges of the Basel Framework for Emerging Market, Developing and Small Economies.* No. 27, Basel.

BCBS (Basel Committee on Banking Supervision). 1988. *International Convergence of Capital Measurement and Capital Standards.* Basel.

———. 1998. *Enhancing Bank Transparency: Public Disclosure and Supervisory Information That Promote Safety and Soundness in Banking Systems.* Basel.

———. 2004. *International Convergence of Capital Measurement and Capital Standards: A Revised Framework.* Basel.

———. 2006. *International Convergence of Capital Measurement and Capital Standards: A Revised Framework.* Basel.

———. 2010. *Basel III: A Global Regulatory Framework for More Resilient Banks and Banking Systems.* Basel.

———. 2011. *Basel III: A Global Regulatory Framework for More Resilient Banks and Banking Systems* (revised version). Basel.

———. 2013. *Basel III: The Liquidity Coverage Ratio and Liquidity Risk Monitoring Tools.* Basel.

———. 2014. *Basel III: The Net Stable Funding Ratio.* Basel.

———. 2015. *Guidelines: Corporate Governance Principles for Banks.* http://www.bis.org/bcbs/publ/d328.pdf.

———. 2016. "Literature Review on Integration of Regulatory Capital and Liquidity Instruments." Working Paper No. 30, Bank for International Settlements, Basel.

———. 2017a. *Basel III: Finalising Post-Crisis Reforms, Bank for International Settlements.* Basel.

———. 2017b. "The Regulatory Treatment of Sovereign Exposures." Discussion paper, Bank for International Settlements, Basel.

———. 2018a. *Global Systemically Important Banks: Revised Assessment Methodology and the Higher Loss Absorbency Requirement.* Basel.

———. 2018b. *Sound Practices: Implications of Fintech Developments for Banks and Bank Supervisors.* Basel.

———. 2018c. *Basel III Monitoring Report.* October 2018. Basel.

———. 2019. *Proportionality in Bank Regulation and Supervision: A Survey on Current Practices.* Basel.

Beck, T., E. Jones, and P. Knaack. 2018. "Basel Standards and Developing Countries: A Difficult Relationship." Vox, CEPR Policy Portal. https://voxeu.org/article/basel-standards-and-developing-countries.

Behn, M., R. Haselmann, and P. Wachtel. 2016. "Procyclical Capital Regulation and Lending." *Journal of Finance* 71 (2): 919–56.

Behn, M., R. Haselmann, and V. Vig. 2016. "The Limits of Model-Based Regulation." Working Paper Series No. 1928, European Central Bank, Frankfurt.

Beltratti, A., and R. M. Stulz. 2012. "The Credit Crisis around the Globe: Why Did Some Banks Perform Better?" *Journal of Financial Economics* 105: 1–17.

Berg, T., and C. Kaserer. 2015. "Does Contingent Capital Induce Excessive Risk-Taking?" *Journal of Financial Intermediation* 24 (3): 356–85.

Berger, A. N. 1995. "The Relationship between Capital and Earnings in Banking." *Journal of Money, Credit and Banking* 27: 432–56.

Berger, A. N., and C. H. S. Bouwman. 2009. "Bank Liquidity Creation." *Review of Financial Studies* 22: 3779–837.

———. 2013. "How Does Capital Affect Bank Performance during Financial Crises?" *Journal of Financial Economics* 109 (1): 146–76.

Berger, A. N., R. DeYoung, M. J. Flannery, D. Lee, and Ö. Öztekin. 2008. "How Do Large Banking Organizations Manage Their Capital Ratios?" *Journal of Financial Services Research* 34 (2–3): 123–49.

Berger, A. N., R. J. Herring, and G. P. Szegö. 1995. "The Role of Capital in Financial Institutions." *Journal of Banking and Finance* 19 (3–4): 393–430.

Berger, A. N., C. P. Himmelberg, R. A. Roman, and S. Tsyplakov. 2018. "Bank Bailouts, Bail-ins, or No Regulatory Intervention? A Dynamic Model and Empirical Tests of Optimal Regulation." https://papers.ssrn.com/sol3/papers.cfm?abstract_id=3179226.

Berger, A. N., T. Makaew, and R. A. Roman. Forthcoming. "Do Business Borrowers Benefit from Bank Bailouts? The Effects of TARP on Loan Contract Terms." *Financial Management.*

Berger, A. N., and R. A. Roman. 2017. "Did Saving Wall Street Really Save Main Street? The Real Effects of TARP on Local Economic Conditions."*Journal of Financial and Quantitative Analysis* 52: 1827–67.

Berger, A. N., R. A. Roman, and J. Sedunov. Forthcoming. "Did TARP Reduce or Increase Systemic Risk? The Effects of Government Aid on Financial System Stability." *Journal of Financial Intermediation.*

Berger, A. N., and G. F. Udell. 1994. "Did Risk-Based Capital Allocate Bank Credit and Cause a 'Credit Crunch' in the United States?" *Journal of Money, Credit and Banking* 26: 585–628.

Bernanke, B. S. 1983. "Non-Monetary Effects of the Financial Crisis in the Propagation of the Great Depression." NBER Working Paper 1054, National Bureau of Economic Research, Cambridge, MA.

Bernanke, B. S., and C. S. Lown. 1991. "The Credit Crunch." *Brookings Papers on Economic Activity* 1991 (2): 205–47.

Berrospide, J., R. Correa, L. Goldberg, and F. Niepmann. 2017. "International Banking and Cross-Border Effects of Regulation: Lessons from the United States." *International Journal of Central Banking* 3: 435–76.

Besanko, D., and G. Kanatas. 1996. "The Regulation of Bank Capital: Do Capital Standards Promote Bank Safety?" *Journal of Financial Intermediation* 5: 160–83.

Bertay, A. C., A. Demirgüç-Kunt, and H. Huizinga. 2016. "Should Cross-Border Banking Benefit from the Financial Safety Net?" *Journal of Financial Intermediation* 27: 51–67.

Bhattacharya, S., and A. V. Thakor. 1993. "Contemporary Banking Theory." *Journal of Financial Intermediation* 3: 2–50.

Black, L. K., and L. N. Hazelwood. 2013. "The Effect of TARP on Bank Risk-Taking." *Journal of Financial Stability* 9: 790–803.

Bliss, R. R., and M. J. Flannery. 2002. "Market Discipline in the Governance of US Bank Holding Companies: Monitoring vs. Influencing." *Review of Finance* 6 (3): 361–96.

Bloomberg. 2018. "China Opens Door to New $450-Billion Bank Funding Buffer." https://www.bloomberg.com/news/articles/2018-04-10/china-opens-door-to-new-450-billion-funding-buffer-for-banks.

Boeddu, G. L., L. B. Newbury, N. L. Kachingwe, L. De Souza Neves Lopes, and D. Randall. 2018. "From Spreadsheets to Suptech: Technology Solutions for Market Conduct Supervision." Working Paper 127577, World Bank, Washington, DC.

Bolton, P., and M. Oehmke. 2018. "Bank Resolution and the Structure of Global Banks." *Review of Financial Studies.*

Bongini, P., L. Nieri, and M. Pelagatti. 2015. "The Importance of Being Systemically Important Financial Institutions." *Journal of Banking and Finance* 50: 562–74.

Borio, C., C. Furfine, and P. Lowe. 2001. "Procyclicality of the Financial System and Financial Stability: Issues and Policy Options." In *Marrying the Macro- and Micro-prudential Dimensions of Financial Stability,* vol. 1, 1–57. Basel: Bank for International Settlements.

Bostandzic, D., and G. N. Weiß. Forthcoming. "Why Do U.S. Banks Contribute More to Global Systemic Risk?" *Journal of Financial Intermediation.*

Boyd, J. H., S. Kwak, and B. Smith. 2005. "The Real Output Losses Associated with Modern Banking Crises." *Journal of Money, Credit and Banking* 37: 977–99.

Braggion, F., A. Manconi, and H. Zhu. 2018. "Can Technology Undermine Macroprudential Regulation? Evidence from Peer-to-Peer Credit in China. CEPR Discussion Paper No. DP12668.

Briault, C., E. Feyen, I. Gonzalez Del Mazo, B. Kwok Chung Yee, J. Rademacher, and I. Skamnelos. 2018. "Cross-Border Spillover Effects of the G20 Financial Regulatory Reforms. Results from a Pilot Survey." Policy Research Working Paper 8300, World Bank, Washington, DC.

Broeders, D., and J. Prenio. 2018. "Innovative Technology in Financial Supervision (Suptech): The Experience of Early Users." Financial Stability Institute Paper No. 9, Bank for International Settlements, Basel.

Brown, C. O., and I. S. Dinç. 2011. "Too Many to Fail? Evidence of Regulatory Forbearance When the Banking Sector Is Weak." *Review of Financial Studies* 24: 1378–1405.

Brun, M., H. Fraisse, and D. Thesmar. 2013. "The Real Effects of Bank Capital Requirements." *Débats économiques et financiers* 8: 3–26.

Brunnermeier, M., A. Crockett, C. A. Goodhart, A. Persaud, and H. S. Shin. 2009. "The Fundamental Principles of Financial Regulation." *Geneva Reports on the World Economy,* No. 11, Geneva.

Buchak, G., G. Matvos, T. Piskorski, and A. Seru. 2018. "Fintech, Regulatory Arbitrage, and the Rise of Shadow Banks." *Journal of Financial Economics* 130 (3): 453–83.

Calem, P., and R. Rob. 1999. "The Impact of Capital Based Regulation on Bank Risk Taking." *Journal of Financial Intermediation* 8: 317–52.

Calomiris, C. W. 2012. "How to Regulate Bank Capital." *National Affairs* 10.

———. 2017. "Reforming Financial Regulation after Dodd-Frank." Manhattan Institute for Policy Research, New York.

Calomiris, C. W., and S. H. Haber. 2014. *Fragile by Design: the Political Origins of Banking Crises and Scarce Credit.* Princeton, NJ: Princeton University Press.

Calomiris, C. W., and R. J. Herring. 2011. "Why and How to Design a Contingent Convertible Debt Requirement." https://papers.ssrn.com/sol3/papers.cfm?abstract_id=1815406.

———. 2013. "How to Design a Contingent Convertible Debt Requirement that Helps Solve Our Too-Big-To-Fail Problem." *Journal of Applied Corporate Finance* 25: 39–62.

Calomiris, C. W., and C. M. Kahn. 1991. "The Role of Demandable Debt in Structuring Optimal Banking." *American Economic Review* 81: 497–513.

Calormiris, C. W., and J. R. Mason. 2003. "How to Restructure Failed Banking Systems: Lessons from the U.S. in the 1930's and Japan in the 1990's." NBER Working Paper 9624, National

Bureau of Economic Research, Cambridge, MA.

Calormiris, C. W., and B. Wilson. 1998. "Bank Capital and Portfolio Management: The 1930's Capital Crunch and Scramble to Shed Risk." NBER Working Paper 6649, National Bureau of Economic Research, Cambridge, MA.

Caprio, G., A. Demirgüç-Kunt, and E. J. Kane. 2010. "The 2007 Meltdown in Structured Securitization: Searching for Lessons, not Scapegoats." *World Bank Researcher Observer* 25: 125–55.

Carlson, M., H. Shan, and M. Warusawitharana. 2013. "Capital Ratios and Bank Lending: A Matched Bank Approach." *Journal of Financial Intermediation* 22 (4): 663–87.

Carmassi, J., and R. Herring. 2016. "The Corporate Complexity of Global Systemically Important Banks." *Journal of Financial Services Research* 49 (2–3): 175–201.

Castro Carvalho, A. P., S. Hohl, R. Raskopf, and S. Ruhnau. 2017. "Proportionality in Banking Regulation: A Cross-Country Comparison." Financial Stability Institute Insights on Policy Implementation No. 1.

Choi, D. B. 2014. "Heterogeneity and Stability: Bolster the Strong, not the Weak." *Review of Financial Studies* 27: 1830–67.

Chu, Y., D. Zhang, and Y. Zhao. Forthcoming. "Bank Capital and Lending: Evidence from Syndicated Loans." *Journal of Financial and Quantitative Analysis.*

Čihák, M., A. Demirgüç-Kunt, E. Feyen, and R. Levine. 2013. "Financial Development in 205 Economies, 1960 to 2010." NBER Working Paper 18946. National Bureau of Economic Research.

Čihák, M., A. Demirgüç-Kunt, and R. B. Johnston. 2013. "Incentive Audits: A New Approach to Financial Regulation." Policy Research Working Paper 6308, World Bank, Washington, DC.

Čihák, M., A. Demirgüç-Kunt, M. S. Peria, and A. Mohseni-Cheraghlou. 2012. "Bank Regulation and Supervision around the World: A Crisis Update." Policy Research Working Paper 6286, World Bank, Washington, DC.

———. 2013. "Bank Regulation and Supervision in the Context of the Global Crisis." *Journal of Financial Stability* 9 (4): 733–46.

Claessens, S. 2014. "An Overview of Macroprudential Policy Tools." IMF Working Paper No. WP/14/214, International Monetary Fund, Washington, DC.

Claessens, S., G. Dell'Ariccia, and L. Laeven. 2010. "Cross-Country Experiences and Policy Implications from the Global Financial Crisis." *Economic Policy* 25: 267–93.

Claessens, S., J. Frost, J. G. Turner, and F. Zhu. 2018. "Fintech Credit Markets around the World: Size, Drivers and Policy Issues." *BIS Quarterly Review* (September).

CNN. 2018. "Six Days after a Ransomware Cyberattack, Atlanta Officials Are Filling Out Forms by Hand." https://www.cnn.com/2018/03/27/us/atlanta-ransomware-computers/index.html.

Cohen, B. H., and M. Scatigna. 2016. "Banks and Capital Requirements: Channels of Adjustment." *Journal of Banking and Finance* 69: S56–S69.

Cosimano, T. F., and D. Hakura. 2011. "Bank Behavior in Response to Basel III: A Cross-Country Analysis." IMF Working Paper WP/11/119, International Monetary Fund, Washington, DC. https://www.imf.org/external/pubs/ft/wp/2011/wp11119.pdf.

Coval, J. D., and A. V. Thakor. 2005. "Financial Intermediation as a Beliefs-Bridge between Optimists and Pessimists." *Journal of Financial Economics* 75: 535–59.

Crotty, J. 2009. "Structural Causes of the Global Financial Crisis: A Critical Assessment of the 'New Financial Architecture.'" *Cambridge Journal of Economics* 33: 563–80.

Cull, R., L. W. Senbet, and M. Sorge. 2005. "Deposit Insurance and Financial Development." *Journal of Money, Credit and Banking* 37: 43–82.

Danielsson, J., P. Embrechts, C. Goodhart, C. Keating, F. Muennich, O. Renault, and H. S. Shin. 2001. "An Academic Response to Basel II." Special Paper, LSE Financial Markets Group.

De Haas, R., and I. Van Lelyveld. 2014. "Multinational Banks and the Global Financial Crisis: Weathering the Perfect Storm?" *Journal of Money, Credit and Banking* 46 (s1): 333–64.

Deli, Y. D., M. D. Delis, I. Hasan, and L. Liu. 2019. "Enforcement of Banking Regulation and the Cost of Borrowing." *Journal of Banking and Finance* 101: 147–160.

Dell'Ariccia, G., E. Detragiache, and R. Rajan. 2008. "The Real Effect of Banking Crises." *Journal of Financial Intermediation* 17: 89–112.

Dell'Ariccia, G., L. Laeven, and R. Marquez. 2014. "Real Interest Rates, Leverage, and Bank Risk-Taking." *Journal of Economic Theory* 149: 65–99.

Demirgüç-Kunt, A., and E. Detragiache. 2002. "Does Deposit Insurance Increase Banking System Stability? An Empirical Investigation." *Journal of Monetary Economics* 49 (7): 1373–1406.

———. 2011. "Basel Core Principles and Bank Soundness: Does Compliance Matter?" *Journal of Financial Stability* 7 (4): 179–90.

Demirgüç-Kunt, A., E. Detragiache, and O. Merrouche. 2013. "Bank Capital: Lessons from the Financial Crisis." *Journal of Money, Credit and Banking* 45: 1147–64.

Demirgüç-Kunt, A., E. Detragiache, and T. Tressel. 2008. "Banking on the Principles: Compliance with Basel Core Principles and Bank Soundness." *Journal of Financial Intermediation* 17 (4): 511–542.

Demirgüç-Kunt, A., and H. Huizinga. 2013. "Are Banks Too Big to Fail or Too Big to Save? International Evidence from Equity Prices and CDS Spreads." *Journal of Banking and Finance* 37 (3): 875–94.

Demirgüç-Kunt, A., E. J. Kane, and L. Laeven, eds. 2008. *Deposit Insurance around the World: Issues of Design and Implementation.* Cambridge, MA: MIT Press.

Demirgüç-Kunt, A., L. Klapper, D. Singer, S. Ansar, and J. Hess. 2018. *The Global Findex Database 2017: Measuring Financial Inclusion and the Fintech Revolution.* Washington, DC: World Bank. doi:10.1596/978-1-4648-1259-0.

Demirgüç-Kunt, A., and L. Servén. 2010. "Are All the Sacred Cows Dead? Implications of the Financial Crisis for Macro- and Financial Policies." *World Bank Research Observer* 25: 91–124.

Dewatripont, M., and J. Tirole. 1994. "The Prudential Regulation of Banks." ULB Institutional Repository, Free University of Brussels.

Dewenter, K. L., and L. A. Riddick. 2018. "What's the Value of a TBTF Guaranty? Evidence from the G-SII Designation for Insurance Companies." *Journal of Banking and Finance* 91: 70–85.

Diamond, D. W., and P. H. Dybvig. 1983. "Bank Runs, Deposit Insurance, and Liquidity." *Journal of Political Economy* 91: 401–19.

Diamond, D. W., and R. G. Rajan. 2000. "A Theory of Bank Capital." *Journal of Finance* 55: 2431–65.

———. 2001. "Liquidity Risk, Liquidity Creation, and Financial Fragility: A Theory of Banking." *Journal of Political Economy* 109: 287–327.

Djankov, S., C. McLiesh and A. Shleifer. 2007. "Private Credit in 129 Countries."*Journal of Financial Economics* 84 (2): 299-329.

Duchin, R., and D. Sosyura. 2014. "Safer Ratios, Riskier Portfolios: Banks' Response to Government Aid." *Journal of Financial Economics* 113: 1–28.

ECB (European Central Bank). 2018. *ECB Annual Report on Supervisory Activities 2017.* Frankfurt.

European Central Bank SDW (Statistical Data Warehouse). 2019. "Number of Monetary Financial Institutions (MFIs) in the Euro Area." Frankfurt.

Faia, E., and B. Weder di Mauro. 2015. "Cross-Border Resolution of Global Banks." SAFE Working Paper Series 88, Research Center SAFE (Sustainable Architecture for Finance in Europe), Goethe University, Frankfurt.

Fang, X., D. Jutrsa, M. S. Martinez Peria, A. Presbitero, L.Ratnovski, and F. Vardy. 2018. "The Effects of Higher Bank Capital Requirements on Credit in Peru." IMF Working Paper WP/18/222, International Monetary Fund, Washington, DC.

Ferguson, R. W. 2003. "Capital Standards for Banks: The Evolving Basel Accord." *Federal Reserve Bulletin* 89 (9): 395–405.

Ferreira, C., N. Jenkinson, and C. Wilson. 2019. "From Basel I to Basel III: Sequencing Implementation in Developing Economies." IMF Working Paper No. WP/19/127, International Monetary Fund, Washington, DC.

FFIEC (Federal Financial Institutions Examination Council) (U.S.). 2019. Commercial Banks in the U.S. [USNUM], retrieved from FRED, Federal Reserve Bank of St. Louis. https://fred.stlouisfed.org/series/USNUM, February 23.

Financial Sector Advisory Center. 2017. "Financial Sector's Cybersecurity: A Regulatory Digest." World Bank, Washington, DC. http://pubdocs.worldbank.org/en/524901513362019919/FinSAC-CybersecDigestOct-2017-Dec2017.pdf.

Financial Stability Forum. 2000. "Grouping of Offshore Financial Centres (OFCs) to Assist in Setting Priorities for Assessment." Press release, May 26.

Fiordelisi, F., G. Pennacchi, and O. Ricci. Forthcoming. "Are Contingent Convertibles Going-Concern Capital?" *Journal of Financial Intermediation.*

Flannery, M. J. 2001. "The Faces of 'Market Discipline.'" *Journal of Financial Services Research* 20: 107–19.

Flannery, M. J., and S. M. Sorescu. 1996. "Evidence of Bank Market Discipline in Subordinated Debenture Yields: 1983–1991." *Journal of Finance* 51 (4): 1347–77.

Francis, B., I. Hasan, L. Liu, and H. Wang. 2019. "Senior Debt and Market Discipline: Evidence from Bank-to-Bank Loans." *Journal of Banking and Finance* 98: 170–82.

Freixas, X. 1999. "Optimal Bail Out Policy, Conditionality and Constructive Ambiguity." Working Paper No. 400. https://papers.ssrn.com/sol3/papers.cfm?abstract_id=199054.

Freixas, X., and J. Rochet. 2008. *Microeconomics of Banking,* 2nd ed. Cambridge, MA: MIT Press.

French, K. R., M. N. Baily, J. Y. Campbell, J. H. Cochrane, D. W. Diamond, D. Duffie, A. K. Kashyap, et al. 2010. *The Squam Lake Report: Fixing the Financial System.* Princeton, NJ: Princeton University Press.

FSB (Financial Stability Board). 2014. *Key Attributes of Effective Resolution Regimes for Financial Institutions.* Basel.

———. 2015. *Total Loss-Absorbing Capacity (TLAC) Principles and Term Sheet.* Basel.

———. 2017a. *Financial Stability Implications from Fintech: Supervisory and Regulatory Issues that Merit Authorities' Attention.* Basel.

———. 2017b. *Review of OTC Derivatives Market Reform: Effectiveness and Broader Effects of the Reforms.* Basel.

———. 2018a. *Evaluation of the Effects of Financial Regulatory Reforms on Infrastructure Finance.* Basel.

———. 2018b. *Implementation and Effects of the G20 Financial Regulatory Reforms: 4th Annual Report.* Basel.

Fungacova, Z., L. Weill, and M. Zhou. 2017. "Bank Capital, Liquidity Creation and Deposit Insurance." *Journal of Financial Services Research* 51: 97–123.

Furlong, F. T., and M. Keeley. 1989. "Capital Regulation and Bank Risk-Taking: A Note." *Journal of Banking and Finance* 13: 883–91.

Gai, P., A. Haldane, and S. Kapadia. 2011. "Complexity, Concentration and Contagion." *Journal of Monetary Economics* 58 (5): 453–70.

Gambacorta, L. 2011. "Do Bank Capital and Liquidity Affect Real Economic Activity in the Long Run? A VECM Analysis for the US." *Economic Notes* 40 (3): 75–91.

Gambacorta, L., and H. S. Shin. Forthcoming. "Why Bank Capital Matters for Monetary Policy." *Journal of Financial Intermediation.*

Gennotte, G., and H. Leland. 1990. "Market Liquidity, Hedging, and Crashes." *American Economic Review* 80: 999–1021.

Gerhardt, M., and R. Vander Vennet. 2017. "Bank Bailouts in Europe and Bank Performance." *Finance Research Letters* 22: 74–80.

Giannetti, M., and A. Simonov. 2013. "On the Real Effects of Bank Bailouts: Micro Evidence from Japan." *American Economic Journal: Macroeconomics* 5 (1): 135–67.

Goldberg, L. S., and A. Meehl. 2019. "Complexity in Large US Banks." FRB of New York Staff Report 880.

Goodhart, C. 2011. *The Basel Committee on Banking Supervision: A History of the Early Years 1974–1997.* Cambridge, U.K.: Cambridge University Press.

Gorton, G. B. 2009. *Slapped in the Face by the Invisible Hand: Banking and the Panic of 2007.* Paper prepared for Federal Reserve Bank of Atlanta's 2009 Financial Markets Conference: Financial Innovation and Crisis, May 11–13.

Gorton, G. B., and A. Winton. 2017. "Liquidity Provision, Bank Capital, and the Macroeconomy." *Journal of Money, Credit and Banking* 49: 5–37.

Gropp, R., T. Mosk, S. Ongena, and C. Wix. 2019. "Banks' Response to Higher Capital Requirements: Evidence from a Quasi-Natural

Experiment." *Review of Financial Studies* 32 (1): 266–99.

Haldane, A. G. 2011. "Capital Discipline." Speech presented to American Economic Association, Denver.

Haldane, A. G., and V. Madouros. 2012. "The Dog and the Frisbee."Speech presented to Federal Reserve Bank of Kansas City's 366th Economic Policy Symposium, "The Changing Policy Landscape," Jackson Hole, WY.

Hancock, D., A. J. Laing, and J. A. Wilcox. 1995. "Bank Capital Shocks: Dynamic Effects on Securities, Loans, and Capital." *Journal of Banking and Finance* 19 (3–4): 661–77.

Hart, O., and J. Moore. 1998. "Default and Renegotiation: A Dynamic Model of Debt." *Quarterly Journal of Economics* 113 (1): 1–41.

Hasan, I., Y. Fang, L. Liu, and G. Zhang. 2017. "Deposit Insurance and the 2008–2009 Global Financial Crisis." *Financial Stability Studies* 18: 1–19.

Hohl, S., M. C. Sison, T. Stastny, and R. Zamil. 2018. "The Basel Framework in 100 Jurisdictions: Implementation Status and Proportionality Practices." Financial Stability Institute Insights on Policy Implementation No. 11.

Holmstrom, B., and J. Tirole. 1997. "Financial Intermediation, Loanable Funds, and the Real Sector." *Quarterly Journal of Economics* 112: 663–91.

Homar, T., and S. J. van Wijnbergen. 2017. "Bank Recapitalization and Economic Recovery after Financial Crises." *Journal of Financial Intermediation* 32: 16–28.

Hong, H., and J. C. Stein. 2003. "Differences of Opinion, Short-Sales Constraints, and Market Crashes." *Review of Financial Studies* 16: 487–525.

Honohan, P., and D. Klingebiel. 2000. "Controlling the Fiscal Costs of Banking Crises." Policy Research Working Paper 2441,World Bank, Washington, DC.

Horvath, R., J. Seidler, and L. Weill. 2014. "Bank Capital and Liquidity Creation: Granger-Causality Evidence." *Journal of Financial Services Research* 45: 341–61.

Hryckiewicz, A. 2014. "What Do We Know about the Impact of Government Interventions in the Banking Sector? An Assessment of Various Bailout Programs on Bank Behavior." *Journal of Banking and Finance* 46: 246–65.

Huizinga, H., and L. Laeven. 2012. "Bank Valuation and Accounting Discretion during a Financial Crisis." *Journal of Financial Economics* 106 (3): 614–34.

IBM. 2018. "IBM X-ForceThreatIntelligence Index." https://public.dhe.ibm.com/common/ssi/ecm/77/en/77014377usen/security-ibm-security-solutions-wg-research-report-77014377usen-20180404.pdf.

Institute of International Finance. 2016. *Regtech in Financial Services: Technology Solutions for Compliance and Reporting*. Washington, DC.

Jackson, P., C. Furfine, H. Groeneveld, D. Hancock, D. Jones, W. Perraudin, L. Radecki, and M. Yoneyama. 1999. *Capital Requirements and Bank Behaviour: The Impact of the Basel Accord,* No. 1. Basel: Bank for International Settlements.

Jiménez, G., S. Ongena, J. L. Peydró, and J. Saurina. 2012. "Credit Supply and Monetary Policy: Identifying the Bank Balance-Sheet Channel with Loan Applications." *American Economic Review* 102 (5): 2301–26.

———. 2017. "Macroprudential Policy, Countercyclical Bank Capital Buffers, and Credit Supply: Evidence from the Spanish Dynamic Provisioning Experiments." *Journal of Political Economy* 125 (6): 2126–77.

Jones, E., and A. O. Zeitz. 2017. "The Limits of Globalizing Basel Banking Standards." *Journal of Financial Regulation* 3: 89–124.

Kashyap, A. K., R. G. Rajan, and J. C. Stein. 2008. "Rethinking Capital Regulation." Proceedings, Federal Reserve Bank of Kansas City Symposium "Maintaining Stability, a Changing Financial System," Jackson Hole, WY.

Kashyap, A. K., and J. C. Stein. 2004. "Cyclical Implications of the Basel II Capital Standards." *Economic Perspectives—Federal Reserve Bank of Chicago* 28 (1): 18–33.

Kashyap, A. K., D. P. Tsomocos, and A. Vardoulakis. 2017. "Optimal Bank Regulation in the Presence of Credit and Run Risk." Working Paper 2017-17, Saïd Business School, University of Oxford, Oxford.

Kim, D., and W. Sohn. 2017. "The Effect of Bank Capital on Lending: Does Liquidity Matter?" *Journal of Banking and Finance* 77: 95–107.

Kishan, R. P., and T. P. Opiela. 2000. "Bank Size, Bank Capital, and the Bank Lending Channel." *Journal of Money, Credit and Banking* 32: 121–41.

Klingebiel, D., R. Kroszner, V. P. Oijen, and L. Laeven. 2001. *Stock Market Responses to Bank Restructuring Policies during the East Asian Crisis*. Washington, DC: World Bank.

Klomp, J., and J. de Haan. 2014. "Bank Regulation, the Quality of Institutions, and Banking Risk in Emerging and Developing Countries: An Empirical Analysis." *Emerging Markets Finance and Trade* 50 (6): 19–40.

———. 2015. "Bank Regulation and Financial Fragility in Developing Countries: Does Bank Structure Matter?" *Review of Development Finance* 5 (2): 82–90.

Kodres, L. E., and M. Pritsker. 2002. "A Rational Expectations Model of Financial Contagion." *Journal of Finance* 57: 769–99.

Koehn, M., and A. M. Santomero. 1980. "Regulation of Bank Capital and Portfolio Risk." *Journal of Finance* 35 (5): 1235–44.

Laeven, L., L. Ratnovski, and H. Tong. 2016. "Bank Size, Capital, and Systemic Risk: Some International Evidence." *Journal of Banking and Finance* 69: S25—34.

Laeven, L., and F. Valencia. 2013. "The Real Effects of Financial Sector Interventions during Crises." *Journal of Money, Credit and Banking* 45: 147–77.

———. 2018. "Systemic Banking Crises Revisited." IMF Working Paper WP/18/206, International Monetary Fund, Washington, DC.

Laffont, J.-J., and J. Tirole. 1993. *A Theory of Incentives in Procurement and Regulation*. Cambridge, MA: MIT Press.

Lagarde, C. 2018. "Ten Years After Lehman—Lessons Learned and Challenges Ahead." IMF Blog, September 5, International Monetary Fund, Washington, DC.

Laux, C., and C. Leuz. 2009. "The Crisis of Fair-Value Accounting: Making Sense of the Recent Debate." *Accounting, Organizations and Society* 34 (6-7): 826–34.

Lei, A. C. H., and Z. Song. 2013. "Liquidity Creation and Bank Capital Structure in China." *Global Finance Journal* 24: 188–202.

Le Leslé, V., and S. Avramova. 2012. "Revisiting Risk-Weighted Assets: Why Do RWAs Differ across Countries and What Can Be Done about It?" IMF Working Paper WP/12/90, International Monetary Fund, Washington, DC.

Li, L. 2013. "TARP Funds Distribution and Bank Loan Supply." *Journal of Banking and Finance* 37 (12): 4777–92.

Lucas, D. 2018. "Measuring the Cost of Bailouts". Annual Review of Financial Economics.

Lucas, D., and R. L. McDonald. 2006. "An Options-Based Approach to Evaluating the Risk of Fannie Mae and Freddie Mac." *Journal of Monetary Economics* 53 (1): 155–76.

Lumb, R., M. Macchi, and J. P. Moreno. 2016. "Bridging the Technology Gap in Financial Services Boardrooms." https://www.accenture.com/t20160118T152822__w__/us-en/_acnmedia/PDF-4/Accenture-Strategy-Financial-Services-Technology-Boardroom.pdf.

Majluf, N. S., and S. C. Myers. 1984. "Corporate Financing and Investment Decisions When Firms Have Information That Investors Do Not Have." *Journal of Financial Economics* 13: 187–221.

Mare, D. S., F. Moreira, and R. Rossi. 2017. "Nonstationary Z-Score Measures." *European Journal of Operational Research* 260 (1): 348–58.

Mariathasan, M., and O. Merrouche. 2014. "The Manipulation of Basel Risk-Weights." *Journal of Financial Intermediation* 23: 300–321.

Masciandaro, D., and D. Romelli. 2018. "Central Bankers as Supervisors: Do Crises Matter?" *European Journal of Political Economy* 52: 120–40.

Mehran, H., and A. Thakor. 2011. "Bank Capital and Value in the Cross-Section." *Review of Financing Studies* 24: 1019–67.

Mishkin, F. S. 1999. "Financial Consolidation: Dangers and Opportunities." *Journal of Banking and Finance* 23 (2–4): 675–91.

Modigliani, F., and M. Miller. 1963. "Corporate Income Taxes and the Cost of Capital: A Correction." *American Economic Review* 53: 433–43.

Myers, S. C.1977. "Determinants of Corporate Borrowing." *Journal of Financial Economics* 5: 147–75.

New York Times. 2017. "Lessons from the Collapse of Banco Popular." June 23. https://www

.nytimes.com/2017/06/23/business/lessons-from-the-collapse-of-banco-popular.html.

———. 2018. "The Billion-Dollar Bank Job." May 3. https://www.nytimes.com/interactive/2018/05/03/magazine/money-issue-bangladesh-billion-dollar-bank-heist.html.

Obstfeld, M., and K. Rogoff. 2009. "Global Imbalances and the Financial Crisis: Products of Common Causes." CEPR Discussion Paper No. DP7606, Centre for Economic Policy Research, London.

Ongena, S., A. Popov, and G. F. Udell. 2013. "'When the Cat's Away the Mice Will Play': Does Regulation at Home Affect Bank Risk-Taking Abroad?" *Journal of Financial Economics* 108 (3): 727–50.

Passmore, W., and A. von Hafften. 2017. "Are Basel's Capital Surcharges for Global Systemically Important Banks Too Small?" FEDS Notes, Board of Governors of the Federal Reserve System, Washington, DC.

Peek, J., and E. S. Rosengren. 1995a. "Bank Regulation and the Credit Crunch." *Journal of Banking and Finance* 19: 679–92.

———. 1995b. "The Capital Crunch: Neither a Borrower Nor a Lender Be." *Journal of Money, Credit and Banking* 27 (3): 625–38.

———. 1997. "The International Transmission of Financial Shocks: The Case of Japan." *American Economic Review* 87 (4): 495–505.

Poczter, S. 2016. "The Long-Term Effects of Bank Recapitalization: Evidence from Indonesia." *Journal of Financial Intermediation* 25: 131–53.

Politico. 2018. "Latvia-Sized Hole in European Banking Supervision." https://www.politico.eu/article/ablv-small-bank-exposes-big-hole-in-ecb-banking-supervision/.

Pyle, D. H. 1986. "Capital Regulation and Deposit Insurance." *Journal of Banking and Finance* 10 (2): 189–201.

Rajan, R. 2010. *Fault Lines: How Hidden Fractures Still Threaten the World Economy*. Princeton, NJ: Princeton University Press.

Rajan, R., and A. Winton. 1995. "Covenants and Collateral as Incentives to Monitor." *Journal of Finance* 50 (4): 1113–46.

Register. 2018. "Equifax Reveals Full Horror of That Monstrous Cyber-Heist of Its Servers." https://www.theregister.co.uk/2018/05/08/equifax_breach_may_2018/.

Repullo, R. 2004. "Capital Requirements, Market Power, and Risk-Taking in Banking." *Journal of Financial Remediation* 13: 156–82.

Repullo, R., and J. Suarez. 2012. "The Procyclical Effects of Bank Capital Regulation." *Review of Financial Studies* 26 (2): 452–90.

Restoy, F. 2018. "Proportionality in Banking Regulation." Speech presented to Financial Stability Institute, Bank for International Settlements, Westminister Business Forum Keynote Seminar, London, July.

Rochet, J. C. 1992. "Capital Requirements and the Behaviour of Commercial Banks." *European Economic Review* 36 (5): 1137–70.

Rose, A. K., and T. Wieladek. 2012. "Too Big to Fail: Some Empirical Evidence on the Causes and Consequences of Public Banking Interventions in the UK." *Journal of International Money and Finance* 31 (8): 2038–51.

Rose, N. L., ed. 2014. *Economic Regulation and Its Reform: What Have We Learned?* Chicago: University of Chicago Press.

Santos, J. A. C. 2001. "Bank Capital Regulation in Contemporary Banking Theory: A Review of the Literature." *Financial Markets, Institutions and Instruments* 10: 41–84.

Schepens, G. 2016. "Taxes and Bank Capital Structure." *Journal of Financial Economics* 120 (3): 585–600.

Schliephake, E. 2016. "Capital Regulation and Competition as a Moderator for Banking Stability." *Journal of Money, Credit and Banking* 48: 1787–1814.

Schwert, M. 2018. "Bank Capital and Lending Relationships." *Journal of Finance* 73 (2): 787–830.

Shleifer, A. 2005. "Understanding Regulation." *European Financial Management* 11(4): 439–451.

Siegert, C., and M. Willison. 2015. "Estimating the Extent of the 'Too Big to Fail' Problem: A Review of Existing Approaches." Financial Stability Paper 32, Bank of England, London.

Sironi, A. 2003. "Testing for Market Discipline in the European Banking Industry: Evidence from Subordinated Debt Issues." *Journal of Money, Credit and Banking* 35: 443–72.

Skeel, D. 2010. *The New Financial Deal: Understanding the Dodd-Frank Act and Its (Unintended) Consequences*. New York: Wiley.

Stames, S., M. Kurdyla, A. Prakash, A. Volk, and S. Wang. 2017. *De-Risking and Other Challenges in the Emerging Market Financial Sector: Findings from IFC's Survey on Correspondent Banking*. Washington, DC: International Finance Corporation.

Stigler, G. 1971. "The Theory of Economic Regulation." *Bell Journal of Economics and Management Science* 2: 3–21.

Thakor, A.V. 1996. "Capital Requirements, Monetary Policy, and Aggregate Bank Lending: Theory and Empirical Evidence." *Journal of Finance* 51 (1): 279–324.

Toronto Centre. 2017. *FinTech, RegTech and SupTech: What They Mean for Financial Supervision.*

Valencia, F. 2016. "Bank Capital and Uncertainty." *Journal of Banking and Finance* 69: S1-S9.

Van den Heuvel, S. J. 2002. "The Bank Capital Channel of Monetary Policy." Unpublished paper, Wharton School, University of Pennsylvania, Philadelphia.

Van Hoose, D. D. 2008. "Bank Capital Regulation, Economic Stability, and Monetary Policy: What Does the Academic Literature Tell Us?" *Atlantic Economic Journal* 36 (1): 1–14.

Violon, A., D. Durant, and O. Toader. 2017. "The Impact of the Identification of GSIBs on Their Business Model." No. 33, Banque de France, Paris.

Von Thadden, E.-L. 2004. "Bank Capital Adequacy Regulation under the New Basel Accord." *Journal of Financial Intermediation* 13: 90–95.

Wall, L. D. 2014. "The Adoption of Stress Testing: Why the Basel Capital Measures Were Not Enough." *Journal of Banking Regulation* 15: 266–76.

Wall Street Journal. 2018. "Banks Say No Thanks to Volcker Rule Changes." August 15. https://www.wsj.com/articles/banks-say-no-thanks-to-volcker-rule-changes-1534353932.

Watanabe, W. 2007. "Prudential Regulation and the 'Credit Crunch': Evidence from Japan." *Journal of Money, Credit and Banking* 39 (2–3): 639–65.

Webel, B., and M. Labonte. 2018. "Costs of Government Interventions in Response to the Financial Crisis: A Retrospective." Congressional Research Service Report, Washington, DC.

World Bank. 2012. *Global Financial Development Report 2013: Rethinking the Role of the State in Finance.* Washington, DC: World Bank.

———. 2016. "Bank Resolution and Bail-In in the EU: Selected Case Studies Pre- and Post-BRRD." Working Paper 112265, World Bank, Washington, DC.

———. 2018. *Global Financial Development Report 2017/2018: Bankers without Borders.* Washington, DC: World Bank.

Yuan, K. 2005. "Asymmetric Price Movements and Borrowing Constraints: A Rational Expectations Equilibrium Model of Crises, Contagion, and Confusion." *Journal of Finance* 60: 379–411.

ZDNet. 2018. "NonPetya Ransomware Forced Maersk to Reinstall 4000 Servers, 45000 PCs." https://www.zdnet.com/article/maersk-forced-to-reinstall-4000-servers-45000-pcs-due-to-notpetya-attack/.

Zeissler, A. G., T. Piontek, and A. Metrick. 2014. "Ireland and Iceland in Crisis C: Iceland's Landsbanki Icesave." Yale Program on Financial Stability Case Study, New Haven, CT.

ECO-AUDIT

Environmental Benefits Statement

The World Bank Group is committed to reducing its environmental footprint. In support of this commitment, we leverage electronic publishing options and print-on-demand technology, which is located in regional hubs worldwide. Together, these initiatives enable print runs to be lowered and shipping distances decreased, resulting in reduced paper consumption, chemical use, greenhouse gas emissions, and waste.

We follow the recommended standards for paper use set by the Green Press Initiative. The majority of our books are printed on Forest Stewardship Council (FSC)–certified paper, with nearly all containing 50–100 percent recycled content. The recycled fiber in our book paper is either unbleached or bleached using totally chlorine-free (TCF), processed chlorine–free (PCF), or enhanced elemental chlorine–free (EECF) processes.

More information about the Bank's environmental philosophy can be found at http://www.worldbank.org/corporateresponsibility.

green press INITIATIVE